Real Music

A Guide to the Timeless Hymns of the Church

Anthony Esolen

TAN Books
Gastonia, North Carolina

Cover design by Caroline Kiser

Cover image: Angels Playing Musical Instruments, right hand panel from a triptych from the Church of Santa Maria la Real, Najera, c.1487-90 (oil on panel), Memling, Hans (c.1433-94) / Koninklijk Museum voor Schone Kunsten, Antwerp, Belgium / Bridgeman Images.

Author portrait by Chris Pelicano

ISBN: 978-1-5051-2659-4

Published in the United States by
TAN Books
P. O. Box 269
Gastonia, NC 28053
www.TANBooks.com

Printed and bound in the United States of America.

Contents

Foreword

THE Church has blessed us with a rich heritage of sacred music to beautify the Sacred Liturgy, to elevate our minds, and to enrich our souls. As St. Augustine teaches us in the *City of God*, beauty is "a good gift from God." Thus, it is crucial that we worship Him with our best music, because the "Liturgy is the most beautiful confession of the true faith" (Pope Sixtus V). Lest we diminish the beauty of the Holy Sacrifice of the Mass by singing "pseudo music" that is substandard or profane, we must insist on the sacred nature of the Liturgy by presenting to the Lord "real music"—a musical offering that is true, good, and beautiful. When music beautifies the Liturgy in this manner, how much more easily is the soul able to enter into intimacy with God. Thus does true sacred music unveil the "beauty of holiness" (Ps 96:9).

While Gregorian chant and sacred polyphony rightly enjoy "pride of place" in the music of the Liturgy, our Holy Mother the Church also exhorts us to raise a fitting melody unto the Lord by singing "psalms, and hymns, and spiritual canticles" (Eph 5:19). The hymns we sing should be a window to the sacred, ushering us into an atmosphere of prayer where the human soul can inhale inspiration from the Holy Spirit. The great hymn-writers of the past, from St. Ambrose to Father Faber, and from Prudentius to G. K. Chesterton, penned their finest hymns with rich allusions to Sacred Scripture and theology. These timeless hymns, the fruit of prayer and mystical contemplation, still inspire us and teach us the Faith. They have stood the test of time.

In the following pages, Anthony Esolen shows how these carefully selected hymns, like gems in the treasure chest, combine the best of poetry with doctrinally sound lyrics and beautiful melodies. As we restore the tradition of singing "real music" to beautify the Sacred Liturgy, we ought to let the Lord make beautiful music in us, so that our lives might be a living sacrifice—a beautiful hymn unto God for He is the Divine Maestro!

Rev. Scott A. Haynes, S.J.C.
Director, St. Cecilia Choir
St. John Cantius Church, Chicago

Author's Note

THE King James Version is not a canonical text, and its modern printings omit the deuterocanonical books. (These were once included at the back as salutary reading; Anglican churchgoers were well aware of them.) But as an English translation, it is incomparable for its beauty and its influence upon English poets and hymnodists. I will be using it throughout, for the simple reason that the authors of the hymns used it, or had its phrasings and its rhythms in mind when they wrote. It will help us see and hear what the poets were doing, and I hope that will in turn inspire Catholic poets, using more authoritative versions of Scripture, to go and do likewise.

Publisher's Note

SIMILARLY, we carefully chose our subtitle—"A Guide to the Timeless Hymns of the Church"—to highlight the catholicity of the hymns in both the "uppercase" and "lowercase" senses of the term. This despite the fact that many of the hymns included were written or translated by non-Catholics and are staples in non-Catholic hymnals. The great hymns, through their orthodox expressions of creedal doctrine, remind us of how much we have in common with our separated brethren. However, as many mainline denominations drift further and further from the faith of their fathers, it may give one pause to wonder how many non-Catholic hymnodists could or would produce such work today. Do the Methodist and Anglican hymnodists of the twenty-first century believe as Wesley and Neale did? It is in this sense that we humbly submit this work as an effort in ecumenism in the hope that all Christians may sing as one.

In order to derive the most benefit and enjoyment from the book and CD, we recommend that you listen to the hymns after or while reading them. The appendix at the back of the book includes a list of hymns by chapter and those that are on the CD are noted by track number. Enjoy!

Introduction

"HE who sings prays twice," says St. Augustine.

"See that panel on the front of the altar," said my friend, the priest, pointing to a wooden relief sculpture of the Lamb of God. "You won't believe where I found it. It was in the basement of a tavern. It had been torn out of some church somewhere, and I have no idea how it ended up where it did. We asked for it for the church here. If you look hard you can faintly see a seam across the sculpture where it had been split in two," Father explained. The rest of the church was grand, filled with impressive works of art in stone and glass. "The parish was too poor in the 1970s to afford any renovation, but the art survived," he said.

Richer parishes were not so fortunate. My own home church, Saint Thomas Aquinas, was built by Irish coal miners in the nineteenth century. They built a large neo-Romanesque structure, one great barrel vault without internal supports. The ceiling, entirely open, was covered with paintings executed by an Italian they hired and brought over from Europe. No square foot was left blank, not even the area between the stained glass windows and the arc of the ceiling. There were painted medallions of ten of the twelve apostles, five on each side, with large hanging medallions of St. Peter and St. Paul in the sanctuary.

The background was a warm, muted purple, decorated with golden fleurs-de-lis.

But the wave of New Iconoclasm hit. Most of the ceiling survived, but Peter and Paul disappeared, leaving the church in the absurd position of commemorating the Ten Apostles, bereft of their chief and of the great apostle to the Gentiles. The delicate background was painted over in icy white. The marble communion rail and the great altar met the jackhammer. The organ in the loft was removed, and no one knows in what landfill its hundreds of pipes have been crushed.

Almost every parish in the United States and Canada has such a story to tell. A priest instructs workmen to take away the statues of saints and throw them in the pond. A bishop orders the removal of wooden pews boasting hand-carved reliefs of the local Appalachian flora and fauna. What is harder to notice, though, is that the same rage for reduction and removal did its work on the very prayers of the Church. It is easy for someone to notice the emptiness of a large sanctuary whose dimensions were set precisely for the altar that used to be there. It is harder to notice words no longer spoken, or melodies no longer heard.

I am writing this book to bring back the words of great Christian hymns, most of which are no longer heard anywhere. These hymns are not pious sentiments (or, worse, self-celebrating sentiments or social propaganda) set to a catchy tune. They are works of art. They are, at their best, profound meditations upon the meaning of Scripture, their artistry serving to help us to see truths we may have missed or to hear in our hearts, not only in our ears, the implications of the Word of God for our lives. They are verbal and melodic icons of Jesus Christ.

I've spent my entire adult life teaching poetry to college students. It is a joy for me to see their eyes open with wonder when they hear the art of poetry for the first time. It certainly is a change from the usual. Most of what we see and hear every day is shabby, slovenly, cynical, brazen, and stupid. The modern is either utterly drab or glaring: A school built like a vast warehouse, or an airport filled with visual and auditory noise. When young people encounter poetry, if they will but open themselves up to it, they are like people tasting wine who have known only oily water. It is as if they cry out, "Here at last is something I can give my heart to!"

The Church, it is true, offers the incomparable wine of the Eucharist. But she offers it, all too often, with the carelessness of the drab or the tastelessness of the glaring. And here I return to St. Augustine's saying above. Why do they who sing pray twice?

Certainly, song requires that we lift up our hearts. "Singing is what the lover does," says Augustine. It is one thing to say the words of a psalm, but to sing them means that we cherish them within us and proclaim them with our whole being. And yet this is not simply an emotional outburst. The hymns that Augustine heard when he was still an unbeliever, and that he sang out in devotion once he had given his life to Christ, were works of theological art. That is to say, human intelligence and the divine teachings are woven together in a sacrifice of praise, as Abel chose the best of his flock to sacrifice to the Lord. And they do so in a *memorable* way. Music and poetry help to form the Christian imagination, resonating in the heart long after we have left the doors of the Church, as we sing, "Pleasant are thy courts above, O Lord of hosts!"

I wish, then, to reintroduce this human and divine poetry to my fellow Christians, to show them how the great hymn-poems work and what they have to teach us. May the Lord

Jesus, who sang the ancient hymns of His people after His last supper with His friends, be also a friend to us and send us that same Holy Spirit who inspired the poets and the composers of our heritage. May we turn in gratitude to the work they did. Few churches can afford a Caravaggio or a Rembrandt, but all can afford a Bach or a Handel. The music is there to be heard, the poetry there to be sung.

Chapter One

The Psalms

THE psalms are the foundational poems of Christian praise. Roman Catholics say or sing verses of one of the psalms at every Mass. Monks pray the psalms all the way through every few days. Protestant congregations have given us such splendid collections as the *Scottish Psalter*. So it is not idle to ask, "Why do we need hymns at all, when we already have the Psalms?" Inspired by a wish to return to the source of Christian hymnody, lyricists in the 1970s simply set the psalms to English free-verse, without rhyme or meter, as if that were more genuine than the older renderings into formal poetry. Many even employed the Anglicized "Yahweh," the holy name of the Lord that faithful Jews do not utter. They thus reduced the mysterious name-and-no-name, the great I AM, to an ordinary tag, like Zeus or Apollo.

The result was neither flesh nor fowl, neither the psalm itself, sung or chanted straightforwardly, nor a work of theology in verse. But the assumption behind it—the less art, the better—was incorrect. It betrays a misunderstanding of the psalms themselves.

The psalms are Hebrew poems, and they reflect the peculiarities of the Hebrew language. Think of a language in the way that a painter thinks of the tools and the stuff of his art. There are things that you might do with oil on canvas that you would not do with watercolor on paper, or with egg tempera on wood, or with earthen paints on wet plaster. Some languages, like Italian, rhyme easily, because there are not so many combinations of consonants at the end of a word, and few vowel sounds that will go along with any one combination. An Italian orders *pasta*, and the *a* before the consonants is a short *ah*, and that is it. But an Englishman can say *past*, with a short *a*, or *paste*, with a "long" *a*, and they don't rhyme. It is harder to rhyme in English because of the hundreds of ways in which an English word can end. But it is easier in English to write poetry with strongly stressed syllables, since we hammer them out, as do our cousins the Germans. Speakers of other languages make their vowels long by, well, making them long—they stretch them out. We in English don't really do that. We make our vowels lax or tense, and that's what accounts for the difference between *past* and *paste*. But the ancient Greeks really did stretch their vowels, so that they heard different kinds of syllables, long ones and short ones, and crafted their poetry accordingly, by fixed patterns of long and short.

What, then, did the ancient Hebrew poets do? Hebrew is remarkably terse, its words placed beside one another like massive blocks of meaning. There are very few "operator" words to show relationships. The words themselves are terse, too, built upon a root of three consonants, with internal vowels varying to show changes of meaning. It's hard to "hear" syllables in Hebrew, because of a frequent breath between two consonants, a breath that isn't quite a vowel. So, for example, we have *b'nai b'rith*, "sons of the covenant," and it's hard to tell whether we should count that as two syllables or four. Rhymes, however, are common—too common, too easy. If you want to say *my son* in Hebrew, you put a little pronoun-suffix after the noun: *beni*. That will rhyme with "my father," *abi*, and "my God," *Eli*, and my everything else. The same sort of thing can be seen in Hebrew verbs.

So Hebrew poets do not count syllables strictly, nor do they rhyme systematically. Instead they take full advantage of the terseness of the language. The poets commonly set two or three words on one side of the line against two or three words on the other side, in a parallel structure, with the second half of the line explaining or amplifying the first half, or providing a result or a contrast. Here's a typical example, the first verse of Psalm 118:

Hodu l'Adonai ki tov,	*ki le'olam chasdo.*
[Give] thanks to-[the]-Lord for [He is] good,	*for forever his-mercy.*

O give thanks unto the Lord; for he is good: because his mercy endureth for ever.

Notice the balance. The everlasting mercy of the Lord (right) is a special instance of his goodness (left). Notice also the impressive concentration in the Hebrew poem. Four words on one side, including the operator *ki*, "because," and four on the other side, with *ki* repeated. Notice also that the name of God (unpronounceable, and so *Adonai*, "Lord," is uttered as a substitute) is set in balance across from the adverb *le'olam*, by the introductory *l'*, "to, unto." Thus *to the Lord* alliterates with *to all ages, for ever*. The form of the words teaches us that the Lord is eternal, and that nothing lasts forever unless by the power of the Lord.

That is straightforward and powerful. It's not the sort of thing that survives translation into English prose, which in the worthy King James Version spins eight words out into sixteen, and thirteen syllables into twenty-two. So what should the

English poet do? If the *poetry* of the psalm is to be honored, we must avail ourselves of the possibilities of English lyric. We must allow rhyme and meter to do some of the work in English that parallelism and balance did in Hebrew.

English poets have understood the point. Great poets such as Philip Sidney and John Milton translated many of the psalms into English verse, often employing the meter of popular ballads. Best known of all is, or used to be, the work of Isaac Watts, who wrought the whole psalter into English. Watts has twenty entries in *The Hymnbook* of the Presbyterian churches in America (1955), fourteen in the Episcopalian *Hymnal* (1940). We will be encountering Dr. Watts later in this work. For now, let us look at an "ordinary" English rendering of the straightforward Psalm 100, attributed to William Kethe (1561). Here is Psalm 100 in the King James prose:

> *Make a joyful noise unto the Lord, all ye lands.*
> *Serve the Lord with gladness: come before his presence with*
> *singing.*
> *Know ye that the Lord he is God; it is he that hath made us,*
> *and not we ourselves;*
> *we are his people, and the sheep of his pasture.*
> *Enter into his gates with thanksgiving, and into his courts*
> *with praise:*
> *be thankful unto him, and bless his name.*
> *For the Lord is good; his mercy is everlasting:*
> *and his truth endureth to all generations.*

Now in Kethe's English:

> *All people that on earth do dwell,*
> *Sing to the Lord with cheerful voice;*

Him serve with mirth, His praise forth tell,
Come ye before Him and rejoice.

Know that the Lord is God indeed;
Without our aid He did us make;
We are His folk, He doth us feed,
And for His sheep He doth us take.

O enter then His gates with praise,
Approach with joy His courts unto;
Praise, laud, and bless His name always,
For it is seemly so to do.

For why? the Lord our God is good,
His mercy is forever sure;
His truth at all times firmly stood,
And shall from age to age endure.

Read them over again, one after the other. As a translation this is really very fine. Not one motif in the original is left out. But it is an impressive poem in its own right. Kethe employs the simple four-line stanza, with four strong beats in a line, rhyming on alternate lines, to bind together in English the thoughts and images of the Hebrew.

Each stanza marks a clear progression. The first, translating the first two Hebrew verses, is a call for praise. The second gives us the principal reason for that praise: We owe our very existence to God, and our welfare. The clearly delineated syllabic lines, and the alternating rhymes, place the ideas in balance with one another. The Lord is God indeed. Why? Well, for one thing, *without our aid He did us make*. Not only did He make us: He feeds us. We are His folk, His sheep. The far-flung nations of the first two lines—*All people that on earth do dwell*—are brought into one universal church, one common fold.

The third stanza draws a conclusion from the second, and deepens the idea of approaching God that is present in the first. Because God has so blessed us, we should not only praise Him but enter His gates and approach His courts. Here the pilgrims sojourn toward a specific place, the courts of God, the heavenly Jerusalem. Kethe inserts the adverb *always* into the stanza: We should never cease to bless the holy name of God. It is *seemly so to do*, he adds, giving himself the opportunity to bind the third stanza to the fourth, and all the stanzas together in one.

Why is it seemly to bless the name of God *always?* Because the mercy and the truth of God are *always*. Our faithful praise is the just response to God's everlasting faithfulness to us. His mercy is *sure*, and His truth stands firm: It will *endure*. The rhymes are exactly right. I cannot imagine a more powerful and more sensitive poetic translation. Sung to the unadorned and mighty melody *Old Hundredth* (note the loving way the melody was remembered by generations of English churchgoers and choristers), the poem sets down deep roots into the heart and mind and soul.

So far I've discussed only a few formal features of the Hebrew psalms. But when we turn to the content, the psalms stand out as unique in ancient literature. They are holy songs that meditate upon the holy *deeds* of the Lord in the lived experience of the Hebrews, and upon the holy *words* of the Lord, already possessed in various books, and also in oral traditions. We take that combination of deeds and words for granted, but we shouldn't.

The Greeks had their religious traditions regarding the beginning of the world. The early poet Hesiod sang of them in his *Theogony*, literally *The Generation of the Gods*. It's from Hesiod that we learn about the wicked god Cronus who devoured his children whole, till his wife tricked him one day, giving him a stone wrapped up in a blanket instead and spiriting their small boy into hiding—the boy who was named Zeus, and who would overthrow his father. Hesiod gives to the sophisticated Greek an allegory about how the world, both the divine world and the human world, works; but it isn't meant to be "historical," and we don't have Greek prophets revealing to mankind the everlasting commandments of Zeus. The Greeks did have their historical writers, long after Hesiod, like the shrewd Thucydides, who wrote against his native city, Athens, in his history of the Peloponnesian War. But Thucydides is not concerned too much with theology. By contrast, the psalms are at once historical in a way that Hesiod's *Theogony* is not, and theological in a way that Thucydides' history is not. It is therefore quite mistaken to treat them as lovely poems to be preserved in some pristine and primitive simplicity.

To see what I mean, let's turn again to the opening line of Psalm 118:

Hodu l'Adonai ki tov, *ki le'olam chasdo.*

The rest of the poem is rich indeed, and well do many Christian churches sing it on Easter. Consider but the verse, "The stone which the builders refused is become the head stone of the corner," cited by St. Peter to refer to Jesus, the Messiah rejected by His own people (1 Pt 2:7). But even this first line may deceive us with its apparent simplicity. Notice the two little words in the first half, *ki tov*, "for [He is] good." The English translation has to supply words that are only implied in the terse Hebrew: *O give thanks unto the Lord; for he is good: because his mercy endureth for ever*. But those supplied words obscure a powerful truth delivered by *ki tov*. When God created the universe, those are the words used to describe His judgment upon it: *w'yar Elohim eth ha'or ki tov*: "And God saw the light, that it was good." When we place the two verses beside one another, we see that the goodness of the world proceeds from the goodness of God. He creates what is good, imparting to it a measure of His own essence: He causes it to be.

So then, it's in the spirit of the psalms themselves when English poets render them as meditations upon scripture or upon the work of God, even when their thoughts may not have been in the psalmist's mind. The result is often a tapestry of scriptural and theological insight. That's what we have in the lovely rendering of Psalm 84, *Pleasant Are Thy Courts Above*, by the hymnodist Henry Francis Lyte (1834). Here is the psalm:

How amiable are thy tabernacles, O Lord of hosts!
My soul longeth, yea, even fainteth for the courts of the Lord:
my heart and my flesh crieth out for the living God.
Yea, the sparrow hath found an house, and the swallow a nest for herself,
where she may lay her young,
even thine altars, O Lord of hosts, my King, and my God.
Blessed are they that dwell in thy house: they will still be praising thee.
Blessed is the man whose strength is in thee; in whose heart are the ways of them.
Who passing through the valley of Baca make it a well; the rain also filleth the pools.
They go from strength to strength, every one of them in Zion appeareth before God.

O Lord God of hosts, hear my prayer: give ear, O God of Jacob.
Behold, O God our shield, and look upon the face of thine anointed.
For a day in thy courts is better than a thousand.
I had rather be a doorkeeper in the house of my God, than to dwell in the tents of wickedness.
For the Lord God is a sun and shield: the Lord will give grace and glory:
no good thing will he withhold from them that walk uprightly.
O Lord of hosts, blessed is the man that trusteth in thee.

That glorious poem gives the translator a lot to work with, many paths to travel. Lyte knows that he cannot do everything, so he chooses to base his poem upon two of the psalm's motifs, and to show them in relationship with one another. The first is the contrast between the house of God and the tents of wickedness. The second is that of the birds finding a nest. When the two meet, we see the psalm as a poem of flight, of pilgrimage, from the world below to the world above:

Pleasant are thy courts above
In the land of light and love;
Pleasant are thy courts below
In this land of sin and woe.
O my spirit longs and faints

For the converse of thy saints,
For the brightness of thy face,
For thy fullness, God of grace.

The parallelism—*pleasant are thy courts above, pleasant are thy courts below*—is quite effective. Lyte does not scorn the Christian life in this world. God's courts—the church, our prayer together—are delightful even here. But their delight whets the appetite for the things above, which Lyte enumerates in a second parallelism, building to a fine climax. We long to be among the saints; we long to dwell within the light of God's countenance; we long for God Himself, His fullness, given to us as a free gift of grace.

Having established the poem's theological structure, Lyte returns to the image of the birds in flight:

Happy birds that sing and fly
Round thy altars, O Most High;
Happier souls that find a rest
In a heavenly Father's breast!
Like the wandering dove that found
No repose on earth around,
They can to their ark repair
And enjoy it ever there.

Again we begin with a parallelism. The birds—angels—that fly about the altars of God are *happy*, but even *happier* are the souls that no longer need to fly, because they have found their rest in the bosom of the Father. That's the first half of the stanza. In the second half, Lyte recalls a bird from Genesis, the dove that Noah sent forth after the rain had ceased. That dove at first could not find a place of rest, so she returned to the ark. Seven days later, as if it were the Sabbath of a new creation, Noah sent the dove forth again, and this time she returned with an olive branch in her beak. The poet brings those two flights of the dove together in one. The dove, a pilgrim, a wanderer, finds no repose on the earth but does find repose in heaven, which is the ark of God. Her motion is not from the ark to the earth but from the stormy and restless earth to the ark—to the Church triumphant, to the courts of God.

That pilgrimage is filled with blessings even here:

Happy souls, their praises flow
Ever in this vale of woe;
Waters in the desert rise,
Manna feeds them from the skies:
On they go from strength to strength
Till they reach thy throne at length,
At thy feet adoring fall,
Who hast led them safe through all.

Notice how the rhyming couplets unite things that belong together: Rhymes are not only for pleasant music but for union and meaning. The pilgrim souls praise God here in the vale of woe. Why not, since God gives them food and drink—the water from the rock that the Israelites drank in the desert, a foreshadowing of the living water that the Messiah brings; the manna that fell like dew upon the ground below, a foreshadowing of the Eucharist, the true bread from heaven. Thus fortified, they go robustly on from strength to strength, till they attain the goal, the throne of God. Then at last they fall in adoration, for God in His grace has led them safely through their joyful trials.

In the final stanza, Lyte applies the lessons of the first three to the individual Christian. Here the theology becomes deeply personal:

Lord, be mine this prize to win;
Guide me through a world of sin;

Keep me by thy saving grace;
Give me at thy side a place.
Sun and shield alike thou art;
Guide and guard my erring heart.
Grace and glory flow from thee;
Shower, O shower them, Lord, on me.

Lyte knows what he is doing. The parallelisms, apparently simple, are quite precise and build to a climax. In the first four lines, we beseech the Lord to guide us, to keep us, and to give us a place at his side. The final four lines employ the pairs *sun and shield* and *grace and glory*, found in the psalm. But here they embrace a pair of alliterating verbs that recall the first four lines: *Guide and guard*. We need the guidance of God because our hearts are *erring*—that is, wandering, straying. We need the guardianship of God because when we wander, we wander into sin, at the prompting of the enemy. The music of the phrase *guide and guard* is echoed by the *grace and glory* of the next line. Justly so, since we yearn for the grace of God to guide us and guard us so that we may finally behold His glory. Finally, the pair *sun and shield* is echoed, and made personal, by the last line, the ultimate petition: *Shower, O shower them, Lord, on me*. The destructive rain that Noah survived in the ark is now a showering of gifts from above, so that we may live well in this world and delight in the glory of God in the next.

That, dear readers, is a poem. The psalmist would heartily approve. Sung to the melody *Maidstone*, composed especially to bring the parallelisms into harmony, it is a hymn of both deep feeling and brave confidence.

It isn't necessary, though, to devote an entire psalm to one hymn. Often the poets will develop the thought of a part of a psalm, writing a wholly new poem founded in the inspiration of the sacred author. Here, for example, are the first few verses of Psalm 90, a penitential psalm that stresses the misery of human life and God's wrath visited upon sinners:

Lord, thou hast been our dwelling place in all generations.
Before the mountains were brought forth, or ever thou hadst formed the earth and the world,
Even from everlasting to everlasting, thou art God.
Thou turnest man to destruction; and sayest, Return, ye children of men.
For a thousand years in thy sight are but as yesterday when it is past, and as a watch in the night.
Thou carriest them away as with a flood: they are as a sleep:
In the morning they are like grass which groweth up.
In the morning it flourisheth, and groweth up;
In the evening it is cut down, and withereth.

The excellent Isaac Watts takes up the psalm's motif of time—its evanescence, the transience of all mortal things—and sees in it a promise of eternity. The trials that beset man on earth are not necessarily the decrees of an angry God. They may be the proving grounds of glory. So it is in Revelation, when the evangelist John asks the angel to identify the souls who sing praises around the throne of God. "These are they which came out of great tribulation," says the angel, "and have washed their robes, and made them white in the blood of the Lamb. Therefore are they before the throne of God, and serve him day and night in his temple; and he that sitteth on the throne shall dwell among them" (Rv 7:14–15).

Let's see then what Watts does in *O God, Our Help in Ages Past*:

O God, our help in ages past,
Our hope for years to come,
Our shelter from the stormy blast,
And our eternal home:

Under the shadow of Thy throne
Thy saints have dwelt secure;
Sufficient is Thine arm alone,
And our defense is sure.

The first two stanzas constitute one sentence. The first is an address to God, named four times. Notice the balance of ideas and images. God is *our help* in the past (Watts is with the psalmist, thinking of the history of salvation, continued into present time), and therefore also *our hope* for years to come. But these two orientations of time, past and future, are resolved into an unchanging present. Without the love of God, this world is a whirl of trouble, of storms and war; God alone is *our shelter*. That means more than that God is a screen against these trials. He is *our dwelling place for all generations*—as Watts puts it, thinking of heaven, *our eternal home*.

Therefore those who give themselves to God, who dwell within the shadow of His throne, are *secure*, literally, free from care, free from trouble, even amid suffering. That's not because they are strong. The arm of the Lord alone is sufficient. We are secure, *our defense is sure* (notice the rhyming words) solely because God has brought us into His dwelling place, which no evil can taint or rebellion disturb.

In the third stanza, Watts returns to the language of the psalm to explain why that dwelling place is so secure:

Before the hills in order stood,
Or earth received her frame,
From everlasting Thou art God,
To endless years the same.

It won't do to say that Watts has simply turned the verses into English. We hear the stanza in the context of what we have just sung. We also see a subtle connection here between the things that change, and the Creator who is beyond change. For the hills stand *in order*, and the earth too receives *her frame*. Order, in the world of time, is a reflection of God's eternity.

Watts highlights the contrast between time and eternity in the next stanza, which again echoes the psalm very closely:

A thousand ages in Thy sight
Are like an evening gone;
Short as the watch that ends the night
Before the rising sun.

The blink of an eye is greater, as compared with the innumerable ages of the universe, than are those ages to the eternity of God. The psalmist expresses the relative nothingness of time with an image—the watch in the night. Watts takes up that image, and then, as if he had nothing to do but end the stanza with a rhyme, he adds, *before the rising sun*. But his choice is deliberate. The ages are not only compared to a short watch in the night. They are *identified* with the night. So we're not just considering their quickness. We consider their shadowiness, their insubstantiality, their failure to attain a full measure of being.

That becomes clear in the poignant stanza that follows:

Time, like an ever-rolling stream,
Bears all its sons away;
They fly, forgotten, as a dream
Dies at the opening day.

Watts here has transferred the agency from God to *Time* and the objects of the action from the psalm's *children of men* to Time's *sons*. He is justified in doing so, since he's not writing a poem about the wrath of God. He's writing about our lives that flee away, and the life of life we long for, the dwelling place of God. So the emphasis is twofold. These sons of Time are like the fleeting shadows of a dream. They die, true. But they die *at the opening day*; thus the stanza ends, as did the previous stanza, with the hopeful image of the rising sun.

The final stanza repeats the first but with a crucial change. Now we entreat God directly for His help in securing our hope; we pray that God will guide us through time to eternity:

O God, our help in ages past,
Our hope for years to come,
Be Thou our guide while life shall last,
And our eternal home.

We see here that it makes as much sense to omit the last verse of a genuine hymn-poem, as it would to read the Gospels without bothering to finish them. What would we miss then? Easter.

I've suggested that the psalms look backward to the Scriptures and to the history of Israel. But what Isaac Watts shows us is that they also look *forward*. They are prophecies of blessing. In particular, they await the coming of the Messiah, the Anointed One.

Jesus Himself affirms this way of reading the psalms. He asks the scribes, "How say they that [the Messiah] is David's son? And David himself saith in the book of Psalms, The Lord said unto my Lord, Sit thou on my right hand, till I make thine enemies thy footstool. David therefore calleth him Lord, how is he then his son?" (Lk 20:41–44; cf. Ps 110:1). Jesus implicitly identifies Himself as the Lord of David alluded to in the psalm. So too the Apostle John, recalling the crucifixion, sees the soldiers throwing dice for Jesus' robe, and reminds us of Psalm 22, traditionally read in the churches on Good Friday: "They said therefore among themselves, Let us not rend it, but cast lots for it, whose it shall be: that the scripture might be fulfilled, which saith, They parted my raiment among them, and for my vesture did they cast lots" (Jn 19:24; cf. Ps 22:18). The Church Fathers are unanimous in reading the "just man" of Psalm 1 as referring to the only man who could stand pure in the sight of the Father: Christ, the Son. No doubt they take their cue from the writer to the Hebrews, referring to the obedience, the passion, and the resurrection of Jesus: "For unto which of the angels said he at any time, Thou art my son, this day I have begotten thee? And again, I will be to him a Father, and he shall be to me a Son? And again, when he bringeth in the firstbegotten into the world, he saith, And let all the angels of God worship him" (Heb 1:5–6; cf. Ps 2:7, 89:26, 97:7).

So it is right and just for us to read the psalms in the light of Christ—and to transform the psalms into hymns composed in the key of Christ. Let's now look at Psalm 23, most beloved of all the psalms:

The Lord is my shepherd; I shall not want.
He maketh me to lie down in green pastures;

he leadeth me beside the still waters. He restoreth my soul:
He leadeth me in the paths of righteousness for his name's sake.
Yea, though I walk through the valley of the shadow of death, I will fear no evil:
For thou art with me; thy rod and thy staff they comfort me.
Thou preparest a table before me in the presence of mine enemies:
Thou anointest my head with oil; my cup runneth over.
Surely goodness and mercy shall follow me all the days of my life:
And I will dwell in the house of the Lord for ever.

Here is the straightforward English rendering in the *Scottish Psalter* (1650):

The Lord's my Shepherd, I'll not want;
He makes me down to lie
In pastures green; He leadeth me
The quiet waters by.

My soul he doth restore again,
And me to walk doth make
Within the paths of righteousness,
E'en for His own name's sake.

Yea, though I walk in death's dark vale,
Yet will I fear none ill;
For Thou art with me, and Thy rod
And staff me comfort still.

My table Thou hast furnished
In presence of my foes;
My head Thou dost with oil anoint,
And my cup overflows.

Goodness and mercy all my life
Shall surely follow me;
And in God's house forevermore
My dwelling place shall be.

The "translation" here is from the unmetered verses of the King James to the simple 4–3–4–3 ballad meter—that is, four strong beats on the first and third lines, and three strong beats on the second and fourth lines. (This meter is called Common Meter, C.M., in the hymnals.) It is so well done, so faithful to the images, the thoughts, and the emphases of the original, that we might miss the rhymes, chosen with great delicacy. Consider the peacefulness implied by the rhyme in the first stanza, which binds together the green pastures and the still waters. Or consider, in the third stanza, the fitness of the final adverb *still*, added by the anonymous poet. I shall fear no evil even in the valley of the shadow of death, no matter what I confront, no matter how long my passage through that valley must be, for the rod and the staff of my Shepherd comfort me, they still my heart, now and always.

This unknown poet knew what he was doing. Look at the fourth stanza. A lesser poet would have written, *Thou dost anoint my head with oil*, not needing to rhyme in any case. But that would have blurred the parallelism and the climax that the poet intends. The first two lines begin with *my table*, and praise the Lord for being a champion against the poet's enemies; then the last two lines, beginning with *my head*, develop the image of the feast and stress the love between the poet and the Lord, who anoints his head with oil and fills his cup with wine: *My cup overflows.*

Look, finally, at the last stanza. It's become commonplace for translators to blunt the force of the final words of the psalm, saying only that we will dwell in the house of God "as long as we live," as if God will ask us to leave the premises once we die. But our English poet rightly balances *all my life* with *forevermore.* We do not wish to visit God now and again, or even to take up squatter's residence on His property till we die. We want to *dwell* with Him, and since He is the eternal God, that implies an everlasting dwelling—even if the certainty of eternal life had not yet been revealed to the psalmist.

So much for an "ordinary" English rendering. The Scottish melody *Crimond* is especially sweet, with an unusual lilting progression at the end, from a very high sixth (high D) down to the peaceful resolution of the tonic (F). Well then, what happens when the rendering is not ordinary? What happens when the poet meditates upon the psalm as it refers to Christ?

What happens, from the pen of the hymnodist Henry W. Baker, is the beautiful and profound *The King of Love My Shepherd Is* (1868). We'll take the poem stanza by stanza:

The King of love my Shepherd is,
Whose goodness faileth never;
I nothing lack if I am His
And He is mine forever.

Note the difference: Baker straightaway identifies the Lord as *the King of love.* He is not just indulging his religious feelings. Baker is aware (we will see this awareness again) of the version of the Psalm in Jerome's Latin Vulgate, based on a Hebrew manuscript that often differs from the one used by the King James translators. In Jerome's version, the opening of the psalm is *Dominus regit me, The Lord governs me*, with the suggestion of kingship (Latin, *rex*, king) present in the verb. So Baker unites the two openings, and adds that this King is a king *of love*, since, as St. John says, "God is love" (1 Jn 4:8). The final two lines develop the implications of the psalm, in the light of Christ. He came among us to give us the greatest conceivable gift—not a land of milk and honey or long life or many children but Himself. Whoever has Jesus needs nothing more.

How does Jesus give us Himself? The second stanza shows us:

Where streams of living water flow
My ransomed soul he leadeth,
And where the verdant pastures grow,
With food celestial feedeth.

Baker has added three motifs to the psalm: The *living* water, the *ransomed* soul, and the food *celestial*. All three come from the New Testament and refer to the self-giving of Christ.

Recall when Jesus and His disciples went to Samaria, and He was thirsty after the long journey. He was alone with the Samaritan woman at the well, and He asked her for a drink. That prompted a remarkable discussion between the two; and Jesus said to her that He could give her *living water*: "Whosoever drinketh of this water shall thirst again: but whosoever drinketh of the water that I shall give him shall never thirst; but the water that I shall give him shall be in him a well of water springing up into everlasting life" (Jn 4:13–14). This water infinitely surpasses the water that Moses struck from the rock in the desert. It also recalls Jesus' discourse upon the bread of life.

For as Jesus said to the Pharisees, their forefathers ate manna in the desert, yet died nonetheless. The manna was heaven-sent, but it was still only earthly food, a substitute for the bread that the Israelites would eat when they finally entered the Promised Land.

But there's something utterly different about the food that the poet enjoys now. It is *food celestial.* It is not simply earthly food sent *from* above, but the very food of heaven: Christ's own self, given in the Eucharist. "For my flesh is true food," says Jesus, "and my blood is true drink." This, the true manna and the living water, is food not only for the body but for the soul also. When the centurion, making sure that Jesus was dead, thrust his spear into the Lord's side, through the lungs and the pericardium and into the heart, blood and water flowed out; and the evangelist suspends the narrative, with urgency and dread solemnity, to testify: He saw it with his own eyes. The point is that the Eucharist, Jesus' great self-gift to man, is one with his self-gift upon the Cross. That is how we sinners are *ransomed*, redeemed, bought back from sin with the inestimable treasure of the blood of Christ.

That leads us to Baker's third stanza:

Perverse and foolish oft I strayed,
But yet in love He sought me,
And on His shoulders gently laid,
And home, rejoicing, brought me.

Of course, this isn't to be found in Psalm 23; and yet it is a brilliant interpolation. In the Old Testament, God is often portrayed as the shepherd of the flock. But Jesus opens out that metaphor and applies it to Himself. When the Pharisees complain that He eats with sinners, He asks which of them, having a hundred sheep, and losing one of them in the desert, would not leave the ninety-nine and search for the lost one? And having found it, he would lay it on his shoulders and bring it home, rejoicing. The poet knows he has *not* walked in the paths of righteousness. He has *strayed*, in his stubbornness and folly. But the Redeemer will not let the sheep wander to destruction. To pick up a cue from the psalm, He does this for His own name's sake. As Christ said in a vision to St. Francis de Sales: "I am not the one who condemns; I am called Jesus," the name meaning *God saves*.

But there's more. The prophet Zechariah had mysteriously foretold the suffering of the Messiah: The Shepherd will be struck down, and the sheep will be scattered. Jesus applies that verse to Himself as He enters Jerusalem for the last time. He is the Good Shepherd; and the Good Shepherd lays down His life for the sheep. So we should see, at once, the image of the Shepherd rejoicing, with the lost sheep gently laid upon His shoulders, and the Shepherd suffering, bearing upon those same shoulders the bitter Cross, the sign of love to the end. The two are one. That is what we Christians must mean when we say, "The Lord is my Shepherd."

And that explains a surprising motif in Baker's fourth stanza:

In death's dark vale I fear no ill
With Thee, dear Lord, beside me;
Thy rod and staff my comfort still,
Thy cross before to guide me.

Baker has here interpreted the psalm's "valley of the shadow of death." It is the hollow of sin. It is where the perverse and foolish sheep wanders. But the valley cannot cause terror now, because the Lord abides with us. The *rod and staff* of the psalm look forward to the wood of the Cross—that is the rod and staff that smite the evil one, who prowls about seeking the destruction of souls. The cross is also our guide. We are not only, then, inoffensive and stupid sheep, but fellow walkers with Christ along the dolorous way of life. We share in His sacrifice, not simply by deriving benefit from it, but by suffering for Him in our own persons.

The whole poem, then, is Eucharistic. We can't understand it without thinking of the sacrifice of Jesus, on the cross, in the sacrament, and in the trials of our lives. Yet that love brings life in abundance. Hence the Eucharistic joy of the fifth stanza:

Thou spread'st a table in my sight;
Thy unction grace bestoweth;
And O what transport of delight
From Thy pure chalice floweth!

The *foes* of the psalm are no more. Sin and death have been defeated. The table is spread in the sight of the believing Christian: It is the Lord's Supper. The bread, the oil, and the wine are all bestowers of grace. Baker has picked up another hint from Jerome's version: "The wine of thy cup, how it doth inebriate me!" It is the holy drunkenness of the soul caught up in the love of God. It ravishes us; it sweeps us up in delight. It is the best of wines, the pure wine of the blood of Jesus, the everlasting love of God.

To dwell in the house of the Lord, to drink of that wine at the wedding feast of the Lamb, to have been redeemed by the blood of Christ shed in love upon the cross, and to have been led home by the Good Shepherd, are all one and the same. So the poem concludes:

And so through all the length of days
Thy goodness faileth never:
Good Shepherd, may I sing Thy praise
Within Thy house forever.

The grateful soul can say no more. Baker has been true to the psalm by being true to the Messiah whom the psalm foreshadows. The poem appears simple enough, but that simplicity belies great subtlety and insight, born of a lifetime of meditation upon the word of God and the Christian life. The sweetest melody for it, fittingly enough, is the apparently simple Irish air, *St. Columba*, with its surprising ascending triplet in the second line, and its calm, solemn whole notes at the end, suggesting the endlessness of our praise: *forever*.

Chapter Two

Who Is Jesus?

THE psalms have always been the primary songs of the Church, but even by the time of St. Paul, there must have been many other hymns. Writing to the church at Ephesus, Paul recommends a mirth that far transcends the giddiness brought on by strong drink: "Be not drunk with wine, wherein is excess; but be filled with the Spirit; speaking to yourselves in psalms and hymns and spiritual songs, singing and making melody in your heart to the Lord; giving thanks always for all things unto God and the Father in the name of our Lord Jesus Christ" (Eph 5:18–20).

What were those first hymns like? Some scholars say we have an example in the mighty words wherein Paul describes the humility of Christ:

> *Let this mind be in you, which was also in Christ Jesus:*
>
> *Who, being in the form of God, thought it not robbery to be equal with God:*
>
> *But made himself of no reputation, and took upon him the form of a servant, and was made in the likeness of men:*

> *And being found in fashion as a man, he humbled himself, and became obedient unto death, even the death of the cross.*
>
> *Wherefore God also hath highly exalted him, and given him a name which is above every name:*
>
> *That at the name of Jesus every knee should bow, of things in heaven, and things in earth, and things under the earth;*
>
> *And that every tongue should confess that Jesus Christ is Lord, to the glory of God the Father.* (Phil 2:5–11)

Let's note first what is *not* here. There's no sentimentality. There is not one reference to any person's feelings. There is no glance at the wonderfulness of us, who do God the honor of thinking about Him now and again. This early Christian hymn is a song of theological drama, even cosmic drama, from beginning to end. We do not say that Jesus is the Son of God or that he is a *son* of God because He was a fine moral teacher; as if Jesus depended on public opinion, that reed in the wind. We say that Jesus is the definitive teacher *because He is the Son of God.* All His gifts to us are inestimably precious because of who He is. I may admire George Washington, but let me never visit upon Jesus the indignity of admiration. I worship Him.

Therefore this early hymn teaches us who Jesus is. He is the eternal Son of God; as St. John puts it, the Word, who *was in the beginning with God* (Jn 1:2). There is no difference between the high theology of John and the theology of this hymn that St. Paul likely learned from the first Christians in Antioch and Jerusalem. Only because Jesus is the Son of God is there any surprising exposé, any stunning revelation about God's love, any real *drama* in the incarnation. Paul's verses insist upon that drama. He *made himself of no reputation.* He *took upon him the form of a servant* (recall the suffering servant of Isaiah 53, that mysterious prophecy of the rejected Messiah). There is a descent, lower and lower: *He humbled himself, and became obedient.* God, the Creator—obedient! Not only obedient, as Athena might obey Zeus when it suited her. This is true obedience, true hearing: Jesus is *obedient unto death.* Nor just any death. Jesus embraced a death that the Romans would not inflict upon a citizen, no matter the crime; St. Paul, who enjoyed the privileges of citizenship, was not crucified, but was beheaded outside the walls of Rome. Christ's was a horrible, protracted death by suffocation, made agonizing by the spikes driven through clusters of nerves, and the scourging that cut him to the spine. It was death *upon a cross.*

The cross is the hinge of the hymn. It is the crux of the world, the ineluctable point where sin and grace meet. Jesus Himself says, "If any man will come after me, let him deny himself, and take up his cross, and follow me" (Mt 16:24). For "blessed are ye, when men shall revile you, and persecute you, and shall say all manner of evil against you falsely, for my sake" (Mt 5:11). The cross represents the daring gift of all, not as a soldier who hopes for his country's esteem, but as a slave, the most despised of men—to toss away not only life but the good name for which pagans in all ages have most desperately longed. But the cross means nothing without Christ. Many people suffer persecution, but they alone are blessed who suffer for the God who loves, and is love.

That's why the hymn changes direction, from descent—even *through* descent—to ascent. "He that humbleth himself shall be exalted" (Lk 14:11), says Jesus. But God does not tack the reward on as an afterthought. It is in the nature of humility to rise, by love. Thus we are meant to understand the two movements of the hymn together, as one. Despite being equal to

God, Jesus humbled Himself; and *because* He was equal to God, He humbled Himself. He is exalted above every creature in the cosmos, all of which bend the knee at the *name* of Jesus, which is now revealed to be equal to the holy name of God, the name the Jewish people dared not utter. We now proclaim that *Jesus is Lord*, not teacher, not great statesman, but the source and the meaning and the goal of the world. "I am the way, the truth, and the life," says He (Jn 14:6).

We see the same pattern of descent and ascent in the ninth-century hymn, *Conditor alme siderum, Creator of the Stars of Night*, best sung to the plainsong melody of the same name, *Conditor Alme*, one of the oldest melodies in existence. It is an Advent hymn that spans all of time, from creation to final judgment. Again, Jesus is not reduced to an admirable person. He is the *conditor* of the stars, the God who set them in their place. Therefore He may shine His incomparably greater light upon us:

Creator of the stars of night,
Thy people's everlasting light,
O Christ, Thou Savior of us all,
We pray Thee, hear us when we call.

To Thee the travail deep was known
That made the whole creation groan
Till Thou, Redeemer, shouldest free
Thine own in glorious liberty.

Creation is marred by the fall of man, who lapses into sin and darkness. So the universe groans, says St. Paul, thinking of a woman in travail, awaiting its deliverance "from the bondage of corruption into the glorious liberty of the children of God"

(Rom 8:19–23). But that yearning for deliverance, the poet sees, was already present in the world before Christ came. That is why He did come, in answer:

When the old world drew on toward night,
Thou camest, not in splendor bright
As monarch, but the humble child
Of Mary, blameless mother mild.

The poet wishes us to compare night with night: the original darkness which the Lord studded with stars; and now the aging night of sin, which the Lord penetrates with Himself, the light of the world, born of a humble woman, and laid in a manger, because there was no room for them in the inn. The ultimate self-giving of Calvary is present here in the seed. The shadow of the Cross falls upon the stable.

Therefore the poet can leap from Bethlehem to the hymn of St. Paul:

At Thy great name of Jesus, now
All knees must bend, all hearts must bow;
And things celestial Thee shall own,
And things terrestrial, Lord alone.

The parallelism of the final two lines highlights the central idea of the poem: The Lord, Creator of the stars, has humbled Himself to be born in the midst of our night, upon the earth. He alone is Lord of both. So we pray that He will come again, not as a little child, but as the great Judge of heaven and earth. Now the poet does not merely say that the old world grew dark. The world is in the *power* of darkness; but the day we long for has no sunset:

Come in Thy holy might, we pray;
Redeem us for eternal day
From every power of darkness, when
Thou judgest all the sons of men.

We have reached the ultimate bound of time. Beyond time there is eternity: The life of God. The old hymnodists understood this. We may be tempted to think they appended to their poems a Trinitarian verse—a doxology, a "glory-word," for tradition's sake. That would be a foolish supposition. They knew that the abundant life we seek is God Himself, and He is love, a communion of Persons. No Trinity, no Son of God; no Son of God, no Spirit of love. We would be left, at best, with the cold beauty of a lonely unitarian deity, an impersonal source of all things. Spiritual life would be for those rare mystics who could undertake what the pagan philosopher Plotinus calls "the flight of the alone to the Alone." But there is no aloneness in God:

To God the Father, God the Son,
And God the Spirit, Three in One,
Laud, honor, might, and glory be
From age to age eternally.

That sweet song overleaps Calvary, even as it builds upon it. But many an ancient hymn dwelt with deep veneration upon the Cross, and justly so. "We preach Christ crucified," said St. Paul, "unto the Jews a stumbling block, and unto the Greeks foolishness; but unto them which are called, both Jews and Greeks, Christ the power of God, and the wisdom of God" (1 Cor 1:23–24). We must not sever the participle from the noun; we must not look to a Christ who only *happened* to have been crucified. When Philip asked Jesus to show him the Father, Jesus replied, a touch exasperated by his friend's sluggish understanding, that any man who sees Him sees the Father. Anyone who looks upon the Cross sees what love means, and who Jesus is.

An ancient hymn that dwells upon Calvary, the great *Vexilla regis prodeunt* of Venantius Fortunatus (569), shows us that we understand Jesus and His kingship only by the Cross.

The royal banners forward go,
The cross shines forth in mystic glow;
Where he in flesh, our flesh who made,
Our sentence bore, our ransom paid:

Where deep for us the spear was dyed,
Life's torrent rushing from his side,
To wash us in that precious flood,
Where mingled water flowed, and blood.

Fortunatus has the Holy Week liturgies in mind. They help him interpret the Cross, and his hymn in turn supports and lends musical beauty to the liturgies. When Jesus spoke with the Samaritan woman at the well, as we've seen, He said that He could give her "living water," water that will quench the thirst forever, because it will be a "well of water springing up into everlasting life" (Jn 4:10–14). This living water recalls the water that Moses struck from the rock, to give to the children of Israel in the desert (Ex 17), and the water that Ezekiel saw in his great vision of Israel restored, water flowing from the right side of the Temple (Ez 47:1–2). The early Christians saw the prophecy of Ezekiel fulfilled in Christ: Hence the traditional antiphon *I saw water*, sung during Eastertide.

Several motifs from the New Testament are united here. When Jesus died, "the veil of the temple was rent in twain from the top to the bottom" (Mt 27:51). The Holy of Holies is now laid bare, not for desecration, but for love. For Jesus Himself is our Temple and our High Priest. The water that Ezekiel saw flowing from the right side of the Temple is the water of baptism, mingled with the blood of the Eucharist, which the apostle John saw flowing from the pierced right side of Jesus (Jn 19:34). This is the same water that John saw in the Apocalypse, "a pure river of water of life, clear as crystal, proceeding out of the throne of God and of the Lamb" in the new Jerusalem (Rv 22:1). It is also the blood of the Lamb, wherein the saints have washed their robes and made them white (Rv 7:14).

We could go on and on here, delving into the Letter to the Hebrews, which explains most powerfully the high priesthood of Jesus, and the tearing of the veil. But we have more than enough to consider already. Fortunatus encourages us to see his opening stanzas in relation to one another. An army is known by its banners; think of the Roman legions, with their eagles. The Christian army is known by the Cross. That is the standard of the King—what looks like a symbol of desolation! But those banners *forward go*. They take the world by storm. Consider what Jesus says to Peter: "Upon this rock I will build my church: and the gates of hell shall not prevail against it" (Mt 16:18). That implies a Church on the offensive, battering down those infernal gates, which are, as C. S. Lewis shrewdly notes, locked on the inside, more to keep God out than to keep sinners in. Yet note what happens to the spear. We expect the triumphant general to be wielding the spear against the enemy; but here the spear is wielded against the victor. Christ is victorious in love: The victor is the victim, the sacrifice.

He, not some Roman emperor, is the King who unites all men:

Fulfilled is all that David told
In true prophetic song of old;
Amidst the nations, God, saith he,
Hath reigned and triumphed from the tree.

The "nations," the pagans, rage against the anointed one of God in vain. Fortunatus recalls these words of the psalmist David:

Yet have I set my king upon my holy hill of Zion.
I will declare the decree: the Lord hath said unto me,
Thou art my Son; this day have I begotten thee.
Ask of me, and I shall give thee the heathen for thine inheritance,
and the uttermost parts of the earth for thy possession.
(Ps 2:6–8)

He interprets the psalm in the light of Christ. It is Christ, the Son in whom the Father is well-pleased, who is established in glory upon Mount Zion, now the sacred mountain of Calvary. The word *triumphed* has a special meaning. When a victorious general returned to Rome, the Senate might vote a triumph for him, a victory parade through the city, passing beneath a triumphal arch, with the captives and the plunder in tow. But Christ triumphs *from the tree*, needing no arch, and no other throne but the Cross.

Christ accomplishes His victory by bearing the weight of sinful man upon the Cross:

O Tree of beauty, Tree of light!
O Tree with royal purple dight!
Elect on whose triumphal breast
Those holy limbs should find their rest:

On whose dear arms, so widely flung,
The weight of this world's ransom hung:
The price of humankind to pay,
And spoil the spoiler of his prey.

Fortunatus imagines the Cross as a royal resting place, clothed with the majestic purple of the blood of Christ. John reclined upon the breast of Jesus at the Last Supper, but Jesus reclines here upon the triumphal breast of the Cross. It is the horrible instrument of His execution, and yet a couch, to repose the arms that bore so heavy a burden. There's more. A Roman soldier who slew the enemy general in battle was awarded the *spolia optima*, the "Best of Spoils"—literally, the armor and robes off the back of the dead man. Jesus, stripped of His garments, spoils the spoiler. He seizes from the devil what the devil had seized, the devil who like a roaring lion "walketh about, seeking whom he may devour" (1 Pt 5:8). We are that prey, saved by Christ from the maw of the enemy.

Therefore the Cross is a place of repose for us too. We can *rely* upon it—we can lean upon it in our weakness:

O Cross, our one reliance, hail!
So may thy power with us avail
To give new virtue to the saint,
And pardon to the penitent.

We recall the penitent thief, crucified at the side of Jesus, who said, "Lord, remember me when thou comest into thy kingdom" (Lk 23:42). Saints derive strength from the Cross, but the rest of us can echo the words of the thief, and plead for pardon. The final stanza binds the image of the Cross to the action of the Trinity in our lives. We may have more moments left to us than did the thief. So we pray for guidance; we pray that the King will reign in our hearts:

To Thee, eternal Three in One,
Let homage most by all be done;
Whom by the Cross thou dost restore,
Preserve and govern evermore.

These are petitions for our lives. But worship never ends; for worship is love. That's why the ultimate aim of the vision of St. John in the Apocalypse is not to tell of the trials we will suffer on earth in the last days, but to reveal the glory beyond the last days. That glory is expressed, again and again, in praise of who Christ is: "Worthy is the Lamb that was slain to receive power, and riches, and wisdom, and strength, and honor, and glory, and blessing" (Rv 5:12). He is "Alpha and Omega, the beginning and the ending, which is, and which was, and which is to come, the Almighty" (Rv 1:8). "Before Abraham was," said Jesus, referring to Himself the holy name of God, "I AM" (Jn 8:58).

It's natural for human beings to consider that a name reveals something essential about the bearer. That's why Moses asked God for a name, if the Israelites should ask which God was sending him to them. The name of Jesus, the Hebrew *Yeshua*, means *God saves*. That denotes more than what God does: It shows who God is and who Jesus is. Thence arises the venerable tradition of meditating upon the name of Jesus, in prayer and song. My favorite among such hymns is Caroline Noel's *At the Name of Jesus*. The brilliant and theologically sensitive composer of sacred music, Ralph Vaughan Williams, wrote a minor-key melody called *King's Weston* for this hymn, to bring out its power, especially in the climactic final lines of every stanza. Vaughan Williams understood, with his musical imagination, a principle of poetry that the inexperienced may miss. We suppose that a line with ten syllables will feel slower than a line with three or four syllables. It isn't so, and poets know this. The poet and the composer understand that we tend to read and hear lines as occupying about the same duration, so that we speed up to read a long line and slow down to read a short line; and the slowing down will be especially pronounced if the short line follows a long line, or *ends the stanza.*

Now then, Noel's stanzas consist of alternating lines of six and five syllables—all short lines, but with the shortest lines carrying the rhymes. To stress those five-syllable lines, Vaughan Williams ends all of them boldly—with a dotted whole note, held for a lung-pressing count of *six* beats—and to make sure we will have the last words of the stanza ringing in our minds, he precedes that long note with two others, a whole note and a half note. In transcribing the poem, I'll mark in boldface all words sung with at least one whole note, so that the reader may *see* the musical "rhyming" along with the poetic rhyming. The first stanza echoes the passage from Philippians, which we have already considered:

At the name of ***Jesus***
Every knee shall ***bow,***
Every tongue confess Him
King of glory ***now;***
'Tis the Father's pleasure
We should call Him ***Lord,***
Who from the beginning
Was the ***mighty Word****.*

"Who is this King of glory?" asks the Psalmist. "The Lord strong and mighty, the Lord mighty in battle" (Ps 24:8). Noel has combined this verse with the hymn from Philippians and the astounding revelation that begins the gospel of John: "In the beginning was the Word, and the Word was with God, and the Word was God" (Jn 1:1). Notice that the name *Jesus* and the title *mighty Word* bracket the stanza: The two are one. That means that the adverb *now*, which ends the first half of the stanza, isn't just tossed in to provide a rhyme with *bow*. Good poets don't search for rhymes; they have them already, and use them for many purposes. Here the *now* of our time is placed in the context of the existence of the Word *from the beginning*.

So in the next stanza—unfortunately omitted from most hymnals—Noel takes us back to the beginning:

> *At His voice* ***creation***
> *Sprang at once to* ***sight****,*
> *All the Angel faces,*
> *All the hosts of* ***light****,*
> *Thrones and dominations,*
> *Stars upon their* ***way****,*
> *All the heavenly orders*
> *In their* ***great array****.*

Christ is the Word of God through whom all things were made (Jn 1:3): "By the word of the Lord were the heavens made; and all the host of them by the breath of his mouth" (Ps 33:6). Noel recalls the mighty words of St. Paul, who expresses in no uncertain terms the divinity of Jesus:

> *For by him were all things created, that are in heaven, and that are in earth, visible and invisible, whether they*

be thrones, or dominions, or principalities, or powers: all things were created by him, and for him:

And he is before all things, and by him all things consist.

And he is the head of the body, the church: who is the beginning, the firstborn from the dead; that in all things he might have the preeminence.

For it pleased the Father that in him should all fullness dwell. (Col 1:16–19)

Notice the "bracket" for this stanza: ***creation*** and ***great array***. All is in order, all under the governance of the providential Lord.

The next two stanzas declare the humility of God the Son, the Word, who humbled Himself that He might be named by sinners as their Savior:

Humbled for a ***season****,*
To receive a ***name***
From the lips of sinners
Unto whom He ***came****,*
Faithfully He bore it
Spotless to the ***last****,*
Brought it back victorious
When from death ***He passed****:*

Bore it up ***triumphant***
With its human ***light****,*
Through all ranks of creatures,
To the central ***height****,*
To the throne of Godhead,
To the Father's ***breast****;*
Filled it with the glory
Of that ***perfect rest****.*

The whole life and death and resurrection of Jesus is compressed into one continued image, that of carrying a name—again, the name *God saves*. The irony is that He had a name already, the name of God: He was and is the Word of God. But now He humbles Himself to receive a name *from the lips of sinners*, from us, who are unworthy to name Him! Yet Jesus takes that sinner-bestowed name and bears it, as He bore our infirmities, as He bore the Cross, without sin, without spot. He passes through death with that name unstained, and bears it up in triumph through all those *ranks of creatures* that He Himself created in the beginning, all the way to the breast of the Father. Notice again the bracketing words: Christ is *triumphant*—as a conquering hero returning to the city in parade—and enjoys the *perfect rest* of God.

Then Noel turns toward us. It's a turn we will see again and again in the old hymns. Once the poet has meditated upon who God is, or upon what God has done, the lesson will be applied to us, in our troubled lives now. The stanzas are cast in the form of exhortation and command:

Name Him, brothers, ***name Him,***
With love strong as ***death,***
But with awe and wonder,
And with bated ***breath;***
He is God the Savior,
He is Christ the ***Lord,***
Ever to be worshipped,
Trusted, ***and adored.***

In your hearts ***enthrone Him;***
There let Him ***subdue***
All that is not holy,
All that is not ***true:***

Crown Him as your captain
In temptation's ***hour;***
Let His will enfold you
In its ***light and power.***

It's unfortunate that the first of those stanzas doesn't appear in every hymnal. Consider the profound prayer it enjoins on us—the urgency of the repeated command underscores it. We are to *name Him*:—with a catch in our breath, with wonder and reverential fear. The very Name of Jesus is a prayer. We are to dwell upon it because of what He has done for us, but more because of who He is. Vaughan Williams' music drives the point home. To *name Him* is to *adore Him*. It is to *enthrone Him* in our hearts, that He might cleanse them and make of them a worthy dwelling place. It is to call upon Him in our need, *in temptation's hour*. It is to derive our will from *His will*. We enthrone Him, yes, but when we do so, we are the ones who are enfolded, in the *light and power* He sheds upon us.

The final stanza takes us to the end of time, and the second coming of Jesus:

Brothers, this ***Lord Jesus***
Shall return ***again,***
With His Father's glory,
With His angel ***train;***
For all wreaths of empire
Meet upon His ***brow,***
And our hearts confess Him
King of ***glory now.***

Tremendous, this poetry. Noel ends the poem by repeating lines from the first stanza, but here in the context of eternity. Every power in heaven and on earth is subject to Christ, and when He comes again it will not be as a humble child, but as the King of Glory. *All wreaths of empire meet upon His brow*. And what do we do? We, dwelling in time, bestow on Him the name that is His from eternity. We confess Him *King of Glory*. When do we do this? *Now*: now and forevermore.

Who is Jesus? The Word of God who was made flesh and dwelt among us; but also, as Catholics and Orthodox believe, the Word who gives Himself again in the sacrament of the altar, not in symbols only but in the flesh. I'll devote a separate chapter to Eucharistic hymns, but here we'd do well to examine a hymn that combines the motifs of Christ as God, Christ as the child born of Mary, and Christ as the gift of the Eucharist. It is *Let All Mortal Flesh Keep Silence*, from the liturgy of St. James, paraphrased and set in verse by Gerard Moultrie (1864). The melody by which it is best known, the French *Picardy*, highlights the meaning and the form of the stanzas in a most remarkable way, as we'll see.

The first stanza is deliberately ambiguous. It refers at once to Christ's becoming incarnate, and to His descent to dwell within the sacrament:

Let all mortal flesh keep silence,
and with fear and trembling stand;
Ponder nothing earthly-minded,
for with blessing in His hand
Christ our God to earth descendeth,
our full homage to demand.

Notice the present tense. He descends *now*. He dwells among us *now*. He comes both to bless us and to demand *our full homage*. The phrase *mortal flesh* is not just a fancy synonym for *man*.

Our flesh is mortal. His flesh is immortal; He in His risen body sits at the right hand of the Father. It is the risen Christ now who comes to meet us.

Each stanza comprises a rhyming triplet, a form that lends itself well to progression and climax. Consider this stanza from "The Sacrifice" by George Herbert. The speaker is Jesus, echoing the words of Jeremiah's lamentation over Jerusalem:

O all ye who pass by, behold and see:
Man stole the fruit, but I must climb the tree;
The tree of life to all, but only me:
    Was ever grief like mine?

Imagine the stanza without the triplet—without the third rhyming line. It would still make good sense. But it would no longer deliver the terrible shock. It isn't that the Tree of Life in the garden has become the Cross. It's that the Cross is the Tree of Life for every man and woman who ever lived, *except* for Jesus, the innocent.

So the melody, *Picardy*, takes advantage of the opportunity that the triplet presents. The melody of the first element (lines one and two) is repeated for the second element (lines three and four), although with a nice change in harmony from a minor to a major chord. What's quite different is the melody for the third element. It takes an additional measure, a whole four-note run on the second-last syllable of the fifth line. That's why I have printed the line with a space to separate the last word: The melody sets that word apart. Then the melody of the sixth line repeats the melody of the first part of the fifth line, before final resolution on the tonic note. That sets off the final pair—the change in the music. (I will mark the musical phrases with letters below, and an asterisk for a variation. So an A line has exactly the same melody as another A, and an A* echoes the melody of an A, but with some change.) But even though the melody has changed, the *rhymes* link all three elements together. Why do we keep silence, and stand with fear and trembling? The final pair relates the wonder: Christ is descending *now*:

A
Let all mortal flesh keep silence,

B
And in fear and trembling stand;

A
Ponder nothing earthly minded,

B
For with blessing in His hand,

C
Christ our God to earth descendeth,

C*
Our full homage to demand.

The second stanza describes from our earthly vantage the character of His descent, and links it with His birth in Bethlehem:

King of kings, yet born of Mary,
as of old on earth He stood,
Lord of lords in human vesture,
in the Body and the Blood

He will give to all the faithful
His own self for heavenly food.

Notice the nice progression. *King of kings* in the first element is echoed by *Lord of lords* in the second: "Keep this commandment without spot, unrebukeable, until the appearing of our Lord Jesus Christ: which in his times he shall shew, who is the blessed and only Potentate, the King of kings, and Lord of lords" (1 Tm 6:14–15). Paul is referring to the coming of Christ in His full glory; not as the little child in the manger. That consummate appearance is anticipated in the sacrament: So we move from *King of kings* and *Lord of lords* to *His own self*, given in Holy Communion. Again the poet echoes scripture: "I am that living bread which came down from heaven" (Jn 6:51).

The third stanza describes the descent but from the vantage of heaven, reminding us that the angels, too, are present as ministers of Christ's precious gift of Himself:

Rank on rank the host of heaven
spreads its vanguard on the way,
As the Light of Light descendeth
from the realms of endless day,
That the powers of hell may vanish
as the darkness clears away.

Christ, as the Nicene Creed affirms, is God of God and Light of Light: "I am the light of the world," said Jesus (Jn 8:12). Christ's coming into the world as a child was the dawning of a new sun: "The people that walked in darkness have seen a great light: they that dwell in the land of the shadow of death, upon them hath the light shined" (Is 9:2). Christ has called us "out of darkness into his marvelous light" (1 Pt 2:9). His light can never be quenched. It does not just drive out the powers of Hell. It makes them *vanish*. They are nothing. They are a night dispelled by the Lord who brings along with Him the *realms of endless day*: "And the city had no need of the sun, neither of the moon, to shine in it: for the glory of God did lighten it, and the Lamb is the light thereof" (Rv 21:23).

The last stanza is located in heaven alone, and we join our voices to those of the angels:

At His feet the six-winged seraph;
cherubim with sleepless eye,
Veil their faces to the Presence,
as with ceaseless voice they cry,
"Alleluia, Alle luia,
Alleluia, Lord most high!"

Here we recall the vision of Isaiah:

> *I saw the Lord sitting upon a throne, high and lifted up, and his train filled the temple. Above it stood the seraphims: each one had six wings; with twain he covered his face, and with twain he covered his feet, and with twain he did fly. And one cried unto another, and said, Holy, holy, holy, is the Lord of hosts: the whole earth is full of his glory*. (Is 6:2–3)

The poet has echoed *sleepless* with *ceaseless*, conveying the full-hearted constancy of true worship. That vigor, that joy cannot be held back. It bursts the divide of the last two lines, so to speak—the three alleluias spill from one line to the next, three, for the thrice-holy God. The angels *veil their faces to the Presence*, their gesture of honor before the unfathomable light of God, returning us to our own *fear and trembling* before the Sacrament.

"Who do men say that I am?" Jesus asked the apostles, and then He asked the question that He still asks all of us. You, what about you? Who do *you* say that I am? He's not asking for our opinions. He is asking for our faith. Simon Peter replies, "Thou art the Christ, the Son of the living God" (Mt 16:13–16).

Many of our contemporary praise'n'worship songs sidle past the question. But that is to betray Jesus all over again. The disciples did not say, "My goodness, what a wise rabbi he is! Let's worship him as a god." The Jewish tradition was full of wise rabbis. The disciples knew that. They also prayed, every day, the definitive prayer of the Jewish faith, the *sh'ma Yisroel*: "Hear, O Israel: The Lord our God is one Lord: and thou shalt love the Lord thy God with all thine heart, and with all thy soul, and with all thy strength" (Dt 6:4–5). Jesus Himself cites that prayer as the first of God's commandments. The scribe with whom He is speaking agrees, saying, "Well, Master, thou hast said the truth: for there is one God; and there is none other but he" (Mk 12:29–34). Imagine a confirmed vegetarian whose civilized disciples, after his death, take solemnly to cannibalism. That's as absurd as the suggestion that these Jewish disciples made Jesus into a divinity because they were impressed with His teachings on the Jewish faith. No, it's the reverse. Because they had experienced the risen Christ, because they were convinced by that stupendous (and utterly unexpected) victory that He was the Lord, they remembered how often He said that He and the Father are one—and they remembered all that He said about how we ought to live on earth. They then took it not as prophecy, not at second-hand, but as coming from God, who alone possesses authority, in Himself, to declare the truth.

Who is Jesus? The mightiest of our hymns that answer this question do not touch upon a single passage here or there from Scripture, but are poetic interpretations of the whole of the message: Everything in Scripture leads us ultimately to Jesus. With this in mind, consider Matthew Bridges' well-known *Crown Him with Many Crowns*:

Crown Him with many crowns,
The Lamb upon His throne,
Hark! how the heavenly anthem drowns
All music but its own:
Awake, my soul, and sing
Of Him who died for thee,
And hail Him as thy matchless King
Through all eternity.

The poem employs a variation on our old friend, the 4–3–4–3 ballad meter, four strong beats in eight syllables, followed by three strong beats in six syllables. But the meter for this poem is called "Short," because the first line of the four has only three strong beats, like the second and fourth lines. And since each stanza is made up of two of these 3–3–4–3 groups, it is called Double Short Meter (hence marked in the old hymnals as D.S.M.). This doubling allows the poet to change the emphasis or the point of view, so that the last four lines may apply the lesson of the first four lines in an unexpected way. This first stanza begins with the end, so to speak—*the Lamb upon His throne*, in the eternal City of God. The music accompanying the crowning of the Lord drowns out all other music—or rather all true music is summed up in it. So in the "turn" of the stanza, Bridges calls on his own soul to wake, to sing with that heavenly anthem. But since Bridges is a man redeemed by Christ, not an angel who had no need of redemption, his "version" of the anthem is to sing *of Him who died for thee*. Christ is the King: But, says Bridges to his soul, He is *thy matchless King*, with the personal pronoun repeated. He is my King in a special and poignant way: He is *my* King, who died for *me*.

The second stanza gives us again this double vision, of Christ as God on high, and of Christ who dwelt among us, so that we might dwell with Him in eternity:

Crown Him the Son of God
Before the worlds began,
And ye, who tread where He hath trod,
Crown Him the Son of man;
Who every grief hath known
That wrings the human breast,
And takes and bears them for His own,
That all in Him may rest.

What a shame it is that this moving and beautiful stanza is omitted in many hymnals because of a foolish and unscriptural desire to avoid the general word *man*, as if *Son of man* were something embarrassing scribbled on a wall, and not a title that Jesus applied to Himself! But let us again consider the poetry. Christ is crowned Son of God not because of something He did to earn the title, but because that's who He is, *before the worlds began*. He came to dwell among sinners, and so, Bridges says, all who walk the ways of suffering upon earth must now crown him *Son of man*. The fourth line is thus exactly parallel with the first—a deft touch.

But why is it important that Christ is also the *Son of man?* The final four lines explain. He has assumed our humanity, meaning that He knows our suffering. He was like us in all things but sin.

There is not one sorrow that He did not know. But He did not reject those sorrows; not He, the man of sorrows Himself! He takes them. He carries them. He claims them as His own, so that we who suffer may find our rest in Him and with Him.

The third stanza specifies the grief: Jesus suffered death, to redeem sinners from the grave. Notice in the third stanza the fine interplay of the images of death and life, reflecting in poetic form the victory the words describe:

Crown Him the Lord of life,
Who triumphed o'er the grave,
And rose victorious in the strife
For those He came to save;
His glories now we sing
Who died, and rose on high,
Who died, eternal life to bring,
And lives that death may die.

Bridges is thinking of the triumphant cry of St. Paul: "O death, where is thy sting? O grave, where is thy victory?" (1 Cor 15:55). He is the Lord of life—and He died! He died—Bridges repeats the phrase, lest we forget. He died to bring life, and that in abundance. He lives, and in His lordship, He puts death to death. Darkness is thrust through with its own sword.

Now Bridges moves from the death and resurrection of Christ to His dwelling place in heaven, as God before time and in time and after time:

Crown Him of lords the Lord,
Who over all doth reign,
Who once on earth, the incarnate Word,
For ransomed sinners slain,

Now lives in realms of light,
Where saints with angels sing
Their songs before Him day and night,
Their God, Redeemer, King.

The two halves of this stanza are bound closely together—the stanza is one continuous sentence, the last six lines depending upon the pronoun *who*. On earth, *once*, He was slain, but *now* He dwells beyond decay and death. There the angels and the saints sing forever, and the stanza ends with the emphatic one-syllable word that sums up the imagery of the whole poem: *King*. For who is to be crowned, if not a king?

Bridges seems well aware that repetition was dear to the Hebrew poets, and no music can sound coherent without it. So he has bound his first four stanzas together by beginning them with the same words: *Crown Him*. Now, in the final stanza, he wants to bind the whole poem together. It stands to reason he will begin this stanza as he began the others. But he does much more. Every other line in the stanza repeats the motif: *Crown Him*:

Crown Him the Lord of heaven,
Enthroned in words above;
Crown Him the King, to whom is given
The wondrous name of Love.
Crown Him with many crowns,
As thrones before Him fall,
Crown Him, ye kings, with many crowns,
For He is King of all.

In the second half of the stanza, Bridges dares to repeat the first line of the poem, not once, but twice—and with a slight variation. It's one thing to repeat a line to the same melody. It's another and more startling thing to repeat it to a *different part* of that melody—here, *two different parts.* Here, when we sing *Crown Him with many crowns* (in the melody *Diademata,* written for the poem), it's as if we are striving ever upward in our praise: *Crowns* is the high note in the line; *fall,* in the next line, is a full tone higher than that; and *Him,* in the line after that, is higher still; all three notes are stressed by being held longer than the notes before them. What is there left to say? All the kings of the world are summoned, not to be crowned, but to crown Him who is King of Kings and Lord of Lords: *For He is King of all.*

Chapter Three

Who Is Christ?

JESUS is the Christ, the Anointed One, the only begotten Son of the Father. We've considered hymns that spring from this glorious and central truth of the Christian faith. Now I'd like to look at it from the other side of the identity. If we wish to know who the Messiah is, we must look to Jesus, in His divinity and His humanity. It's one thing to say that Jesus is our only Savior; another, to say that our Savior is and only could be none other than Jesus.

The poets, then, will regard moments in the life of Jesus, not as biographers regard an interesting period in the life of an inventor or a politician, but as believers, as theologians, dwelling upon what such moments reveal to us about God. The human face of Jesus reveals the face of God; the life of Jesus reveals the pattern of our salvation, through Him and in Him. The poets will not reduce Jesus to a social worker or revolutionary, one who, according to one dreadful contemporary hymn (*Who Is This Who Breaches Borders*), "subverts the social orders." They will not reduce Jesus to a chum, or to somebody preaching the current popular "wisdom," a guru whose fame is like the light of a firefly. He is our Savior, and our Savior is none but He. Most especially, the poets will not let us turn from His act of deepest love for us, on Calvary.

In this light, let's look at Jesus' fast in the desert, through the eyes of an unknown Latin poet of the sixth century, whose poem in translation we know as the Lenten hymn *The Glory of These Forty Days* (sung to the solemn minor-key melody *Spires*, also known as *Erhalt Uns, Herr*, harmonized with chaste simplicity by Johann Sebastian Bach):

The glory of these forty days
We celebrate with songs of praise;
For Christ, by Whom all things were made,
Himself has fasted and has prayed.

The poetry is so straightforward that we might miss the artistry. Notice the word *glory*. That should surprise us. When Jesus went forth into the desert, what glory accompanied Him? No train of disciples, no fanfare, no parade, no earthquake. The *glory*, then, must subsist in the very absence of the manifestations of glory. It subsists in loving humility—a glory the world misses.

Thus we can understand the first part of the stanza only in the context of the last part. This is what's glorious: Christ, by Whom the world was brought into being (cf. Jn 1:3), *Himself has fasted and has prayed*. He Himself has done so. The pronoun is emphatic. The richness of the world's being—*all things*—is placed in contrast with Jesus' depriving Himself of food, and His attitude of complete openness, complete self-emptying, in prayer before the Father.

The example for us is obvious, but first the poet reminds us that prophets before Jesus did the same:

Alone and fasting Moses saw
The loving God who gave the law;
And to Elijah, fasting, came
The steeds and chariots of flame.

That is really a magnificent stanza. The participle *fasting*, picked up from the verb in the first stanza, is repeated, once before the proper name and once after it: *Fasting Moses* and *Elijah, fasting*. These two, the greatest prophets of the Old Testament, appeared beside Jesus on the Mount of Transfiguration. They indicate Jesus as the giver of the New Law and the establisher of the New Israel. But they were inspired in the midst of fasting: Moses on Mount Sinai, Elijah on Mount Horeb. Each man felt the hand of God. Moses received the tablets of the law, and Elijah was taken from the earth by a "chariot of fire" (2 Kgs 2:11).

The poet then turns to Daniel, who spoke of the coming of the Son of Man, and to John the Baptist, the great forerunner:

So Daniel trained his mystic sight,
Delivered from the lions' might;
And John, the Bridegroom's friend, became
The herald of Messiah's name.

Daniel refused the rich (and, for Jews, unclean) food provided by King Nebuchadnezzar of Babylon, and instead asked only for water and a gruel of lentils (Dn 1:12), and therefore, the poet suggests, the Lord granted him *mystic sight*. John went into the desert to preach the coming of the Kingdom of God, "and he did eat locusts and wild honey" (Mk 1:6).

Now the poet applies the lesson to us, who long to be with our Savior. Then we must join Him in the desert:

Then grant us, Lord, like them to be
Full oft in fast and prayer with Thee;
Our spirits strengthen with Thy grace,
And give us joy to see Thy face.

Who is our Savior? There He is, Jesus, entering the wilderness to fast and pray. Do we want to see His face? Then we must go where He has gone before. We cannot do so by our own strength, so we pray for the grace of Christ to give us the heart to endure the fast and prayer. Then we will not simply sweat it out. We'll have, in the very desert, the *joy* of seeing the face of God, in the face of Jesus. The poem ends by praising the Trinity to whom we pray:

O Father, Son, and Spirit blest,
To Thee be every prayer addrest,
Who art in threefold Name adored,
From age to age, the only Lord.

Who is our Savior? There He is, in the Garden of Gethsemane, suffering in anticipation the anguish of bearing upon His shoulders the sins of the world. The pagan Celsus, writing against Christianity in the third century, scoffed. What kind of hero can this man be? Where's the steely contempt for suffering that a good stoic would show?

Well, stoic silence in the face of evil is not triumph but resignation and despair. It is a firm refusal to embrace suffering. The sage Epictetus tells us what should be on the good stoic's lips if someone should cry, "Your son is dead!" "And when did I ever say he was immortal?" comes the response. But when Jesus heard Mary and Martha say, "Lord, if you had been here our brother would not have died," He was struck to the heart. St. John gives us the shortest verse in all of Scripture: "Jesus wept."

So, rather than imitate the drowsiness of Peter, James, and John, let us accompany Jesus to the garden and keep watch with Him there. He, in His humanity, will teach us to be truly human. Here is the scene as presented by James Montgomery (1825), in *Go to Dark Gethsemane*:

Go to dark Gethsemane,
Ye that feel the tempter's power;
Your Redeemer's conflict see,
Watch with Him one bitter hour;
Turn not from His griefs away,
Learn of Jesus Christ to pray.

The verse is simplicity itself—but it is *not* simplistic. Who is our Savior? He is the One who took our poor humanity to Himself. "For we have not an high priest which cannot be touched with the feeling of our infirmities," writes the apostle, "but was in all points tempted like as we are, yet without sin" (Heb 4:15). That is a statement of astounding depth. It isn't that Christ showed us up, to gloat. He, unlike the proud stoic, is *touched with the feeling* of our weaknesses. If we are tempted, He does not shake His head. He too was tempted. He too engaged the evil one in conflict. Then we watch with Him. That's not because we wish to lend Him moral support, out of the goodness of our hearts, but because we wish to unite ourselves with Him and learn from Him. Do we suffer? Our Savior suffered. He, maker of all things, fell to His knees and prayed, teaching us to do the same when trials come.

Then the poem walks with Christ to His condemnation:

Follow to the judgment hall;
View the Lord of life arraigned;
O the wormwood and the gall!
O the pangs His soul sustained!
Shun not suffering, shame, or loss;
Learn of Him to bear the cross.

The terrible irony, that the Lord of life should submit to the judgment of sinful man and be arraigned in a corrupt court on a charge motivated by political tactics and hatred, causes the poet to suspend his series of imperative verbs, for the two parallel exclamations. "They gave me also gall for my meat," sang the psalmist, "and in my thirst they gave me vinegar to drink" (Ps 69:21). The *wormwood and the gall* are the hyssop that someone beneath the Cross soaked a sponge with, when Jesus cried, "I thirst" (Jn 19:28). But we have not yet come to Calvary. The poet has concentrated the bitterness of that gall in the shame that Christ suffered *before* He was nailed to the Cross. He does so to bring the point home, in all its implications. The first stanza ended with the commands *turn not away* and *learn*; this stanza likewise ends with the commands *shun not* and *learn*. Our Savior is He who did not shun suffering, shame, or loss. Nor should we, for He Himself has said, "Blessed are ye, when men shall revile you, and persecute you, and shall say all manner of evil against you falsely, for my sake" (Mt 5:11).

But the third and final stanza, continuing the pattern of imperatives, turns suddenly from sorrow to wonder:

Calvary's mournful mountain climb;
There, adoring at His feet,
Mark the miracle of time,
God's own sacrifice complete;

"It is finished!" hear Him cry;
Learn of Jesus Christ to die.

Notice the nice play of alliteration—which a good poet uses carefully, to join words and ideas that otherwise might remain separate. We climb the *mournful mountain* of Calvary, but not to mourn! Rather to fall to our knees in adoration, to *mark the miracle* of time—the miracle of love that flings wide the gates of eternity. The *miracle* is inseparable from the mourning, and the *mountain* becomes at once a peak of desolation and the summit of triumphant love. For here is *God's own sacrifice complete.*

Let's take a closer look at that line. The grammar is ambiguous. If we say "my sacrifice," we mean either "that which I sacrifice" or "the sacrifice of me." So it is here too. The sacrifice is established by God—it is His; but God Himself *is the sacrifice.* He is God and priest and sacrifice, all at once. It is *complete,* meaning that it has reached its fullness, its perfection. *Consummatum est,* says Jesus, in Jerome's Latin translation: It has been fulfilled, it has reached its summation. Here Montgomery does not advise us against turning away or shunning. We are to *hear* and, again, to *learn.* That dying man is the Lord. He passed through the strait we fear most. He died in complete surrender to the Father.

At the end of the medieval poem *Sir Gawain and the Green Knight,* the good Sir Gawain approaches the Green Chapel where he is certain he must die. It's New Year's Day, the snow lies deep, and a grindstone hums nearby. As far as Sir Gawain knows, it's sharpening the ax that will shear off his head. "I'll be with you right away," calls the demonic Green Knight from behind the chapel. Exactly one year ago, that same Green Knight had ridden into King Arthur's court, with his green flesh and his green horse and his enormous ax. He had challenged the knights to a game. He'd take one swipe of the ax on his neck, on condition that the knight who gave it to him would take one just like it in turn, on the next New Year's Day, at the mysterious Green Chapel. But when Gawain chopped the man's head off and it rolled among the feet of the knights and the ladies at their tables, the Green Knight didn't collapse. He stood straight up, found the head, held it aloft, opened his eyes, and said—I am paraphrasing—"Gawain, I'll see you next year!" So Gawain expects to die. The Green Chapel, too, is a place of foreboding. There are things missing from it. There is no Cross.

I have been to a church without a cross. It was converted from an old factory. The large windowless inner room where services were held boasted electronic equipment for music and videos and preaching, but no cross. I felt, there, a little like Gawain. Or like Sir Bors in *The Quest of the Holy Grail*, who follows a demon disguised as a hermit into his hermitage and looks about and sees no cross on the walls. I'm not suggesting anything personal here about the preacher or the congregation. I am suggesting that there is something *wrong*, in the old sense of being crooked, off-kilter, bent, about a chapel without a Cross. It cannot lead to good.

Quite different is the wisdom of a remarkable hymn by an otherwise unknown poet named Edward Monro: *The Story of the Cross* (1864). The *English Hymnal* (1933) divides it into five parts. The first is "The Question":

See Him in raiment rent,
With His blood dyed:
Women walk sorrowing
By His side.

Heavy that Cross to Him,
Weary the weight:
One who will help Him stands
At the gate.

Multitudes hurrying
Pass on the road:
Simon is sharing with
Him the load.

Who is this travelling
With the curst tree—
This weary prisoner—
Who is He?

The lines could hardly be more tersely concentrated. The meter accentuates the terseness and provides, at the end of each stanza, a moment of extraordinary power and pathos. For the last line doesn't simply complete the third line. They can't be printed as one, because the last line is, so to speak, "missing" its first syllable. It's a mere three-syllable line, beginning on a strong beat, set apart from the meter of the rest of the stanza. The women are walking in sorrow, where? *By His side*. Who is this weary prisoner? *Who is He?* That is the question of Christianity, right there.

The 1933 Hymnal uses a hauntingly tender melody for parts one, two, and five of the poem. *Bridgwater* is a traditional English air with exactly the right structure for the poem. Played through once, the melody will cover two of Monro's stanzas, but that works well, since each half of the melody ends on the same three notes—two half notes and a whole note, stressing the three syllables as strongly as music can. In fact, it is one note for one syllable throughout; simplicity itself. But the simplicity belies an intricate and subtle structure. Let me illustrate, again, by labeling each line of music with a letter, and asterisks to note a variation:

A	B	A*	C
See Him in raiment rent,	*With His blood dyed:*	*Women walk sorrowing*	*By His side.*

A**	B*	A*	C
Heavy that Cross to Him,	*Weary the weight:*	*One who will help Him stands*	*At the gate.*

We see here that the music not only reflects the pattern of the stanza, but links one stanza to the next with its two variations, followed by an exact return to the final two lines of the first. It's as if one stanza was in conversation with the other—just as the poem intends.

The second part of the poem is aptly called "The Answer":

Follow to Calvary,
Tread where He trod;
This is the Lord of life—
Son of God.

Is there no loveliness—
You who pass by—

In that lone Figure which
Marks the sky?

You who would love Him, stand,
Gaze at His face;
Tarry awhile in your
Worldly race.

As the swift moments fly
Through the blest week,
Jesus, in penitence,
Let us seek.

This is poetry worthy of Emily Dickinson; spare, laconic, immensely suggestive. The pronoun *this*, from "The Question," is now supplied in "The Answer." If you want to know who *this weary prisoner* is, you must follow in His steps, up the bitter mountain. Then you will learn what seems impossible to the world. This weary prisoner, this man, battered and despised, is the Lord of life—*Son of God*, as the centurion who beheld His death professed (Mk 15:39). How powerful is the break in the sentence, and the omission of the definite article! The reply comes with a clutch in the throat—we are to see the essential sonship of Jesus, as He suffers. This is what it means to be *Son of God*.

The next stanza concentrates in four short lines two most powerful allusions to Scripture and to the traditional liturgy of Good Friday. Isaiah says thus of the Suffering Servant: "He hath no form or comeliness; and when we shall see him, there is no beauty that we should desire him" (Is 53:2). That shouldn't surprise us. Spiritual beauty, as Francois Mauriac wrote, is like that. It will attract one man irresistibly, while others don't notice it at all or are repelled by it; as to some people the deeply human countenance of the aged Mother Teresa was only withered and ugly. The poet begs us to find the beauty of Jesus and not simply to pass Him by. That alludes to the Lamentations of Jeremiah, after the destruction of Jerusalem by the Babylonians, a text that foretells the suffering of the Messiah: "It is nothing to you, all ye who pass by? behold, and see if there be any sorrow like unto my sorrow" (Lam 1:12). Why are the people simply passing by? The *worldly race* preoccupies them. Here Monro has in mind another verse from George Herbert's "The Sacrifice":

O all ye who pass by, whose eyes and mind
To worldly things are sharp, but to me blind,
To me, that took eyes that I might you find:
Was ever grief like mine?

The world races to its dissolution, and people race to attain things that perish, "for what hath man of all his labor?" (Eccl 2:22). Our days fly "swifter than a weaver's shuttle" (Jb 7:6). Therefore, in this *blest week* at least, we should leave that race, and tarry awhile, to gaze upon the countenance of Jesus, seeking Him out in penitence and finding in Him our salvation.

In the third part of the poem, we address the Lord personally:

On the Cross lifted up,
Thy face I scan,
Scarred by that agony—
Son of Man.

Thorns form Thy diadem,
Rough wood Thy throne,

To Thee Thy outstretched arms
Draw Thine own.

Nails hold Thy hands and feet,
While on Thy breast
Sinketh Thy bleeding head
Sore opprest.

Loud is Thy bitter cry,
Rending the night,
As to Thy darkened eyes
Fails the light.

Shadows of midnight fall,
Though it is day;
Friends and disciples stand
Far away.

Loud scoffs the dying thief,
Mocking Thy woe;
Can this my Savior be
Brought so low?

Yes, see the title clear,
Written above,
'Jesus of Nazareth'—
Name of love!

What, O my Savior dear,
What didst Thou see,
That made Thee suffer and
Die for me?

The poet combines motifs from the crucifixion with those that look forward to it and those that recall it. "When ye have lifted up the Son of man," said Jesus to the Pharisees, "then shall ye know that I am he" (Jn 8:28; cf. Jn 3:14). That elevation is to the *throne* of the Cross, with the crown of thorns as His *diadem*, fulfilling, in a mysterious and startling way, the prophecy of Daniel: "I saw in the night visions, and, behold, one like the Son of man came with the clouds of heaven, and came to the Ancient of days, and they brought him near before him. And there was given him dominion, and glory, and a kingdom, that all people, nations, and languages, should serve him" (Dn 7:13–14). "And I," said Jesus, "if I be lifted up from the earth"—He is speaking cryptically about both the crucifixion and the ascension to the right hand of the Father—"will draw all men unto me" (Jn 12:32). Those arms stretched to their uttermost are flung wide to embrace all who would come to Him.

But notice, besides all of these scriptural echoes, and besides the skillful way in which Monro tells the story of the crucifixion—the nails, the cry of desolation, the darkness upon the earth, the jeering of the thief, the sign that Pilate had nailed to the top of the cross—notice how he has employed the final lines of his stanzas. *Friends and disciples stand*—where? Where should friends stand? Not where they do stand, *far away*. Can this man lifted high on the cross be the Savior of the world—*brought so low?* Yes, it is; there is the sign. It reads *'Jesus of Nazareth.'* What does that mean? One thing above all: *Love.* What, from your exalted vantage, Jesus, did you see that moved you to grant me the greatest gift of your love—to *die for me?*

The fourth part gives us the Lord's response:

Child of my grief and pain!
From realms above,

I came to lead thee to
Life and love.

For thee my blood I shed,
For thee I died;
Safe in thy faithfulness
Now abide.

I saw thee wandering,
Weak and at strife;
I am the Way for thee,
Truth and Life.

Follow my path of pain,
Tread where I trod:
This is the way of peace
Up to God.

A whole theology of love is bound up here. Jesus came for the speaker, for each of us, because He saw us *wandering, weak and at strife*: "But when he saw the multitudes, he was moved with compassion on them, because they fainted, and were scattered abroad, as sheep having no shepherd" (Mt 9:36). Again and again in the verses above, Jesus uses the personal pronoun *thee*; He does not save a generalized mankind; He saves persons. Hence the emphatic reversal of word order: *For thee my blood I shed, / For thee I died*. Hence the insertion of the pronoun in the famous verse from St. John: "I am the way, the truth, and the life" (Jn 14:6). Here it is *I am the way for thee*: I am the way *you* must go. That is in the spirit of the Gospel passage. For Jesus had said to the disciples, "I go to prepare a place for you," but

Thomas, the doubter, replied, "Lord, we know not whither thou goest; and how can we know the way?" (Jn 14:2, 5).

What is that way? The last stanza uttered by Jesus shows it. The words repeat and yet alter those of a previous stanza. Let's place them side by side:

Follow to Calvary,
Tread where He trod:
This is the Lord of life—
Son of God.

Follow my path of pain,
Tread where I trod:
This is the way of peace
Up to God.

The road up to the summit of Calvary is no mere memorial walk. It is *the way*, a way of love, even in suffering and even unto death. When Jesus told the apostles that He must go to Jerusalem and be put to death by wicked men, St. Peter rebuked Him. Peter loved Jesus and did not want to see Him suffer; but Peter had not fathomed the depths of Jesus' love. He was thinking as a man, not as God. Jesus told him so, bluntly, and then applied the lesson to all the disciples and to us: "If any man will come after me, let him deny himself, and take up his cross, and follow me" (Mt 16:24). Only at the side of the Lord is peace to be found; and the Lord's is the way of the cross.

So in the fifth and final part of the poem, the speaker replies to Jesus with willing and eager love:

O, I will follow Thee,
Star of my soul!

Through the great dark I press
To the goal.

Yea, let me know Thy grief,
Carry Thy cross,
Share in Thy sacrifice,
Gain Thy loss.

Daily I'll prove my love
Through joy and woe;
Where Thy hands point the way,
There I go.

Lead me on year by year,
Safe to the end,
Jesus, my Lord, my Life,
King and Friend.

Not one word is idle; all is concentrated with meaning and feeling. The vocative *O* repeats the loving address from the stanza that called for a response from Jesus: *What, O my Savior dear, / What didst Thou see?* The auxiliary verb *will* is emphatic: I *will* follow, I am resolved upon it, I am eager to do so. The verb *follow*, appearing for the third time, echoes the words of Jesus and is the touchstone of the poem. Jesus is the *star of my soul*, and that is no poetic window dressing. The star is the polestar or lodestar, the North Star, fixed in place, while all the other stars turn about it. It is *the star to sail by*, in the darkness of life.

The interjection *yea*, which might strike a modern reader as superfluous, heightens the promise: *Yes, so willingly shall I follow you, that I am begging you to let me know even your grief, to carry your Cross, to share in your sacrifice!* A series of verbs, *know, carry, share*, culminates in the paradox of the line, *Gain Thy loss*. What can that mean? How can a loss be a gain? But Monro still has the scene from Matthew in mind. After Jesus has told the disciples that they must take up their cross if they wish to follow Him, He says, "For whosoever will save his life shall lose it; and whosoever will lose his life for my sake shall find it" (Mt 16:25). That is the law of love, which timorous human beings do not want to understand. We gain all things only by giving ourselves away; and we gain God by giving ourselves without reservation to Him, who is the giver of all good things, even Himself.

The last two stanzas apply the resolution to the course of our lives. We promise to prove our love *daily*, in good times and bad, traveling on the path pointed out to us by the outstretched hands of the Savior. We pray that He will lead us on *year by year*, until the *end* comes, and we are in the port at last. The last lines address Jesus in words of praise: He is our *Lord*, our *Life*, our *King*. And what is the title that surpasses that of the *King*? Our *Friend*. "Greater love hath no man than this," says Jesus, "that a man lay down his life for his friends" (Jn 15:13).

What remains for us in this chapter is to bind the language of the Gospels as they apply to Jesus with the language of the Psalms as they apply, not to the Messiah, but to *the Father*. That's not because Jesus is the Father; we do not collapse the Trinity. It is because Jesus and the Father are one: "He that seeth me seeth him that sent me" (Jn 12:47). The prophet cried out in terror, "Woe is me! for I am undone; because I am a man of unclean lips, and I dwell in the midst of a people of unclean lips: for mine eyes have seen the King, the Lord of hosts" (Is 6:5). But we need not cry out. Jesus shows us the Father's face.

John Henry Newman—best known for his immense learning, his treatises on the nature of faith and on liberal education, and his homilies, at once profoundly human and theologically exact—was also a fine poet, and several of his works appear in the old hymnals, both Protestant and Catholic. One of these is *Praise to the Holiest in the Height* (1865), sung to the melody *Newman*, composed by Richard Runciman Terry (1912) specifically for this poem.

The first verse resounds with echoes of Scripture from the Psalms and the prophets:

Praise to the Holiest in the height,
And in the depth be praise;
In all His words most wonderful,
Most sure in all His ways.

"For the Lord is a great God, and a great king above all gods," says the psalmist. "In his hand are the deep places of the earth: the strength of the hills is his also" (Ps 95:4). There is no binding God to a locale, as Zeus upon Mount Olympus or Hades beneath the earth: "If I ascend up to heaven, thou art there: if I make my bed in hell, behold, thou art there" (Ps 139:8). God is to be praised in all His words and works, the lofty and the lowly. "Praise ye the Lord from the heavens: praise him in the heights," we sing, but also, "Praise the Lord from the earth, ye dragons, and all deeps: fire and hail; snow, and vapors; stormy wind fulfilling his word: mountains, and all hills; fruitful trees, and all cedars; beasts, and all cattle; creeping things, and flying fowl" (Ps 148:1, 7–10).

These heights and depths are also *interior* to us sinners. Hence we sing in times of joy, and we rely on God's protection in times of sorrow. The God who dwells in His infinitude within the tiniest seed knows our inmost hearts: "Thou knowest my downsitting and mine uprising, thou understandest my thought afar off" (Ps 139:2). That, for us, is most astonishing: "For thou hast possessed my reins: thou hast covered me in my mother's womb. I will praise thee; for I am fearfully and wonderfully made: marvelous are thy works" (Ps 139:13–14). From the *height* of God's glory to the *depth* of human sin, His grace is all-embracing. The embodiment of this grace is the Incarnate Word. Hence the Messianic prophecy, when Isaiah approached King Ahaz: "Ask thee a sign of the Lord thy God; ask it either in the depth, or in the height above" (Is 7:11). When Ahaz declined to ask, Isaiah gave the prophecy anyway: "Behold, a virgin shall conceive, and bear a son, and shall call his name Emmanuel" (Is 7:14), meaning God-with-us.

We must keep these heights and depths firmly in mind as we sing the rest of the hymn, which is composed of three praises, each beginning with the vocative interjection *O*:

O loving wisdom of our God!
When all was sin and shame,
A second Adam to the fight
And to the rescue came.

"I heard thy voice in the garden," said the skulking Adam after he ate the forbidden fruit, "and I was afraid, because I was naked; and I hid myself" (Gn 3:10). Everything, without God's grace, is *sin and shame*. But God does not unmake man, dismissing him as a bad job. He enters the depths. The Son is born into the world as a man like us, to be the *second Adam*. Christ's obedience triumphs over our disobedience, and His resurrection triumphs over our death, as St. Paul says: "The first man Adam was made a living soul; the last Adam was made a quickening spirit" (1 Cor 15:45). He comes to our *rescue*—not as a distant benefactor paying a debt, but as a warrior entering what looks like a lost battle, delivering us from the power of darkness (Col 1:13).

The phrase *loving wisdom of our God* is Trinitarian: Christ, the *wisdom* of God the Father (1 Cor 1:24), is one with Him in the Holy Spirit of love. Newman begs us to consider both the wisdom of God's love and the lovingness of God's wisdom, as seen in His most marvelous work, the Incarnation, and Christ's pouring out His blood for us:

O wisest love! that flesh and blood,
Which did in Adam fail,
Should strive afresh against the foe,
Should strive, and should prevail;

And that a higher gift than grace
Should flesh and blood refine:
God's presence and His very self,
And essence all-divine.

The word *that* in the first line above is not a demonstrative adjective (*that* flesh), but a conjunction governing the pair of stanzas: *How wise is God's love, that the very same flesh and blood which failed in Adam should strive once more against the foe, and prevail.* Mere *flesh and blood* once failed before the enemy, but now, in Christ, flesh and blood fight again and win—and note the emphatic repetition of the phrase, *should strive.* Yes, they strive again, certainly they strive, they wrestle, but this time they *prevail.*

But there is an even *higher gift* in store for us. How is it possible? Can there be a *higher gift than grace*? Yes, because it is a gift that plumbs the depths. This higher gift descends to the depths of our being. It is the Eucharist. In the sacrament, the Most High God, His *presence*, His *very self*, and His *essence all-divine*, penetrates even our lowly *flesh and blood*, to make it pure.

That Sacrament is inseparable from the Cross:

O generous love! that He who smote
In Man for man the foe,
The double agony in Man
For man should undergo;

And in the garden secretly,
And on the cross on high,
Should teach His brethren, and inspire
To suffer and to die.

Here we see how inadequate are all squeamish substitutes for the word *man*. Newman needs a word that is universal (it embraces every man, woman, and child), singular (it embraces them all in one), concrete (it names not an abstraction like *humanity*, but a figure we can imagine), and personal. Christ the man saves Man the sinner. *He shows us the Father: and He shows us Man*, as Man, redeemed, will be. He undergoes for us a *double agony*, with the noun retaining its ancient Greek sense: It is a double *battle*, a double *strife*. Newman is still thinking of height and depth. In secret, in the garden, He suffered the anguish of the soul; and on Calvary, *on high*, He suffers publicly the rending of soul from body. He teaches us the way: The way of the Cross.

What is left to say? The psalmist praised the Father for His mighty deeds. This deed is the mightiest of all. So Newman repeats the first stanza, but now its meaning has been deepened by our meditation upon the love of Jesus:

Praise to the Holiest in the height,
And in the depth be praise;
In all His words most wonderful,
Most sure in all His ways!

Who is the Father? He who loves: "For God so loved the world, that he gave his only begotten Son, that whosoever believeth in him should not perish, but have everlasting life" (Jn 3:16).

Chapter Four

The Nativity

IMAGINE a strain of a beautiful melody. Not the whole of it, but a few notes here, a trill there, a suggestion of a movement of tremendous power, and then silence, and a memory, or the mere memory of a memory. "I once heard a song, or a part of it, and it brought me joy and trouble at once, but I cannot recall it now." The Nativity of the Lord is that melody, which the world hears from so great a distance, and with all the blurring of time and disappointment.

Every newborn child comes into the world like an invader, almost, says Chesterton, as if the old folk tales were true, and the baby were dropped down the chimney upon an unsuspecting family. That's as it should be. The child declares that the world hasn't won, not yet. There is no knowing what will happen now that *he* or *she* is here. The grandmother cradles the child in her arms and is a girl again, and her old husband, stumping along on his cane, looks upon it with glittering eyes, and imagines flinging a fishing line out onto the lake, the child at his side, a basket of bread and cheese broken into, the sun glowing yellow, and all things new.

Yet for all that, there is nothing like the birth of the Word Incarnate. God dwells with us. He shows us in the flesh of His son that true authority and power are inseparable from love. He shows us the frolic *youth* of holiness and goodness, a youth endearingly manifest in the saints—Philip Neri, making a priest-penitent carry the saint's pet dog through the streets, to the knowing laughter of the people, or Corrie ten Boom, evangelist on the run, from whose lips not even her years in the concentration camps of the Nazis nor the death there of her beloved sister could wipe away the blessed smile.

The season of the Nativity has rung with the merriment of gifts and feasts, but it is not really a season of *pleasure*. It's made the mountains reecho with songs of joy, and yet when we think of the event, it is dark night, and an evil king lurks in the shadows with murder in his heart. The best of our Christmas hymns do not bring pleasure. They bring joy—the joy that can embrace the world's trouble and darkness and grief, which pleasure must ignore or anaesthetize. They are theological and human at once. They sing out to God; they look with tender regard upon the God-made man, the little child born in the manger. The hymns that are most theological still remember the babe in swaddling clothes; the hymns that are most human tremble with gratitude that God should come among us. All are musical variations upon the thundering declaration of St. John:

> *In him was life; and the life was the light of men.*
>
> *And the light shineth in darkness; and the darkness comprehendeth it not.* (Jn 1:4–5)

Let's begin with an ancient hymn fit for both Advent and the Nativity: *Of the Father's Love Begotten*. When St. Francis, the little poor man of God, thought of the birth of Jesus, he pictured the humble appearance of the Savior of the world, in the cattle stall, with the lowly oxen and sheep nearby. Francis built the first crèche, and from then on, that quiet birthplace has entered the Christian imagination: the beauty of the small boy, the rapt adoration of Mary, the weary Joseph, and the simple shepherds. It's hard for us to think of Christmas without that scene, and that is right and just, but of course, there is more. The child in the manger is the Son of God, through whom all things were made. In Him, we find the mystery of mankind fallen and redeemed, and the fulfillment of time in eternity.

That's why Prudentius (b. 348), the first great Latin Christian poet, begins his hymn to the birth of Christ with the first and eternal "birth." I shall give both Prudentius' Latin and the English translation by John Mason Neale (1854):

Corde natus ex parentis
ante mundi exordium,
A et O cognominatus,
ipse fons et clausula
omnium quae sunt, fuerunt,
quaeque post futura sunt,
saeculorum saeculis.

Of the Father's love begotten,
Ere the worlds began to be,
He is Alpha and Omega,
He the source, the ending He,
Of the things that are, that have been,
And that future years shall see,
Evermore and evermore.

The first time I heard this hymn, sung to the chant *Divinum Mysterium*, those words *evermore and evermore*, the final line of every stanza, moved me nearly to tears. How simple they are, yet how well they capture the meaning of Christ's dwelling among us! Before that night in Bethlehem, before there was a universe at all, Christ was begotten of the Father's love: *corde natus*, born from the heart. Prudentius knew there was no time before the Son of God was begotten. But the word *natus* expresses the intimate relation of the Son to the Father, for He is begotten from the Father's *heart*, His inmost being. Then if all things past and present and to come spring from the One begotten in love, and have their *clausula* or completion also in Him, they too partake of this love, not only for a time, but *saeculorum saeculis*, for the ages of ages, eternity.

Prudentius then, in a stanza omitted from the hymnals, turns to the creation of the world, and the Son's desire to assume our form, a body prone to fall and die, lest the Law that had drowned us in the depths of hell condemn us *evermore and evermore*. It's a stirring and surprising use of the refrain. In his fourth stanza he turns to Christmas night:

O beatus ortus ille,
virgo cum puerperal
edidit nostram salutem,
feta Sancto Spiritu,
et puer redemptor orbis
os sacratum protulit,
saeculorum saeculis.

O that birth forever blessed,
When the virgin, full of grace,
By the Holy Ghost conceiving,
Bore the Savior of our race,
And the Babe, the world's Redeemer,

First revealed His sacred face,
Evermore and evermore.

The birth is an *ortus*, a rising, like the dawn. Then was the Redeemer of the world first made manifest. He *revealed His sacred face*. The good Christian longs to behold the face of Jesus, our merciful judge. If we fear His severity, we should recall this poem and remember that His is also the face of that little boy, the *puer*, and the revelation of the child is not for a time, but *evermore*.

What has this child come among us to accomplish? Prudentius devotes two stanzas to the question, one set in the past and the other in the future. Jesus is the *promissus*, the Promised One, foretold by the prophets to be the Savior of His people. He is also *venturus*, the One who is to come, judge of the dead, king of the living, vindicator of righteousness, forever. Such glory should be sung by all the mighty ranks of angels, so Prudentius precedes these stanzas with the powers and dominions extolling the Lord. But what about lowly mankind? Again we touch the human heart of Christmas, the beauty of that child. "Let the little children come to me," Jesus said, who never lost the innocence of the babe, and who offers us a new birth, the refreshment of our innocence. So the poet issues this wonderful invitation to all of us children, no matter the age:

Te senes et te juventus,
parvulorum te chorus,
turba matrum, virginumque,
simplices puellulae,
voce concordes pudicis
perstrepant concentibus,
saeculorum saeculis.

Thee let old men, thee let young men,
Thee let boys in chorus sing,
Matrons, virgins, little maidens,
With glad voices answering:
Let their guileless songs re-echo,
And the heart its music bring,
Evermore and evermore!

The opening pronoun, *te*, tells us why we sing: It is, Lord, for *Thee, Thee!* We sing with abandon. The old men sing, the youths and maidens sing, the mothers sing, the boys sing, in voices as pure as childhood, without embarrassment, without guile. It is music from the heart. We wish it would never end.

Nor shall it. Those ancient Christian hymns, bless them, end with no end. As we've seen, their doxologies, their glory-words, return to the beginning:

Christ, to Thee with God the Father,
And, O Holy Ghost, to Thee,
Hymn and chant with high thanksgiving
And unwearied praises be:
Honor, glory, and dominion,
And eternal victory,
Evermore and evermore.

From these theological heights let's consider the holy Child again. For Christmas is also the great feast of the Child. What does it mean to be a child?

Behold a little child, a boy. He has only a few words, but within the wondrous dome of his head, tousled with a wisp of wild hair, a whole world is coming into being. Sometimes he regards things with a settled seriousness, as if he were a metaphysical scholar, batting a toy swing back and forth, investigating the principles of motion. Sometimes he crouches to the earth to make finger-marks in the soil. Sometimes he gazes into the eyes of a stranger and breaks into a smile, the two teeth on the bottom making him look like a rakish old man who's just downed a swig of cider.

If we knew, in advance, that the child would "amount to nothing," as we say in our ruthlessness—that he'd be the first dumped overboard in the surreality television show of modern life, the first sent packing with half a talent—indeed, if we knew he would die before the age of reason, shouldn't that make him all the more precious in our eyes? The good of the child is beyond quantity. It is like the good of love, and beauty.

Our Lord says that unless we become as little children, we shall not enter the Kingdom of God. The child must receive all things as gifts, because on his own he can do nothing. Yet the child is also himself a gift of incomparable beauty, a grace that takes the breath away. We come to Jesus then with the poverty and the dignity of children, and He meets us, on the feast of Christmas, in the same way. What cheer for the heart! The gears of the world grind on, the smokestacks belch, and politicians speak, scientists distill medicines and poisons, producers produce, and consumers consume, but the true world is here, at the side of the Christ child, in stillness and joy.

That is the insight of Christina Rossetti's hymn, *In the Bleak Midwinter*. It's nonsense to suggest that her verses are sentimental. She sees the emptiness of a world without Christ. The month of His birth does not matter. If it was July, it was winter—man's winter, the world's winter:

In the bleak midwinter,
Frosty wind made moan,

Earth stood hard as iron,
Water like a stone;
Snow had fallen, snow on snow,
Snow on snow,
In the bleak midwinter,
Long ago.

The child-like irregularity of the meter should not deceive us. Rossetti knows what she's doing. The repetition of *snow on snow*, like the quiet fall of snow on a windless day, suggests the cold of the world, inexorable, deaf to appeal. Nothing changes, nothing *can* change, until the Word is made flesh and dwells among us.

This happens because God is too great for greatness; He is the Lord who will come in majesty, and who came, long ago, in the royal flesh of a little child. He is beyond the world's imagining, and beneath the world's notice:

Our God, heaven cannot hold him,
Nor earth sustain;
Heaven and earth shall welcome him
When he comes to reign.
In the bleak midwinter
A stable-place sufficed
The Lord God incarnate,
Jesus Christ.

Never has the name of the Lord been so tenderly and beautifully uttered in a poem. He is the little boy, named Jesus by His mother, and a stable suffices to house Him at His birth; and He is the Christ, the Son of God, who rules at the right hand of the Father. His name embraces the whole mystery of our faith. It is the truth. The line needs no more.

The next verse, too, brings together the grand and the small, the mighty and the intimate:

Angels and archangels
May have gathered there,
Cherubim and seraphim
Thronged the air;
But his mother only,
In her maiden bliss,
Worshipped the almighty
With a kiss.

Omnipotence, in the limbs of a babe; and the eternal Love submits to the lips of a maiden girl and her loving kiss. We shouldn't think there is power on display in the heavens above the stable, and weakness and humility within. For the *meaning* of true power is to be seen in the kiss between Mary and the child. The act of worship that was granted to her alone shows us the essence of all adoration of the Lord.

Thinking of that kiss, Rossetti asks, simply, "What do I have to give?" Again, it is no sentimental question. It's precisely because the child has *nothing* to give, and knows he has nothing, that he can give the most important gift of all. A wise man, says the poet with a wry vagueness, might do *his part*, whatever that might be, but what Jesus really wants from us is what the child alone, no matter his age, has to offer:

What can I give Him,
Poor as I am?
If I were a shepherd,

I would give a lamb;
If I were a wise man,
I would do my part;
Yet what I can I give him,
Give my heart.

It would be fine to place Rossetti's and Prudentius' hymns in dialogue, and that's what we find in a remarkable Latin carol written by one Jean Mauburn (1494). In this poetic jewel, *Dost Thou in a Manger Lie?*, the singer addresses the Lord directly:

Dost Thou in a manger lie,
  Who hast all created?
Stretching infant hands on high,
  Savior, long awaited?
If a monarch, where Thy state?
Where Thy court on Thee to wait?
  Royal purple, where?
Here no regal pomp we see;
Naught but need and penury:
  Why thus cradled here?

Mauburn begs us to look with wonder, even puzzlement, upon the love of God. Christ is the Creator of *all*—yet He lies in a *manger*, a feeding trough. How is it possible? The *infant hands* stretch forward, and we see the utter weakness of God-made-Man: Those hands that strewed the heavens with stars now can only move vaguely toward the sky, and the Word is speechless. Is this the long-awaited Savior? The great Son of David, come to "restore again the kingdom to Israel" (Acts 1:6), as the apostles even after the Resurrection supposed, still thinking in political terms? If a king, where are the trappings of royalty? Where is the *royal purple?* In those times, purple was the color of royalty, because its deep rich dye was rare and costly to produce. But Jesus will wear the royal purple, as the poet and we singers know well. He will be arrayed in the purple of His blood.

The second stanza, as far as I know, is unique among Christmas hymns. For the *infant*—literally, the *speechless*—replies:

"Pitying love for fallen man
Brought me down thus low;
For a race deep lost in sin,
Came I into woe.
By this lowly birth of mine,
Sinner, riches shall be thine,
Matchless gifts and free;
Willingly this yoke I take,
And this sacrifice I make,
Heaping joys for thee."

The *need and penury* of the first stanza are man's, not God's. Because man was *fallen*, Christ fell, so to speak, from His glory down *thus low*. Because man was *lost* in the misery of sin, Christ came into that same misery, yet sinless. Because man set himself up as a god, Christ came down as a little child. Because man had made himself destitute of grace by his arrogance, Christ came in humility to grant him *riches*, indeed *matchless gifts and free*. Christ assumes the yoke of suffering *willingly* (cf. Jn 10:18), to heap joys for us: "I am come that they might have life, and that they might have it more abundantly" (Jn 10:10).

In the third and last stanza, the poet responds to the Child and tries to unite his voice with the voices of the angels:

Fervent praise would I to Thee
Evermore be raising;
For Thy wondrous love to me
Thee be ever praising.
Glory, glory be forever
Unto that most bounteous Giver,
And that loving Lord!
Better witness to Thy worth,
Purer praise than ours on earth,
Angels' songs afford.

Mauburn echoes that beloved verse from the Christmas narratives, so often heard in our carols: "And suddenly there was with the angel a multitude of the heavenly host praising God, and saying, Glory to God in the highest, and on earth peace, good will toward men" (Lk 2:13–14).

I'd like here to glance at a fifteenth-century melody to which this poem is set: *Dies est laetitiae*. As in many medieval melodies, its phrases are simple, yet they are delicately varied and woven together in an intricate pattern, in this case perfectly modulated for the poem. Notice that the stanzas divide into two parts, each of which in turn is divided in half. The first part consists of four lines, in a 4–3–4–3 pattern (four stresses, three stresses, and so forth), with alternating rhymes. The second part consists of six lines, in a 4–4–3–4–4–3 pattern, with the longer lines rhyming as couplets, and the short lines rhyming with one another. Any melody for such a poem must hold all ten lines together in some recognizable form, lest by the end of the stanza we forget what we've sung in the beginning. Ten lines—a lot to hold together. Here's how *Dies est laetitiae* solves the problem. As always, I'll mark separate melodic phrases by letters, and variations upon them with asterisks:

A	B	
Dost Thou in a manger lie,	*Who hast all created,*	
A	B	
Stretching infant hands on high,	*Savior, long awaited?*	
C	C*	D
If a monarch, where Thy state?	*Where Thy court on Thee to wait?*	*Royal purple, where?*
A	B*	D*
Here no regal pomp we see;	*Naught but need and penury;*	*Why thus cradled here?*

It is simply brilliant. We see in the first four lines that the music rhymes as the lines rhyme. Then in the second part, when the poem's structure changes, the music changes: We have a new musical phrase entirely, C. But the melody doesn't spin out of control. Like the lines, C "rhymes" on itself, with a variation, followed by yet another new line, D. At this point the composer *returns to the first phrase*, A, followed by a variation upon the second phrase, B*. These phrases "rhyme" in our ears because we have heard them together twice before. They bind the second part of the stanza to the first. All that remains is to bind the last three lines with the previous three, and that is clinched by the final phrase, D*, "rhyming" upon

D, as the words themselves do. It's a far cry from contemporary songs that veer this way and that, without form or coherence. But then, it wasn't meant for trained soloists but for ordinary people singing together.

What about the familiar carols we cherish? They too provide us with much fine poetry, sweet or pensive, rousing or quiet, merry or solemn, and sometimes all of these by turns. And that is fitting. Listen to the account in St. Luke:

> *And there were in the same country shepherds abiding in the field, keeping watch over their flocks by night.*
>
> *And lo, the angel of the Lord came upon them, and the glory of the Lord shone round about them: and they were sore afraid.*
>
> *And the angel said unto them, Fear not: for, behold, I bring you good tidings of great joy, which shall be to all people.*
>
> *For unto you is born this day in the city of David a Savior, which is Christ the Lord.*
>
> *And this shall be a sign unto you: Ye shall find the babe wrapped in swaddling clothes, lying in a manger.*
>
> *And suddenly there was with the angel a multitude of the heavenly host praising God, and saying,*
>
> *Glory to God in the highest, and on earth peace, good will toward men.* (Lk 2:8–14)

We have the stillness of the night, and the simple huddling shepherds. Then a power breaks in upon them and terrifies them. The angel must allay their fears before he announces the good tidings. It is a day of joy for *all people*—it's hard to imagine how the shepherds could have understood that—and especially for Israel, waiting for the Messiah. The angel does not say

"Bethlehem" but *the city of David*, linking Jesus with the great king and affirming that He is the one so long foretold by the prophets and awaited by the Jews. The whole history of God's relationship with the chosen people is concentrated in this moment, and the shepherds, being Jews, *would* have had some flickering notion of that. Then the tidings turn to praise: *Glory to God in the highest.*

The poet Nahum Tate set himself to render this suggestive prose into simple English verse, using the old ballad meter, rhyming on lines two and four. The result is the beloved carol *While Shepherds Watched Their Flocks by Night* (1700). The first stanza sets the scene:

While shepherds watched their flocks by night,
All seated on the ground,
The angel of the Lord came down,
And glory shone around.

What has Tate added? The line *seated on the ground.* He specifies what Luke means by the lovely phrase *abiding in the field.* The shepherds are awake, but they are resting. They have no regal thrones, or even homely chairs. They are rough and simple men. To them, however, comes the glory of the Lord; the contrast is striking.

The next three stanzas take up the angel's words. I shall score in bold the motifs that Tate has added:

"Fear not," said he, for mighty dread
Had seized their troubled mind;
"Glad tidings of great joy I bring
To you and all mankind.

"To you, in David's town, this day
Is born of David's line
The *Savior, who is Christ the Lord;*
And this shall be **the** *sign:*

"The ***heavenly*** *Babe you there shall find*
To human view displayed,
All ***meanly*** *wrapped in swathing bands,*
And in a manger laid."

A poor versifier searches somewhere, anywhere, for a rhyme. A good poet has them well in hand, and follows the advice of John Keats, to "load every rift with ore." Consider the second line of the first stanza above: *had seized their troubled mind.* It is *not* simply Tate's way of embellishing *mighty dread* and providing himself with a rhyme for *mankind.* He is subtly linking this scene with others before. The angel Gabriel came to Zachariah in the temple to announce the birth of the Baptist, and the old priest "was troubled, and fear fell upon him" (Lk 1:12). Gabriel then was sent by God to Nazareth, to Mary:

> *And the angel came in unto her, and said, Hail, full of grace, the Lord is with thee: blessed art thou among women.*
>
> *And when she saw him, she was troubled at his saying, and cast in her mind what matter of salutation this should be.* (Lk 1:28–29)

The irruption of the power of God brings fear, and how should it not? It *troubles* the minds of Zachariah and Mary and the shepherds: It stirs them up, it shakes them. Hence the angel must soothe the trouble, and Tate does well to begin the second stanza with the command *fear not*, set apart from the rest of its sentence (consider how much more pallid the line would be, had Tate simply written, *He said, "Fear not,"* and so forth). Those are the same words the angel spoke to Zachariah (1:13) and to Mary (1:30).

Why did Tate add *born of David's line?* It identifies not where Jesus is but *who He is*. So Luke and Matthew trace Jesus' lineage back to King David, to fulfill the prophecy the Lord gave to David through Nathan the prophet: "Thine house and thy kingdom shall be established for ever before thee: thy throne shall be established for ever" (1 Sm 7:16). That's why the Pharisees and scribes were outraged when people cried out to Jesus, as He entered Jerusalem on Palm Sunday, "Hosanna to the son of David" (Mt 21:15). They knew it was a title for the Messiah. What they did not know was that the Messiah was to be the Son of God, not figuratively, but truly, essentially, from all eternity. Jesus makes the point with characteristic directness:

> *How say the scribes that Christ is the son of David?*
>
> *For David himself said by the Holy Ghost, The Lord said to my Lord, Sit thou on my right hand, till I make thine enemies thy footstool.*
>
> *David therefore himself calleth him Lord; and whence is he then his son?* (Mk 12:35–37)

The Christ, the Messiah, is the son of David by blood, but *not* the son of David by authority; he is instead David's Lord or, as the Palm Sunday hymn *All Glory, Laud, and Honor* puts it, *great David's greater Son*. He is not just *a savior* but *the Savior*.

And the angel gives the shepherds not just *a sign*, but *the sign*. What's the difference? *The sign* suggests that it is the definitive sign. The angel is not just giving the shepherds directions, saying, "Turn right at the crossroads, look to your left, and check out the stable by the inn." The sign is meaningful in its own right. So in the next stanza Tate has added the words *heavenly* and *meanly* to underscore the point. The former is an adjective, the latter an adverb, but their forms echo one another in counterpoint. The Babe who is *heavenly* and thus beyond the perception of man has now come down among us, displaying Himself *to human view*, and how? *All meanly wrapped in swathing bands.*

The final two stanzas complete the account. Again I'll accent what Tate has added:

> ***Thus spake the seraph,*** *and forthwith*
> *Appeared a* ***shining*** *throng*
> *Of angels praising God, who thus*
> ***Addressed their joyful song:***
>
> *"All glory be to God on high*
> *And on the earth be peace;*
> *Good will* ***henceforth*** *from heaven to men*
> ***Begin and never cease."***

It's odd to consider, but the gospel of Luke does not actually say that the angels were singing. We assume so; if ever there was something to sing about, surely it was the birth of the Redeemer! For this night marks a re-creation of the world, and the angels sing, as when God made the world in the beginning, and "the morning stars sang together, and all the sons of God shouted for joy" (Jb 38:7). So the morning stars are here again—the *shining throng* of God's loyal warrior angels, to announce a new world. That's why Tate interprets their song not as a wish but as a prophetic blessing, to be bestowed upon man in time, *henceforth* and forever, as the hymn ends with the brave words, *begin and never cease.*

Now let's turn to a more theologically incisive hymn based on the same text from Luke's gospel: Charles Wesley's mighty *Hark, the Herald Angels Sing* (1739), revised slightly by his friend and fellow missionary George Whitefield. The first stanza, like Tate's, sets the scene, but then shifts to the universal meaning of the birth of Christ:

Hark! the herald angels sing
Glory to the newborn King!
Peace on earth and mercy mild,
God and sinners reconciled!
Joyful, all ye nations, rise,
Join the triumph of the skies;
With the angelic host proclaim
Christ is born in Bethlehem!
Hark! the herald angels sing
Glory to the newborn King!

The "new" word here is *nations*. What does it mean?

The term is common in the Old Testament, and is used with deep ambivalence. Often it denotes peoples set against Israel, the *heathen*, to use the old English word. "Why do the heathen rage," cries the psalmist, "and the people imagine a vain thing?" (Ps 2:1). "The nations," says Jeremiah, have drunk of the wine of the wicked Babylon, and "therefore the nations are mad" (Jer 51:7). All the heathen, the nations, will be wakened and summoned to the Valley of Jehosophat, "for there," says the Lord, "will I sit to judge all the heathen round about . . . for their wickedness is great" (Jl 3:12–13). But God also made His covenant with Abraham, promising to make of him a great nation and extending that blessing to all mankind: "In thy seed shall all the nations of the earth be blessed" (Gn 22:18). "Make a joyful noise unto the Lord, all ye lands," cries the psalmist (Ps 100:1). The nations rebel against the Lord—that's the way of this sinful world—but the world also longs for Jesus. Therefore one of His titles, in the carol *O Come, O Come, Emmanuel*, is *Desire of Nations*: "I will shake all nations, and the desire of all nations shall come; and I will fill this house with glory, saith the Lord of hosts" (Hg 2:7). Now the nations are to rise up in joy, because God and sinners have been reconciled, and they too join the song of the angels. They too turn toward Bethlehem.

In the second stanza Wesley addresses the meaning of the Incarnation, weaving together motifs from all over the Bible:

Christ, by highest heaven adored,
Christ, the everlasting Lord;
Late in time behold Him come,
Offspring of the Virgin's womb.
Veiled in flesh the Godhead see;
Hail the incarnate Deity,
Pleased as man with man to dwell,
Jesus, our Emmanuel!
Hark! the herald angels sing
Glory to the newborn King!

He begins by naming Christ: The Anointed One, and *the everlasting Lord*, adored and served by angels on high. Christ is infinitely greater than they: "For unto which of the angels said he at any time, Thou art my son, this day have I begotten thee? And again, I will be to him a Father, and he shall be to me a Son?" (Heb 1:5, referring to Ps 2:7; 89:26). He comes to us *late in time*, in the fullness of God's plan: "When the fullness of time was come, God sent forth his Son, born of a woman" (Gal 4:4). Not any woman, but a virgin: "Behold, a virgin shall conceive, and bear a son, and shall call his name Immanuel" (Is 7:14). That name means God-with-us, and indeed, God is with us in a most astounding way. He dwells among us, a man among men: "And the Word was made flesh, and dwelt among us" (Jn 1:14).

The phrase *veiled in flesh* is particularly suggestive and works in several ways. Only the High Priest, once a year, could enter behind the veil of the Holy of Holies and pronounce the sacred name of God, during the feast of Atonement, of reconciliation between God and sinful man. That veil was torn in two by the tremors of the earth when Jesus died. Now, says the writer to the Hebrews, we need no longer sacrifice bulls at the Temple, because we have the one supreme High Priest who has entered the sanctuary once and for all. We enter it boldly by the blood of Jesus, "by a new and living way, which he hath consecrated for us, through the veil, that is to say, his flesh" (Heb 10:20). So the *veil* of flesh, the flesh given for us, unites us with the God who deigns to dwell with us in the flesh. Christ's body *is the new Temple, the new Holy of Holies*. The veil both hides His Deity and makes it manifest. It is a veil that unveils. The people of Israel could not bear even to look upon the face of Moses, but veiled it against the light that shone from him. We need no longer do so, because the veil, in Christ, has been taken away, and we, "with open face beholding as in a glass the glory of the Lord, are changed into the same image from glory to glory" (2 Cor 3:18).

Then comes the triumphant third stanza with its key word, *born*:

Hail, the heaven-born Prince of Peace,
Hail, the Sun of righteousness!
Light and life to all He brings,
Risen with healing in His wings.

Mild He lays His glory by,
Born that man no more may die,
Born to raise the sons of earth,
Born to give them second birth.
Hark! the herald angels sing
Glory to the newborn King!

We recognize in the first line the grand summative title of the Messiah: "His name shall be called Wonderful, Counselor, the mighty God, the everlasting Father, the Prince of Peace" (Is 9:6). Wesley then leaps to the end of the prophecy of Malachi, the last of the Old Testament prophets, applying the prophecy of the Day of Judgment and the second coming of Christ to His first coming. Says the Lord: "But unto you that fear my name shall the Sun of righteousness arise with healing in his wings" (Mal 4:2). He brings *light and life*: "In him was life; and the life was the light of men" (Jn 1:4). He lays aside His glory, *born that man no more may die*. Notice the balance here between birth and death: We know that Christ will also *die* so that those who believe in Him may live.

Many hymnals efface the masculine language of this stanza, but that's a dreadful mistake. It's not only like scribbling on a corner of the painting to deface it; it's like painting away the very things that make the painting what it is. Jesus was not born that *we no more may die*, as one bad revision has it. For the pronoun *we* is not universal: It denotes only the people intended by the speaker. Here, it denotes the singers of the carol. But that's not the point. Jesus, who is *God*, was born that *man*, the whole race, summed up in that universal, singular, personal term, need die no more. That balance between the divine being and the human being, between God and man, continues in the next two lines. He, the Son of God, is born *to raise the sons of earth*—not to *raise us from the earth*, as the foolish revision suggests, implying an unscriptural rejection of the earth and lending the scene the comic effect of a science-fiction show. We are sons of the first Adam, the sinner, who was taken from the earth; we are now raised by the second Adam, the obedient Christ, who came to unite the sons of earth with the sons of the morning, the herald angels we have been hailing all along. He is *born* to give men a new birth: "Except a man be born again, he cannot see the kingdom of God" (Jn 3:3).

I'd like here to include the two additional stanzas that Wesley wrote, which I have yet to find in any hymnal. They too take us all the way back to Genesis and the fall of man, and point us forward to the end of time, when God shall be all in all:

Come, Desire of nations, come,
Fix in us Thy humble home;
Rise, the woman's conquering Seed,
Bruise in us the serpent's head.
Now display Thy saving power,
Ruined nature now restore;
Now in mystic union join
Thine to ours, and ours to Thine.
Hark! the herald angels sing
Glory to the newborn King!

Adam's likeness, Lord, efface,
Stamp Thine image in its place;
Second Adam from above,
Reinstate us in Thy love.
Let us Thee, though lost, regain,
Thee, the Life, the inner man:
O, to all Thyself impart,

Formed in each believing heart.
Hark! the herald angels sing
Glory to the newborn King!

To which the good Christian, and the lover of good art, can only say, "Let it be so!"

We shouldn't leave the season of the Nativity without a hymn for Epiphany—for the *manifestation* to the world of the Word made flesh. The one element of that account that most moves the heart is the star that the wise men, stargazers from Persia in the east, followed to Palestine and to the city of David, Bethlehem.

All Christians are called to follow that star. That's the theme of Charles Coffin's Latin hymn, *Quae stella sole pulchrior* (1736), translated into English by John Chandler (1837). I will use the revised (and slightly superior) version appearing in the 1940 Hymnal. The form of the stanza is simple and straightforward, four lines of four strong beats each, rhyming in couplets. (This stanza is also called Long Meter, abbreviated L.M.) That simple form is well set forth by Michael Praetorius' jaunty Christmas melody, *Puer nobis*, with its pattern of alternating quarter notes and half notes (one TWO, one TWO), the half notes striking the strong stresses in the meter, reminiscent of a mother rocking her baby. It is easy for a congregation of men and women, old and young, to sing this melody with abandon. The first stanza begins with a question:

What star is this, with beams so bright,
More beauteous than the noonday light?
It shines to herald forth the King,
And Gentiles to His crib to bring.

The question is not astronomical but theological. Certainly the star above Bethlehem did not illuminate all the surroundings as if it had been broad day. But the beams are more beautiful than the rays of the noon sun. Their beauty arises from what the star is and why it shines: *to herald forth the King*, even unto Gentiles far away. "Where is he that is born King of the Jews?" they ask Herod, because they have come to give Him homage (Mt 2:2). Thus even from His birth, the sign is given that the Jews were chosen by God to be a blessing to all mankind; and therefore the King of the Jews is to be the King of all peoples.

That's the message of the second stanza:

Thus spake the prophet from afar
Who told the rise of Jacob's star;
And eastern sages with amaze
Upon the wondrous token gaze.

Coffin recalls the words of Balaam, prophet for hire, who foretold the ascendancy of the people of Israel, against the wishes of his paymaster Balak: "There shall come a star out of Jacob, and a scepter shall rise out of Israel" (Nm 24:17). The prophet spoke *from afar*: "I shall see him," said Balaam, "but not now; I shall behold him, but not nigh." The star stands for something that comes to us from both the distance of space and the distance of time. It comes from the eternal God who transcends the world. Its beauty surpasses that of any other star because it is a sign, a *wondrous token*. The eastern sages—wise men from the land of the rising sun—do not simply chart its movement. They *gaze* upon it. They contemplate it.

That means that their gazing upon the star is a form of prayer, and in the third stanza Coffin directs our attention to a more powerful star that guides them:

The guiding star above is bright;
Within them shines a clearer light,
And leads them on with power benign
To seek the Giver of the sign.

The light of the Holy Spirit burns in their hearts. His fire stirs them from their comfortable homes, the fire of a love that will not be denied:

Their love can brook no dull delay,
Though toil and danger block the way;
Home, kindred, fatherland, and all,
They leave at their Creator's call.

Notice how neatly the stanza is balanced. The first line describes their hearty love; the second dispenses with the obstacles in their path; the third dispenses with attachments that could not hold them back; and the fourth simply declares what they do: *They leave at their Creator's call.*

Time to apply the lesson to ourselves:

O Jesus, while the star of grace
Impels us on to seek Thy face,
Let not our slothful hearts refuse
The guidance of Thy light to use.

"If we had been there," we say, boasting of our piety and fidelity, "we'd have set out from Persia too!" But we're in Persia right now. The star *is shining*. It is *the star of grace*. It drives us forth to seek the face of Jesus. So we pray for more grace, more light, more of that impelling fire, to vanquish the dull delay our *slothful hearts* might weigh upon us. On to the eternal Epiphany:

To God the Father, heavenly Light,
To Christ, revealed in earthly might,
To God the Holy Ghost we raise
Our equal and unceasing praise.

Chapter Five

The Cross and the Resurrection

WHEN Jesus stood upon the mount of the transfiguration and His garments became "shining, exceeding white as snow; so as no fuller on earth can white them" (Mk 9:3), St. Peter, not in his right senses, offered to build three booths or tabernacles upon the site—three dwelling places, one for Jesus, one for Moses, and one for Elijah. That hour on the mountain seems to have stirred Peter to the depths of his being. He recalls it when he writes, years later, that he and his fellow apostles were eyewitnesses of the Lord's majesty (2 Pt 1:16–19).

Yet they were not to remain upon that mountain. We find the apostles eager to bring on a political "salvation" for Israel, but otherwise it is always Jesus on the move, Jesus hastening, while they stood in the way. So too when they descended the mountain, and Jesus said, "The Son of man is delivered into the hands of men, and they shall kill him; and after that he is killed, he shall rise on the third day" (Mk 9:31).

The apostles didn't know what to make of that, and after two thousand years, we still stumble, understanding a little, by fits and starts. To say that Jesus was a profound moral teacher put to death by his envious enemies is to miss the point. There is no separating the person of Jesus from His mission, and no separating His mission from His death; and His death has meaning only in the morning light of the Resurrection.

Many a theologian can illuminate these truths better than I can. My task is to turn our attention to the hymns that portray in language and music what theologians must struggle to express with precisely delineated ideas and painstaking analysis of sacred scripture. Jesus, not by happenstance but by the mission that is His very soul, hastens toward His sacrifice of love. Let us accompany Him.

I have first in mind the heartrendingly tender hymn *Herzliebster Jesu*, written in German by Johann Heermann (1630), set to a deceptively simple and solemn minor-key melody of the same name by the great composer Johann Crueger (1640), and translated into English by Robert Bridges (1899). I call the melody deceptively simple because there are no fancy runs of notes, no striking intervals, no surprising harmonization in the bass lines; yet each phrase of the melody *echoes every other phrase*, and never twice in the same way.

The melody uses half notes (H) and whole notes (W), nothing else. There are only two patterns for their use: W H H W W and H H H H W W. These alternate through the melody, simply: A B A B A B A. So much for the *length* of the notes, but what the notes *are* is something else. Each B phrase plays upon the pattern of the preceding A phrase, without repeating it. All the phrases end with two whole notes of falling pitch, appropriate for the subject, the suffering and death of our Lord. There is only one note to a syllable, regardless of length, so the A phrases have five syllables, and the B phrases have six. But because the A phrases take as much time as the B phrases, the effect, especially at the end of the stanza, is to slow down a melody that is already slow, and to highlight those final words.

For a sense of the power that such a pattern can impart, let us look at the poetry. The first stanza begins with a heartfelt but unanswerable question:

Ah, holy Jesus, how hast Thou offended,
That man to judge Thee hath in hate pretended?
By foes derided, by Thine own rejected,
O most afflicted.

At first glance it seems we have three strung-out lines, followed by a short tag. If we look closer, though, we notice that Bridges *has the melody of the hymn in mind*, just as the composer Crueger had the rhythm of Heermann's poem in mind when he composed the melody. Bridges has made sure there is a pause or *caesura* after the fifth syllable (with *falling stress*, as the melody is falling in pitch) in every line. I'll mark the pause with a space:

Ah, holy Jesus,   *how hast Thou offended,*
That man to judge Thee   *hath in hate pretended?*
By foes derided,   *by Thine own rejected,*
O most afflicted.

In other words, the division in each line corresponds exactly to the melodic phrasing: The five-syllable A phrase, followed by the six-syllable B phrase. This would be but a curiosity, except that it is poetically productive. It creates parallels and contrasts, it suspends ideas to bring them to climax, and it sets off most powerfully the last short line, the odd A phrase that ends the stanza. To hear how this is so, set one A against the following B. Jesus is *by foes derided*. That is bad, but to be expected from enemies. What's not to be expected is what follows: *By Thine own rejected*. Or set one A against a following A. Jesus is *holy*, but man sets himself up as his Lord's *judge*. The last line, with its slant rhyme on *rejected*, is the climax of all the past tense verbs and participles in succession: *offended, pretended, derided, rejected, afflicted*. But it is grammatically dependent upon the name that ends the first phrase in the first line: *Jesus*. Musically and semantically the whole stanza is a meditation upon this identity: *holy Jesus, most afflicted*.

The second stanza begins with another question, and now the question is answered. It is the most powerful use of the first-person pronoun that I know of, in any hymn:

Who was the guilty? Who brought this upon Thee?

Alas, my treason, Jesus, hath undone Thee.

'Twas I, Lord Jesus, I it was denied Thee:

I crucified Thee.

I, Thee, I Thee: The pronouns carry the poetry. It is excruciatingly personal. Each line ends with *Thee*, the object of a terrible verb, building to the climax: *brought-upon Thee, undone Thee, denied Thee, crucified Thee*. The interrogative pronoun *who* quickly yields to the confession: It was *my treason*, it was *I, I* it was, *I*. Yet Bridges utters the name of Jesus twice, as if speaking to Him, a beloved friend. So then, it is not simply "I did this to thee," but, "It was I, Lord Jesus, I was the one who did this to thee." The final five-syllable line—again, the slowed-down A phrase—sums it all up: *I crucified Thee.*

The third stanza brings out the reversal of man's expectations, and the indignity to which God submits Himself, in love for sinful man:

Lo, the Good Shepherd for the sheep is offered;
The slave hath sinned, and the Son hath suffered;
For man's atonement, while he nothing heedeth,
God intercedeth.

"I am the Good Shepherd," says Jesus, "and I lay down my life for the sheep" (Jn 10:14–15). But it's one thing to interpose one's body between the sheep and the wolf. It's another to be put to death by those you came to save. "He is brought as a lamb to the slaughter," says Isaiah of the Suffering Servant (Is 53:7). The second line is equally devastating. Notice the sibilance linking the nouns and verbs across the break in the line: The slave sins, and the Son suffers. The line recalls Jesus' parable of the wicked tenant farmers who slew their master's son, saying, "This is the heir; come, let us kill him, and seize on his inheritance" (Mt 21:38). In bondage to our sins, we slaves put the Son of God to death. Man is heedless, oblivious of his sins and of God's love. Man hears nothing, but *God intercedeth* for him; the Son entreats the Father on man's behalf, man the deaf and foolish. Those two words, making up the entire last line, are a powerful summary of the paradox of the Christian faith: God intercedes.

The fourth stanza turns from mankind to the individual who prays the prayer and sings the hymn:

For me, kind Jesus, was Thy incarnation,
Thy mortal sorrow, and Thy life's oblation;
Thy death of anguish and Thy bitter passion,
For my salvation.

That, poetically, is perfect. Again Bridges builds a stanza around the interplay of pronouns. The phrase *for me* begins it, and the phrase *for my* concludes it. Everything in between belongs to Jesus, *kind Jesus*; and the possessive *Thy*, sung five times in succession, tolls like a solemn bell. One after another, *incarnation, sorrow, oblation, death, passion*, all belong to Jesus and all are *for me, for my salvation*. All the lines rhyme: All are directed toward that final word.

Such love demands a response, and Bridges delivers it in the final stanza:

Therefore, kind Jesus, since I cannot pay Thee,
I do adore Thee, and will ever pray Thee,
Think on Thy pity and Thy love unswerving,
Not my deserving.

The first stanza had begun with an address to the *holy Jesus*, but this last stanza repeats the address of the previous stanza, to *kind Jesus*. Such kindness cannot be repaid. We have nothing to weigh in the scales with the love of Jesus. What is left? Only the adoration of a loving and grateful heart. For the last time we hear the pronouns, *I Thee*; and the poet begs Jesus to think about *Thy pity, Thy love unswerving*, and not—here we find the last of the possessives—*not my deserving.*

In *Ah, Holy Jesus* we acknowledge our guilt in nailing Jesus to the Cross. But in perhaps the best known of all the Passiontide hymns, *O Sacred Head, Sore Wounded*, we plead for the grace to join Jesus at the Cross, to look upon the beauty of His love, and to be embraced by Him when we die.

The hymn has an interesting history. The original Latin poem on which the hymn is based, *Sacre caput cruentatum*, is attributed to St. Bernard of Clairvaux, in the twelfth century. Bernard was a mystic, a powerful theologian, and a tireless reformer of the Church, and that reforming zeal, along with his insistence upon the soul's utter worthlessness apart from the grace of God, endeared him to the Protestant reformers. So it's no surprise that his Latin poem inspired a German poet, Paulus Gerhardt, in the seventeenth century (1656). Then Bach united the poem with a melody by Hans Leo Hassler and, providing his own astonishingly complex and delicate harmonizations, made it the centerpiece of his oratorio, the *Saint Matthew Passion*. To this day the melody is known as the *Passion Chorale*.

I'd need many pages to illustrate the intricacy of the Hassler melody and the adornment by Bach. A few points are in order, to show how the music binds together the lines of the rather long eight-line stanzas, and how it lays an unusual stress upon the final line—a stress that is both resolved and unresolved, like an object at rest but suspended in space, between earth and heaven.

Here is the first stanza, with melodic phrases marked by letters, and variations by an asterisk:

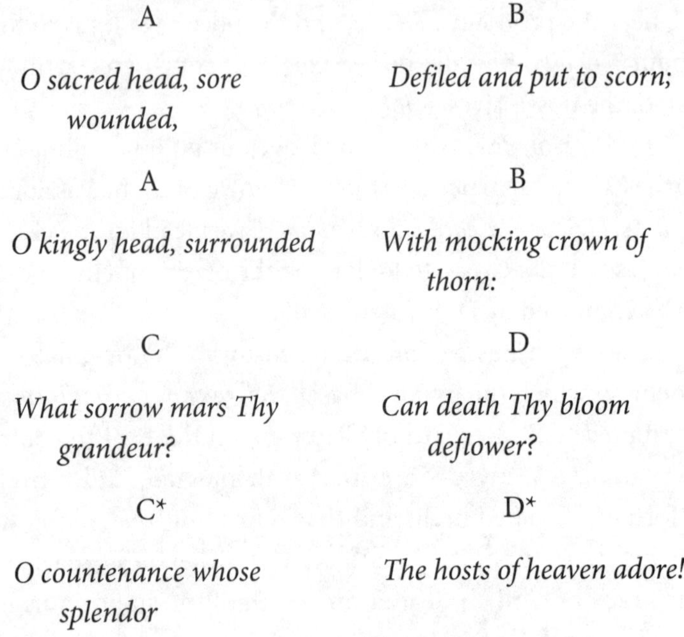

A	B
O sacred head, sore wounded,	*Defiled and put to scorn;*
A	B
O kingly head, surrounded	*With mocking crown of thorn:*
C	D
What sorrow mars Thy grandeur?	*Can death Thy bloom deflower?*
C*	D*
O countenance whose splendor	*The hosts of heaven adore!*

So designated, the melody seems to divide neatly in half. Lines one and two are repeated exactly in lines three and four, and lines five and six are repeated with variations in lines seven and eight.

But if we look more closely, we see all kinds of elements crossing over from one half to the other. It isn't just that the C and D phrases themselves echo the A and B phrases. If we designate each phrase by the note on which it ends—a whole note, held a long time in this solemn melody and, therefore, well stressed—another pattern appears. Still more patterns appear if we take note of the *chord* of that final note in each phrase, as Bach harmonized them in the version that appears most commonly in the hymnals. I'll designate that chord in parentheses:

E (C)	A (Am)
O sacred head, sore wounded,	*Defiled and put to scorn;*
E (C)	A (Am)
O kingly head, surrounded	*With mocking crown of thorn:*
C (C)	E (E)
What sorrow mars Thy grandeur?	*Can death Thy bloom deflower?*
B (G)	E (C)
O countenance whose splendor	*The hosts of heaven adore!*

Now let's consider how the music illumines and even helps to determine the meaning of the poetry. We see from the pattern above that the first phrases in each line always end on the calm of a major chord, usually C major. The first two lines, however, end on A minor—as befits the sorrow of the scene, and the *scorn* heaped upon Christ, the *crown of thorn* pressed upon His brow in mockery. The third line ends on an E major chord, which is still typical for music written in A minor, so that in the end we expect to return to A minor—but we don't. We return instead to the peace of the C major chord. Not only that, but the note itself is suspended, so to speak. The chord is C, but the note is E, just as it was in the opening phrases of lines one and two. It's an unusual and haunting way to end the stanza, but it fits quite well. For the *hosts of heaven* are not only adoring the splendor of Christ's countenance, they are also adoring the *sacred head, sore wounded*. In other words, the music with its crisscrossing patterns throws into high relief the paradox of the beauty of Christ crucified, fulfilling the prophecy of Isaiah:

> *Who hath believed our report? and to whom is the arm of the Lord revealed?*
>
> *For he shall grow up before him as a tender plant, and as a root out of a dry ground: he hath no form nor comeliness; and when we shall see him, there is no beauty that we should desire him.*
>
> *He is despised and rejected of men; a man of sorrows, and acquainted with grief: and we hid as it were our faces from him; he was despised, and we esteemed him not.* (Is 53:1–3)

But it is this very Savior, bleeding and dying, in whom we see the glory of God revealed, the glory of love.

The second stanza builds from this paradox and applies it to the plight of the poet, who still longs for the light of Christ's countenance. I'll highlight two significant progressions of motifs, one in boldface, one in normal type:

> ***Thy beauty***, *long desired,*
> *Hath* vanished *from our sight;*
> ***Thy power*** *is all expired,*
> *And* quenched *the light of light.*
> *Ah me! for whom Thou diest,*
> Hide not *so far* ***Thy grace***:
> Show me, *O Love most highest,*
> *The brightness of* ***Thy face***.

That is remarkable. The *beauty* of Christ has vanished; He is a man in the throes of an agonizing death. His *power* is expiring, as He surrenders His spirit. He is *light of light*, as the Nicene Creed puts it, the divine light of the Son begotten by the light of the Father. That light now is *quenched*. But the stanza turns: If Christ's beauty is hidden, if His power is surrendered, if the light is extinguished, let not His *grace* be hidden! *Show me*, cries the poet, *the brightness of Thy face!* That brings us to the heart of Christ's love. *There* is to be found true beauty, true power, and the splendor of God.

In the third stanza, unfortunately omitted from most hymnals, the face of Jesus is not only something for the poet to behold; it is, when Jesus turns toward him, a sign that he is numbered among the flock:

I pray Thee, Jesus, own me,
Me, Shepherd good, for Thine;
Who to Thy fold hast won me,
And fed with truth divine.
Me guilty, me refuse not,
Incline Thy face to me,
This comfort that I lose not,
On earth to comfort Thee.

He longs for the comfort of comforting the Crucified—the assurance that he will be saved, as he stands by his dying Lord. More than comfort, though; he cries out in an agony of longing to take part in the sufferings of Jesus. True love would wish no less:

In Thy most bitter passion
My heart to share doth cry,

With Thee for my salvation
Upon the cross to die.
Ah, keep my heart thus moved
To stand Thy Cross beneath,
To mourn Thee, well-beloved,
Yet thank Thee for Thy death.

But the poem ends with the embrace of Jesus. Now it is not that the soul willingly accepts the Cross, but that Jesus, His arms thrown wide, takes us to Him, because the Cross is none other than the Tree of Life:

My days are few, O fail not,
With Thine immortal power,
To hold me that I quail not
In death's most fearful hour:
That I may fight befriended,
And see in my last strife
To me Thine arms extended
Upon the Cross of life.

Easter morning penetrates the dread darkness of Good Friday. To that morning we turn, and to Charles Wesley's triumphant hymn, *Christ the Lord is Risen Today* (1742), straightforward and bold in meter, and easy to set to a wide variety of melodies, with and without the *alleluia* often appended to each line. The lines have seven syllables each, beginning on the strong beat; it's impossible to sing this poem *without* the power of joy:

Christ the Lord is risen today,
Sons of men and angels say:

Raise your joys and triumphs high,
Sing, ye heavens, and earth reply,
Alleluia!

The second line has lately been emended to the sexless and impersonal *all creation join to say*. This is most unfortunate. Wesley is calling upon *all beings made in the image and likeness of God*; he is calling upon two choirs, the *sons of men* and the *angels*. We fallen but redeemed human beings join with the never-fallen angels to praise God: Imagine two choirs in the loft of a church, one choir to the left and one to the right, singing together and in response to one another. The angels are the *sons of God* (Jb 38:7), while men (and women, and children) are the sons of Adam. Those differences make the harmony all the sweeter, as we unite in praise: *Sing, ye heavens, and earth reply!*

Most hymnals stitch together the first two lines of the second stanza with the last two lines of the third stanza. Let me present them as Wesley wrote them:

Love's redeeming work is done,
Fought the fight, the battle won:
Lo, our Sun's eclipse is o'er!
Lo, He sets in blood no more!
Alleluia!

Vain the stone, the watch, the seal,
Christ has burst the gates of hell;
Death in vain forbids Him rise;
Christ has opened Paradise.
Alleluia!

"I have fought [the] good fight," says St. Paul (2 Tm 4:7), and Wesley applies the words to the battle Christ has won: This is the definitive fight, the definitive battle. No longer will the darkness of the tomb eclipse the light of Christ, *our Sun*, punning upon the *Son of God*. Wesley compresses several scriptural "eclipses" into those two powerful lines. When Christ was crucified, "from the sixth hour there was darkness over all the land unto the ninth hour" (Mt 27:45). But he is also thinking of Christ's prophecy of the last days, when "shall the sun be darkened" (Mt 24:29). St. John describes those days most vividly: "And I beheld when he had opened the sixth seal, and lo, there was a great earthquake; and the sun became black as sackcloth of hair, and the moon became as blood" (Rv 6:14). The victory of Christ upon Calvary has already secured that victory at the end of time. In other words, on Good Friday the tumultuous battle was engaged, and the Sun, the Son of God, indeed set *in blood*, the red of the skies at nightfall, the red of His precious blood. No more: It is all sunrise now.

Hence the bold exclamation of the following stanza: *vain!* That is the key word; all the shifts and strategies of the realm of death are in vain, useless, empty. "So they went," says St. Matthew of the Jewish leaders, "and made the sepulcher sure, sealing the stone, and setting a watch" (Mt 27:68). All in vain. Christ bursts the gates of His tomb, and bursts *the gates of hell*: We think of both at once. Those gates of hell, the seal, the stone, and the watch set upon the tomb, cannot hold Him back, cannot prevail against His might. *Death in vain forbids Him rise*; Death like a feeble soldier standing guard over the entrance to life eternal. The shattering of hell's gates leads us to the climactic image of a gate, not shattered, but flung wide: *Christ hath opened Paradise.*

The fourth stanza is an ebullient defiance of death, applying the words of St. Paul to this most joyous day:

Lives again our glorious King;
Where, O Death, is now Thy sting?
Dying once, He all doth save;
Where Thy victory, O grave?
Alleluia!

The first and third lines echo Paul's application of Christ's death to the death and resurrection of all believers:

> *If we have been planted together in the likeness of his death, we shall be also in the likeness of his resurrection:*
>
> *Knowing this, that our old man is crucified with him, that the body of sin might be destroyed, that henceforth we should not serve sin.*
>
> *For he that is dead is freed from sin.*
>
> *Now if we be dead with Christ, we believe that we shall also live with him:*
>
> *Knowing that Christ being raised from the dead dieth no more; death hath no more dominion over him.*
>
> *For in that he died, he died unto sin once; but in that he liveth, he liveth unto God.* (Rom 6:5–10)

These verses will be the basis of the fifth stanza also, as we'll see. Meanwhile, the second and fourth lines echo Paul's declaration of Christ's triumph: "Death is swallowed up in victory. O death, where is thy sting? O grave, where is thy victory?" (1 Cor 15:54–55). Wesley interlaces the four lines to great effect. Christ lives: So, O death, where's your sting? He has died to save us all: Well then, O grave, where's your victory?

The fifth stanza renders the victory personal. We rise with Christ, as Paul has said, because we have been conformed to His death and resurrection:

Soar we now where Christ has led,
Following our exalted Head;
Made like Him, like Him we rise;
Ours the cross, the grave, the skies.
Alleluia!

Christ is not simply our example. He is our *exalted Head*, the Head of His body, the church. We have been incorporated into Christ, *made like Him*. Wesley draws the inevitable conclusion. If we have been made like Christ, then like Christ we will rise: Notice the deft repetition of the phrase. The fourth line begins most emphatically: *Ours* will be those things we have associated with the death and resurrection of Jesus. We will take up the Cross. We will enter into the death of Christ; we will meet the grave. And we will rise.

Where can Wesley go from here? We might expect the standard doxology to conclude the hymn, the praise of the Holy Trinity. But instead Wesley devotes his final lines to praise of the risen Christ, and in a way that admits of no further addition:

Hail the Lord of earth and heaven!
Praise to Thee by both be given:
Thee we greet triumphant now;
Hail, the Resurrection Thou!
Alleluia!

The final verb *hail* gives homage not simply to the Lord who *gives us* resurrection, but to the Lord who is in His own Person that resurrection. When He told the grieving Martha that her brother Lazarus would rise again, Martha replied that she knew he would rise again "in the resurrection at the last day" (Jn 11:24). But that could hardly console her now. It was a distant and shadowy hope. The body rotting in the tomb was all too near. Jesus, however, was also near, and in a few short words, He transformed that hope forever, transformed it into assurance, personal, witnessed in the flesh. "I am the resurrection, and the life," said Jesus (Jn 11:25). Again we turn from what Jesus has done to who Jesus is—to the final word of the poem, *Thou.*

Wesley's hymn proclaims the meaning of Easter; others meditate joyously upon the events of that day. One of these even meditates upon the fear and confusion of the disciples. It is Jean Tisserand's Latin hymn, *O Filii et filiae* (1494), usually translated into English as *O Sons and Daughters.* John Mason Neale's nineteenth-century translation has formed the basis for many alternate versions, some of them slightly and happily revised, others mangled to modernize the language. I shall choose a version that remains close to Neale. The hymn has been set to many melodies, all of them with alleluias sung before or after the verse or both. The best known, a deeply moving minor-key air filled with lilting spills of notes, is named for the poem: *O Filii et Filiae.* But the boldest, to my ear, is the sixteenth-century *Gelobt Sei Gott*, breaking the silence of the tomb with its initial high C.

The stanzas are composed of rhyming triplets—as we have seen, an ideal form for the ironic turn or the surprising climax:

O sons and daughters, let us sing!
The King of heaven, the glorious King
O'er death and hell rose triumphing.
Alleluia! Alleluia! Alleluia!

Why do we *sing?* Because the *King*—note the proud repetition of that title of honor—rose *triumphing* and we break into the three alleluias, as if we could not endure their absence for long.

Those alleluias punctuate every stanza, even when nothing glorious seems to have happened to justify them. That's because every detail of that Resurrection morning is precious to us. We cry alleluia in happy anticipation:

That Easter morn at break of day,
The faithful women went their way
To seek the tomb where Jesus lay.
Alleluia! Alleluia! Alleluia!

How fine it is to be accompanying them in that early light! We know from Scripture that they were so absorbed in their grief, they had forgotten to see to the most obvious problem: "Who shall roll us away the stone from the door of the sepulcher?" (Mk 16:3). No need:

An angel clad in white they see,
Who sat and spake unto the three,
"Your Lord doth go to Galilee."
Alleluia! Alleluia! Alleluia!

"Tell his disciples and Peter that he goeth before you into Galilee," said the angel (Mk 16:7). The poet does not dally, as we imagine the women did not, and immediately we are with the disciples huddling in their room:

That night the apostles met in fear;
Amidst them came their Lord most dear
And said, "My peace be on all here."
Alleluia! Alleluia! Alleluia!

We don't need words like "when" and "then" and "after that"—the lines hasten us in joy to the moment when Jesus suddenly appeared before them and said, "Peace be unto you" (Jn 20:19).

He showed them His wounds, but Thomas was not with them then:

When Thomas first the tidings heard,
How they had seen the risen Lord,
He doubted the disciples' word.
Alleluia! Alleluia! Alleluia!

I've long thought that the alleluias at the end of this stanza are the sweetest in all our hymnody. Why should we be singing alleluia, just after the description of Thomas' doubt? But we know what is going to happen. We are enjoying Thomas' embarrassment, and we anticipate his joy. We also disarm the most dreadful weapon in the arsenal of doubt—that we should take it too seriously. Thomas doubts. Well then, he doubts! The Lord will not let him rest there. So without the slightest announcement or preparation, the Lord is suddenly with Thomas:

"My pierced side, O Thomas, see;
My hands, my feet, I show to thee;
Not faithless, but believing be."
Alleluia! Alleluia! Alleluia!

That last line is directed to all of us. Have confidence! Believe! Thomas responds, with a *greater profession of faith* than we have yet heard in all of the Gospels:

No longer Thomas then denied,
He saw the feet, the hands, the side;

"Thou art my Lord and God," he cried.
Alleluia! Alleluia! Alleluia!

The next stanza brings that moment to the present, now, to us who declare that Jesus is the Lord (cf. Jn 20:29):

How blest are they who have not seen,
And yet whose faith has constant been,
For they eternal life shall win.
Alleluia! Alleluia! Alleluia!

We end the poem by returning to the beginning, in an outburst of joy:

On this most holy day of days,
Our hearts and voices, Lord, we raise
To Thee, in jubilee and praise.
Alleluia! Alleluia! Alleluia!

Chapter Six

Our Love for Jesus

THE great St. Thomas Aquinas was praying, his eyes fixed upon a crucifix before him. He was alone, but one of his fellow Dominicans, passing by the door, overheard a conversation from within.

"Thomas," said a voice, "you have written well of Me. What do you wish for a reward?"

"*Solum te*," Thomas replied. "Thee alone."

The Christian faith is not simply a bundle of propositions but an invitation to a personal relationship with Jesus Christ, who has bridged the abyss between the Creator and the creature, between God all-holy and sinful man. Many Christian hymns, then, are songs of love for Jesus. They are filled with expressions of desire, such as may be found in the Psalms, for a bond of friendship that no one on earth can earn or forge on his own. Friends on earth are usually of equal station, but here we are talking about God, who emptied Himself to be born as a man, and who said to His apostles at the Last Supper—the apostles, only one of whom would stay with Him on Calvary—"Henceforth I call you not servants; for the servant knoweth not what his lord doeth; but I have called you friends; for all things that I have heard of my Father I have made known unto you" (Jn 15:15).

Imagine being held worthy of friendship by Jesus. That's what motivated Johann Franck to write *Jesu, Meine Freude* (1650), beautifully rendered into English as *Jesus, Priceless Treasure* by the great translator of hymns, Catherine Winkworth (1863):

Jesus, priceless treasure,
Source of purest pleasure,
Truest friend to me;
Long my heart hath panted,
Till it well-nigh fainted,
Thirsting after Thee.
Thine I am, O spotless Lamb,
I will suffer nought to hide Thee,
Ask for nought beside Thee.

Notice that the stanza is divided into two very different parts, marked by the rhymes. The first part, comprising the first six lines, rhymes AABCCB, with the B rhymes knitting the whole together. The baroque composer Johann Crueger, writing for the poem a melody known by his name, appropriately repeats the music for the first three lines in the next three lines. But for the second part, the final three lines, the meter changes abruptly—and so does the melody. Line seven, with seven syllables, contains an internal rhyme, and could really be written as two separate lines: *Thine I am, / O spotless Lamb*. Line eight is the longest in the stanza, with eight syllables, introducing a new rhyme, one with two syllables, just as in lines one and two. That gives Franck the opportunity, though, to use line nine, the last in the stanza, to bring the poem round to the beginning—for the last line is, in its meter, just like the first line. Crueger, who saw what the poet had done, thus repeats, with a small flourish, the stately melody of the first line, a simple descent, note by note, sol-fa-mi-re-do, ending on the minor chord.

The structure of the stanza reflects the meaning. Jesus is addressed as the *priceless treasure*, an allusion to the parable:

> *The kingdom of heaven is like unto a treasure hid in a field; the which when a man hath found, he hideth, and for joy thereof goeth and selleth all that he hath, and buyeth that field.* (Mt 13:44)

The poet transfers the simile. Now it's not simply *the kingdom of heaven* that the man finds, but Jesus Himself, the King, in whom the kingdom of heaven wholly subsists. Jesus is a treasure beyond price, like the *pearl of great price* in the parable immediately following. He is worth everything, the surrender of all that we have and all that we are.

Jesus is the poet's *truest friend*, because He never will cease to love us, but He is also infinitely beyond our possession, unless He gives Himself as a grace. Nor do we yet behold Him as He is. So Franck turns to the psalms for the language of longing:

> *As the hart panteth after the water brooks, so panteth my soul after thee, O God.*
>
> *My soul thirsteth for God, for the living God: when shall I come and appear before God?* (Ps 42:1–2)

Then he declares the commitment of his whole self. *Thine I am*, he says, with the emphasis on the predicate nominative: *Thine*. Jesus is the *spotless Lamb*, the One seated upon the throne of God. He is not a pagan god *in a temple*, as Zeus dwelt on Olympus or Odin in Valhalla. He Himself is the kingdom and the temple, the city and the light:

> *And I saw no temple therein: for the Lord God Almighty and the Lamb are the temple of it.*
>
> *And the city had no need of the sun, neither of the moon, to shine in it: for the glory of God did lighten it, and the Lamb is the light thereof.* (Rv 21:21–22)

Unlike the merchant in the parable who hid the treasure lest it be found and stolen, the poet has no need to hide Jesus. He *will suffer nought to hide* that spotless Lamb, but will proclaim Him to all who wish to hear and see. A merchant might use his treasure to buy what he wants, but the kingdom of heaven cannot be so used; it is itself the aim of all our desires. So the poet concludes the first stanza with the words of Thomas Aquinas. What does he want? Only Jesus.

The second stanza applies the wisdom of the first to the troubles of our lives:

> *In Thine arm I rest me;*
> *Foes who would molest me*
> *Cannot reach me here.*
> *Though the earth be shaking,*
> *Every heart be quaking,*
> *God dispels our fear;*
> *Sin and hell in conflict fell*
> *With their heaviest storms assail us:*
> *Jesus will not fail us.*

Again the poet has turned to the language of the psalms. The foes against whose wicked designs David so commonly begs the Lord to protect him are identified with the ultimate foes, *sin and hell.* Their actions are symbolized by the earthquake that causes hearts to tremble with fear, and by the assailing storms. They may remind us of the storm and earthquake that accompanied the climax of the terrible battle upon Calvary, when it seemed that evil had triumphed: "And behold, the veil of the temple was rent in twain from the top to the bottom; and the earth did quake, and the rocks rent" (Mt 27:51). But we are not to fear. "Be not afraid," says Jesus, "for I have overcome the world" (Jn 16:33). *Jesus will not fail us.*

Why then should we be troubled?

Hence, all thoughts of sadness!
For the Lord of gladness,
Jesus, enters in:
Those who love the Father,
Though the storms may gather,
Still have peace within;
Yea, whate'er we here must bear,
Still in Thee lies purest pleasure,
Jesus, priceless treasure.

Here the poet combines the motifs of two psalms with the triumph that follows upon the Cross. First, he banishes *thoughts of sadness*, as does the poet in Psalm 42:

> *Why art thou cast down, O my soul? and why art thou disquieted within me? hope thou in God: for I shall yet praise him, who is the health of my countenance, and my God.* (Ps 42:11)

Then he envisions the triumphant entry of Jesus into glory:

> *Lift up your heads, O ye gates; and be ye lift up, ye everlasting doors; and the King of glory shall come in.* (Ps 24:7)

So no matter what crosses we must bear in this life, as long as we have Jesus, we enjoy some measure of "the peace of God, which that passeth all understanding" (Phil 4:7). And the poem, like a pearl, comes round to its beginning in sweet perfection: *Jesus, priceless treasure.*

Here let's glance at another translation of the same German poem, by J. W. Wotherspoon (1912):

Jesus, all my gladness,
My repose in sadness,
Jesus, heaven to me:
Ah, my heart long plaineth,
Ah, my spirit straineth,
Longeth after Thee!
Thine I am, O holy Lamb;
Only where Thou art is pleasure,
Thee alone I treasure.

Hence with earthly treasure:
Thou art all my pleasure,
Jesus, my desire!
Hence, for pomps I care not,
Even as though they were not
Rank and fortune's hire.
Want and gloom, cross, death and tomb;
Naught that I may suffer ever
Shall from Jesus sever.

Flee, dark clouds that lower,
For my joy-bestower,
Jesus, enters in!
Joy from tribulation,

Hope from desolation,
They who love God win.
Be it blame or scorn or shame,
Thou art with me in earth's sadness,
Jesus, all my gladness!

Wotherspoon has used repetition to fine effect. All great poets do, but repetition in a hymn gains added power from the fact that there's also a melody to accentuate the echo. Knowing the melody for which he is translating the lyrics, Wotherspoon, like Winkworth, makes sure that the final line of the first stanza echoes the first line—they will be sung to the same notes—and that the final line of the entire hymn will repeat the first line exactly. But he also dares to repeat the rhymes on *pleasure* and *treasure*, linking the first stanza with the second. That's a clever move. For the words are repeated but in a different context, revealing the gulf between the pleasures of the world and the joy that the love of Jesus brings. The music underscores the difference. Let me print the final lines of the first stanza beside the first lines of the second stanza, using boldface to denote what is sung to exactly the same melody line:

ONLY WHERE THOU ART IS PLEASURE,
Thee alone I treasure.
Hence with earthly treasure:
THOU ART ALL MY PLEASURE.

Hence with it all, cries the poet! Against the treasure that Jesus is, all the pomps and glamour of the world, even if they were not dependent upon mere fortune or social rank, are nothing. We care not for them. How can we, when we know the gladness of Jesus?

This longing to see Jesus is the theme of an anonymous eleventh-century Latin hymn, translated into English by Edward Caswall (1849) as *Jesus, the Very Thought of Thee*:

Jesus, the very thought of Thee
With sweetness fills my breast;
But sweeter far Thy face to see,
And in Thy presence rest.

The poem is in the common English ballad meter we've seen before, with alternating rhymes. It's a simple, unsophisticated meter, which in unskillful hands can degenerate into singsong. But Caswall knows what he's doing. Look at the first line, beginning with the beloved name of Jesus. The Lord is the whole aim of the poet's heart. Even to think of Him fills his breast with sweetness. Thus the word *very* is the key to the stanza. It is not inserted to fill up a couple of metrical spaces. Caswall is setting up an argument: If the very *thought* of Jesus brings so much pleasure, how much more delightful will it be to look upon His face? The longing contemplation broached by the first two lines is answered by an infinitely greater fulfillment in the last two lines, fulfillment which is also *rest* in the presence of Christ.

St. Paul, alluding to Isaiah 64:4, says that the glory we are made for is wholly unknown to the world:

Eye hath not seen, nor ear heard, neither hath it entered into the heart of man, the things which God hath prepared for them that love him. (1 Cor 2:9)

The poet adopts that language in his meditation upon the name of Jesus, which means, as we've seen, "God saves":

Nor voice can sing, nor heart can frame,
Nor can the memory find
A sweeter sound than Thy blest name,
O Savior of mankind!

The motif of sweetness links this stanza to the first, but now the focus has shifted to the name, which implies the mission, what Jesus has come to do for us. Hence the final line, with its joyful address beginning with the exclamation *O*, is developed in the next stanza:

O hope of every contrite heart,
O joy of all the meek,
To those who fall, how kind Thou art!
How good to those who seek!

A simple stanza? Yes and no. It's simple enough for a small child to understand. But it is a small work of art. Lines one and two are bound by the parallel grammar; so are lines three and four. But line one is also bound to line three: The contrite are those who fall and are truly sorrowful. And line two is bound to line four: The meek are those who humbly seek the kingdom of God and find it. "Blessed are the meek," says Jesus, "for they shall inherit the earth" (Mt 5:5). "Seek," says Jesus, "and ye shall find; knock, and it shall be opened unto you" (Mt 7:7). Thus we build toward a climax. The contrite have *hope*, but the meek have *joy*. The Lord is *kind* to those who fall, as the Samaritan was kind to the man who had fallen among thieves; but He is *good* beyond description, bounteous, to those who seek. We move from contrition to meekness, from hope in distress to an energetic pilgrimage toward the kingdom of God.

The fourth stanza picks up the motif of seeking and fulfills it in finding:

But what to those who find? Ah, this
No tongue nor pen can show:
The love of Jesus, what it is
None but His loved ones know.

Again we have what cannot be described in words. But there's a nugget of philosophical wisdom here. How can anyone know what love is by description? Only the lover can know; it is knowledge gleaned from a whole way of being. The same is true of the beloved; all the more, infinitely more, when the other is Jesus.

The final stanza returns to the first, again beginning with the sweet name of Jesus:

Jesus, our only Joy be Thou,
As Thou our Prize wilt be;
Jesus, be Thou our Glory now,
And through eternity.

We mustn't think that the final word, *eternity*, is there to provide a standard ending for a hymn. The whole poem has been structured by anticipation, or foretaste, and fulfillment. We move from the thought of Jesus, to the sight of Jesus face to face. We move from contrition and forgiveness to meekness and joy. We move from seeking to finding. So in this last stanza, we move from the joy we experience in Jesus now to the *prize* that Jesus will be for us when our joy is fulfilled. Both now and in that day that knows no sunset, Jesus will be our *Glory*, our only boast—both now and *through eternity*.

So far we have looked at feelings of longing, gratitude, love, and joy. Now let us look at deeds. How can we repay Jesus for His love for us? That's the question asked by the American revivalist, Robert Lowry, in his hymn *Savior! Thy Dying Love* (1871):

Savior! Thy dying love
Thou gavest me,
Nor should I aught withhold,
Dear Lord, from Thee:
In love my soul would bow,
My heart fulfill its vow,
Some offering bring Thee now,
Something for Thee.

This first stanza shows how well the poet understood the usefulness of the old second person singular pronoun, especially in the accusative case: *thee*. Unlike *you*, it allows for rhymes upon a wealth of English words, among them the important verbs *be* and *see*, and the pronouns *we, he, she*, and here, *me*. Rhyme isn't employed for sound alone but for structure and meaning. Lowry's hymn is a meditation upon an exchange of gifts, between the Lord and the human soul—between *Thee* and *me*. We see this in the first stanza. Jesus has given to the poet His love, even unto death. What can the poet give the Lord in return? The second half of the stanza builds up tension in the triple rhyme: The soul must *bow*, the heart must fulfill its *vow*, the poet must bring some offering to the Lord *now*—but what? The tension is resolved, but not entirely, by the last line—*something for Thee. Something*—what shall that something be?

If we expect the poet to boast of the feats he is going to perform for Jesus, we miss his point altogether. For Jesus continually gives, and Lowry needs those gifts:

At the blest mercy seat,
Pleading for me,
My feeble faith looks up,
Jesus, to Thee;
Help me the cross to bear,
Thy wondrous love declare,
Some song to raise, or prayer,
Something for Thee.

His faith is feeble, and pleads to Jesus for mercy. Jesus, then, will be to Lowry what Simon was for Jesus, when Simon helped Him carry the cross. That is the decreed burden of each mortal saint. But we cannot carry it without Jesus to help us! Nor, without Jesus, can we even declare His wondrous love for us. Our arms are strengthless. We cannot, without Jesus, raise the small burden of a single song or prayer—a simple *something*, as the poet repeats the indefinite pronoun, suggesting that nothing could ever be sufficient.

In the third stanza, Lowry begs the Lord to create a new heart in him, to give him the courage of faith, so that he may accomplish something—and now the pronoun *some* takes over the poetry:

Give me a faithful heart,
Guided by Thee,
That each departing day
Henceforth may see
Some work of love begun,

Some deed of kindness done,
Some wanderer sought and won,
Something for Thee.

With a deft sense of the accumulating power of his plea, Lowry for once *does not* divide the stanza. There's no pause in the middle; the departing day is to see something, some work, some deed, some wanderer sought, *something.*

A lesser poet would end the hymn on that same line, *something for Thee.* But for the final stanza Lowry abandons *some* altogether. A more potent pronoun begins the verse:

All that I am, and have—
Thy gifts so free—
In joy, in grief, through life,
Dear Lord, for Thee;
And when Thy face I see,
My ransomed soul shall be,
Through all eternity,
Offered for Thee.

The first four lines seem to complete the thought of the previous stanza. The *something* is now identified as *all.* What does Lowry want to give to Jesus? All he is, all he has. But he is nothing and has nothing by himself; all the good things he owns are the Lord's gifts to him. His soul has been ransomed by the Lord's love. Jesus does not want our works, merely, as if He were a labor contractor. He wants ourselves, our hearts. He does not hire us; He invites us to the feast. So what do we offer? The last line of a beautiful Eucharistic hymn puts it well: *Thou didst give Thyself to me; now I give myself to Thee.*

Many hymns express the same longing, not specifically for Jesus, but for God. The language, as we've seen, may be found throughout Scripture: "With my soul have I desired thee in the night; yea, with my spirit will I seek thee early" (Is 26:9). St. Augustine knew that longing, when he wrote this most poignant passage in his *Confessions*:

> *Late have I loved you, Beauty so ancient and so new, late have I loved you! Lo, you were within, but I outside, seeking there for you, and upon the shapely things you have made I rushed headlong—I, misshapen. You were with me, but I was not with you. They held me back far from you, those things which would have no being, were they not in you. You called, shouted, broke through my deafness; you flared, blazed, banished my blindness; you lavished your fragrance, I gasped; and now I pant for you; I tasted you, and now I hunger and thirst; you touched me, and I burned for your peace.*

There we have the aching paradox of human life. God has showered us with beauty, the skies, the sea, the meadows, the trees and flowers and animals with which we share this world; and then the beauty of children, and of men and women. They all cry out, with the psalmist, "It is He that hath made us, and not we ourselves!" (Ps 100:2). But when we seek our fulfillment in them, they disappoint us. Then we know the bitterness of the Preacher, who, speaking in the person of the rich and glorious King Solomon, says that all the gardens he planted, the silver and gold he treasured up, the singers he enlisted at his court, the houses he built and the vineyards he stretched across the hills, amounted to nothing: "Then I looked on all the works that my hands had wrought, and on the labor that I had labored to do; and, behold, all was vanity and vexation of spirit, and there was no profit under the sun" (Eccl 2:11). The man who seeks his good in the Lord gains all the good of these things, and infinitely more: "Seek ye first the kingdom of God, and His righteousness; and all these things shall be added unto you" (Mt 6:33). But if we seek those things first, we lose heaven, and earth into the bargain. "Fool," said the Lord to the man who sought fulfillment in stuffed granaries, "this night thy soul shall be required of thee" (Lk 12:20). "Our hearts are restless," says Augustine, "until they rest in Thee."

That longing is expressed with beautiful simplicity by the poet John Byrom (1773), in *My Spirit Longs for Thee*. It's printed in either two stanzas or four, depending on the melody. I prefer the minor key *Fingal*, an Irish air well adapted to the intricate repetitions of the poem:

My spirit longs for Thee
Within my troubled breast,
Though I unworthy be
Of so divine a Guest.
Of so divine a Guest
Unworthy though I be,
Yet has my heart no rest,
Unless it come from Thee.

Unless it come from Thee,
In vain I look around;
In all that I can see
No rest is to be found.
No rest is to be found
But in Thy blessed love:

O let my wish be crowned,
And send it from above.

Make no mistake. These aren't ordinary pious sentiments. The trouble weighing upon the poet's heart is that he at once longs for God and that he is quite unworthy of God. He wishes to invite God into his heart, but it is not a fit place. He would resign himself to disappointment and settle for less, but the heart is *made by God and for God* and cannot be filled by anything else. Consider the gallimaufry of luxuries with which a man will try to fill the vacuity in himself—houses, boats, cruises, fine food, sex, money, glitter—and yet the prospect of death remains, and in his quiet moments, he understands that it is all pointless, a vexation of the spirit.

Therefore the rest cannot come from within, and cannot be provided by the transient things of the world. It must come from God. But it must come *from* God; it must be a gift. That is, the heart cannot be a fit tabernacle for the Most High unless God makes it so. No strenuous spiritual striving will suffice, without the grace of God. So Byrom surveys the world and finds no rest, and fairly pleads with God, "You must send me rest, because if You do not, I never will find it!" The key word is *love*. We do not worship a principle, a force, or a solution to an equation, but the source and fulfillment of all personal being—the God who is, the God who loves.

"Herein is love," writes St. John, "not that we loved God, but that he loved us, and sent his Son to be the propitiation for our sins" (1 Jn 4:10). He recalls the words of the Master, who, after He called His apostles His friends, said, "Ye have not chosen me, but I have chosen you" (Jn 15:16). "Can a mother forget her sucking child," says the Lord through the prophet, "that she should not have compassion on the son of her womb? Yea, they may forget, yet will I not forget thee" (Is 49:15). The ancient pagans could not ascribe love to God, because that would imply a lack or a need; they did not grasp the superabundance of being that divine love expresses. More than we seek God, God seeks us, stray sheep and pitiful sinners though we are.

That is the gist of a beautiful nineteenth-century hymn, *I Sought the Lord*, written by an anonymous poet and set to the gentle melodies *Artavia* and *Peace*:

I sought the Lord, and afterward I knew
He moved my soul to seek Him, seeking me;
It was not I that found, O Savior true;
No, I was found of Thee.

The crucial word is the adverb *afterward*. The poet speaks retrospectively, from the vantage of someone who sees more and knows more than he did during the days of his seeking. When he was in the midst of that search, he thought he was looking for God, and did not yet know that God, seeking him, had moved him to seek. Now he draws the conclusion that would have surprised him at that time. Did he find God? No, that's not quite right. For the Savior is *true*—the word isn't tossed in to clinch the rhyme. Because Jesus is *true*, faithful, He never gave up on the poet. Jesus *found him*.

The second stanza takes the idea of seeking and finding and renders it in a moment of dramatic intensity:

Thou didst reach forth Thy hand and mine enfold;
I walked and sank not on the storm-vexed sea;
'Twas not so much that I on Thee took hold,
As Thou, dear Lord, on me.

How fine that first line is! We can feel the flesh of Jesus as, with sudden firmness, He takes us by the hand. Then the second line, metaphorical and literal at once, places us upon the tossing waves of the Sea of Galilee:

> *But the ship was now in the midst of the sea, tossed with waves: for the wind was contrary.*
>
> *And in the fourth watch of the night Jesus went unto them, walking on the sea.*
>
> *And when the disciples saw him walking on the sea, they were troubled, saying, It is a spirit; and they cried out for fear.*
>
> *But straightaway Jesus spake unto them, saying, Be of good cheer; it is I; be not afraid.*
>
> *And Peter answered him and said, Lord, if it be thou, bid me come unto thee on the water.*
>
> *And he said, Come. And when Peter was come down out of the ship, he walked on the water, to go to Jesus.*
>
> *But when he saw the wind boisterous, he was afraid; and beginning to sink, he cried, saying, Lord, save me.*
>
> *And immediately Jesus stretched forth his hand, and caught him, and said unto him, O thou of little faith, wherefore didst thou doubt?*
>
> *And when they were come into the ship, the wind ceased.* (Mt 14:22–32)

The poet has helped us see something we might miss. Jesus didn't happen to be walking in the direction of the disciples. He was walking on the sea to *seek them out*, knowing their trouble. He could have rebuked the wind and the waves from the shore, but He joined them in their hour of distress. Before they knew to pray for His assistance, He was on the way, approaching them, and saying, "Don't be afraid. I am here." He would say the same when He appeared to them after He had risen from the dead.

Think of those words: *Be of good cheer; it is I; be not afraid.* When the storms thunder upon us and we believe we are alone, Jesus is there. We walk—and if it were not for the Lord, we would sink. We cry, with St. Peter, "Lord, save me!" And we fling out our hands wildly. Even that is an act of faith. Jesus does not say to Peter, "O faithless man!" Our faith is a weakling, but a weakling at least can cry for help, hoping, though with but a crippled hope, that the Lord will save us. We do not give up and drown in despair. But it is not so much that we grasp hold of Jesus, but He that takes us to Him. He is there, before we pray.

The third and final stanza sums up the previous two:

I find, I walk, I love, but O the whole
Of love is but my answer, Lord, to Thee;
For Thou wert long beforehand with my soul,
Always Thou lovedst me.

The series of verbs that begin the stanza, with the repeated pronoun, expresses the futility of the speaker's actions without Christ. "I do this, I do that, I do the other," he seems to say, and it is all in vain, it amounts to nothing, because the *whole of love* is no more than our answer to God's love. The adverb that led the poem—*afterward*—is now reversed. The Lord is *beforehand* with our souls. He is the provident God: He sees from all eternity. But *beforehand* is then fulfilled in the last adverb, in that simple and profound declaration of faith and gratitude: *Always thou lovedst me.*

Chapter Seven

The Holy Eucharist

IN Tolkien's *The Lord of the Rings*, when Frodo and his companions embark upon the perilous quest to cast the last ring of power into the volcanic crater of Mount Doom, and save Middle Earth, the elves of Rivendell provide them with food for the journey. It is *lembas*, which, translated from Elvish into English, means *waybread*. It is light and sweet, baked into thin wafers, like the manna that fed the children of Israel in the desert: "It was like coriander seed, white; and the taste of it was like wafers made with honey" (Ex 16:31). It keeps fresh, too, as nourishing after many weeks as it was before. Its name renders into an old-fashioned English compound the inner meaning of the Latin *viaticum*, the Eucharist given to someone on the verge of making the final voyage over the waters of death: Bread for the *via*, "the way."

But this bread is also, as Catholics and Orthodox believe, and (with some qualifications) many Protestants also, the body and blood of Jesus. This belief in the Real Presence of Christ is not a theological add-on, like a flourish on top of a column. It is the literal fulfillment of Christ's parting words to His disciples, "Lo, I am with you always, even unto the end of the world" (Mt 28:20). It is the principal means by which St. Peter is to fulfill the command of the risen Christ: "Feed my sheep"

(Jn 21:17). It is the extension of the miracle of the loaves and the fishes, whereby the crowds, not in one place, but everywhere, are fed with imperishable food. It is our real foretaste of heaven: "Blessed are they which are called unto the marriage supper of the Lamb" (Rv 19:9).

All this implies what we might find in a truly excellent Eucharistic hymn. Piety, no doubt, and a loving meditation upon the words of Jesus, when He instituted the sacrament: "This is my body, which is broken for you: this do in remembrance of me" (1 Cor 11:24). But we might also expect an attempt to range across the whole of Scripture, seen as concentrated in the meaning of the Sacrament. And we might expect a sense of personal urgency, because this is *our* food, without which we perish in the wilderness.

Thomas Aquinas (1225–74) sets the gold standard for Eucharistic hymns. That theologian of vast learning turned his heart occasionally toward poetry, singing of the Eucharist. Let us look at his *Adoro Te*, translated into English as *Lost, All Lost in Wonder*, by the great Jesuit poet, Gerard Manley Hopkins:

Godhead here in hiding, whom I do adore,
Masked by these bare shadows, shape and nothing more,
See, Lord, at thy service low lies here a heart
Lost, all lost in wonder at the God thou art.

Seeing, touching, tasting are in thee deceived:
How says trusty hearing? that shall be believed;

What God's Son has told me, *take for truth I do;*

Truth himself speaks truly *or there's nothing true.*

I've inserted a space in the middle of each line, to reflect the Latin meter, which includes a *caesura* or pause after the word that ends on the sixth syllable. The result provides a subtle interplay between each half of the line, reflected by the melodies to which the hymn is sung (*Adoro Devote*, a plainsong melody from Aquinas' own time, is the loveliest). We see this interplay quite clearly in the first line. Aquinas adores God—but a God in hiding. That paradox is the poem's touchstone. In a fine reversal of expectations, Aquinas asserts that what he can see with his eyes, the bread and the wine, are *figuris*: Shape and nothing more, as Hopkins bravely renders it. It isn't God's presence that is shadowy; that is the bedrock reality here. God's presence is the substance, literally what stands beneath the appearances. To that presence Aquinas offers his heart in humility and love. He is not beholding a cracker, as one of our contemporary village idiots has scornfully put it. He is, in the Latin, *contemplans*, "contemplating"; beholding in wonder. In that contemplation, his heart and mind must submit themselves to God in love, because on their own they cannot comprehend Him: *Totum deficit*, says Aquinas, which Hopkins renders from within the experience, repeating the adjective to emphasize our helplessness—lost, all lost in wonder.

Why does he believe he is beholding the Lord? Notice the gerunds in the first line: *seeing, touching, tasting*. They involve the senses as they experience the bread and wine. We see the host, we feel it on the tongue, we taste it. But we know the Lord by *hearing*: because the Lord Himself has spoken to His apostles and, through them, to us. "Faith cometh by hearing, and hearing by the word of God," says St. Paul (Rom 10:17). Jesus gives witness: "I am the way, the truth, and the life" (Jn 14:6). So the presence of Jesus in the Eucharist is vouched by Truth Himself, who testifies that His flesh is true bread and His blood is true drink (Jn 6:55).

Modern hymns sometimes turn the Eucharist into an opportunity to celebrate the divinity of the singers. Consider the refrain from *I Myself Am the Bread of Life*:

I myself am the bread of life.
You and I are the bread of life,
taken and blessed, broken and shared by Christ.

That would have struck Aquinas as flat blasphemy. It's pretty bad poetry too. But in the third stanza, Aquinas does make the Eucharist personal, by bringing us to a most dramatic moment in Scripture:

On the cross thy godhead made no sign to men,
Here thy very manhood steals from human ken:
Both are my confession, both are my belief,
And I pray the prayer of the dying thief.

Hopkins hasn't been able to include the Latin *latebat*, it hid, which links this stanza to the first, and to the controlling theme of the poem. But he has rendered the idea quite well. When Jesus was dying upon the cross, it was His divinity that no one but the Blessed Mother could see. The crowds jeered. The Roman soldiers, all in a day's work, played dice for His robe.

The elders jeered, "He saved others; let him save himself, if he be Christ, the chosen of God" (Lk 23:35). One of the thieves took up that tune. But the other thief rebuked him and turned to Jesus to say, "Lord, remember me when thou comest into thy kingdom" (Lk 23:42).

That is the *prayer of the dying thief* that Aquinas alludes to. Why? Consider the thief's situation. He was dying. He knew nothing certain about life beyond this life. He did not expect to be taken down from the cross alive. He knew that Jesus was dying. In fact, Jesus, having been scourged within an inch of His life, was much closer to death than the thief was. And yet, who knows by what breath of the Holy Spirit, the thief calls Jesus "Lord," and begs to be remembered. When we receive the Sacrament, we sinners are in the position of that repentant thief. He could not see the divinity of Jesus, but professed it in one magnificent act of faith. We can see, in the host, *neither the divinity nor the humanity* of Jesus. Yet we believe. We too seek what the thief sought, to hear that tremendous promise: "Today shalt thou be with me in paradise" (Lk 23:43).

Then Aquinas turns to another moment of not seeing:

I am not like Thomas, wounds I cannot see,
But can plainly call thee Lord and God as he;
Let me to a deeper faith daily nearer move,
Daily make me harder hope and dearer love.

We recall the words of the Apostle Thomas, patron saint of pessimists: "Except I shall see in his hands the print of the nails, and put my finger into the print of the nails, and thrust my hand into his side, I shall not believe" (Jn 20:25). Thomas (Aquinas) is *not like* Thomas (the Apostle), because he is not at hand to see and to touch the flesh of Jesus. What has risen from the dead is not some disembodied spirit. It is not an apparition. It is Jesus Himself, the man, flesh and blood, now glorified. The experience of the apostle is impossible to explain without reference to that glory. He does not say, "Teacher, you are alive! I thought you had died!" He says, "My Lord and my God" (Jn 20:28). Thomas Aquinas, beholding the sacrament, cannot see the wounds, but he can, like the apostle, call Jesus *Lord and God*, thus becoming one of those of whom Jesus says, "Blessed are they that have not seen, and yet have believed" (Jn 20:29).

Modern Eucharistic hymns, so eager to celebrate the oneness of the congregation, shun the loneliness of Christ upon the cross and our responsibility for nailing Him there. But Aquinas will not allow our attention to stray from Calvary. For Jesus said, "This cup is the new testament in my blood" (1 Cor 11:25). So we recall that sacrifice:

O thou our reminder of Christ crucified,
Living Bread, the life of us for whom he died,
Lend this life to me then: feed and feast my mind,
There be thou the sweetness man was meant to find.

Hopkins has woven two principal motifs into his stanza: *Life* and the *mind*. Jesus is the living bread come down from heaven (Jn 6:51). That phrase, like the similar *living water* (Jn 4:10), means not just bread that has life, but bread that *gives life*. Bread is the staff of life (cf. Lv 26:26), but the life Jesus gives is eternal. That's not to be considered in terms of duration only. It is a completely new life; a transcendent life. That is why Aquinas pleads for it. It is a life of the *mind*, a life that fulfills all the desires of our rational and intellectual nature. It is the life of seeing God as He is (cf. 1 Jn 3:2). Then will we know the joy that the psalmist knows only in shadow: "O taste and see that the Lord is good; blessed is the man that trusteth in him" (Ps 34:8).

When I was a boy, in the vestry of our Saint Thomas Aquinas Church stood a wardrobe carved with a strange bird and the inscription: *Pie pellicane, Jesu Domine*. I didn't know it then, but that was the first line of Aquinas' next stanza. It refers to a bit of medieval folk wisdom. From a distance, a pelican seems to be feeding its young from its own substance. Medieval people didn't see pelicans in their neighborhood, so they trusted the report from afar, and used the pelican as a symbol of Christ. In the Cistercian *Quest of the Holy Grail* (twelfth century), the good Sir Bors is venturing across the wilderness when he sees a bird in a nest, whose offspring are dead. Then the bird stabs itself in the breast and its nourishing blood brings the chicks to life again. All Aquinas needed to do was to use the word *pelican*, and his fellows would know what he meant. Hopkins can't rely on the understanding of his audience, so he alerts us to the fact that there's a mythological tale in play here, and he hopes that we may find out what it is:

Bring the tender tale true of the Pelican;
Bathe me, Jesu Lord, in what thy bosom ran—
Blood whereof a single drop has power to win
All the world forgiveness of its world of sin.

Aquinas' Latin plays upon the chance similarity between the verb to cleanse, *mundare* (also the adjective for unclean, *immundus*) and the noun for world, *mundum*. Thomas is unclean, a sinner. So he pleads, *me immundum munda tuo sanguine*: Cleanse me, who am unclean, by your blood. That is a most effectual remedy, because one drop of it, *una stilla*, can bring healing—the inner meaning of the Latin *salvus*—to the whole world, *mundum*, which is, alas, a world of sin.

We long for this healing, so that we may see the Lord:

Jesu, whom I look at shrouded here below,
I beseech thee send me what I thirst for so,
Some day to gaze on Thee face to face in light
And be blest for ever with thy glory's sight. Amen.

Aquinas ends the hymn by bringing it round to the beginning. He now sees the Lord with the eyes of faith. Love wants more. Love wants to behold the Lord, face to face. In this last stanza he plays upon the image of a veil. In the Eucharist, Jesus is *velatum*, "veiled," or, to use Hopkins' happy participle, *shrouded*. We await the final revelation of the glory of the Lord—literally the unveiling, suggested by the participle *revelata*, that will be at the eternal banquet of the Lamb.

When Jesus said, "This is my body which is given for you: this do in remembrance of me" (Lk 22:19), He meant that we should keep both parts of His commandment in mind at once. If we remember Jesus in the Eucharist, we remember that He gave up His body for us. Let us now look at two poems, one "modern" (nineteenth century) and one ancient, which do precisely that.

The first, in ballad meter, is *According to Thy Gracious Word*, by James Montgomery (1825). It places upon the lips of the singer a direct and personal address to Christ:

According to Thy gracious word,
In meek humility,
This will I do, my dying Lord,
I will remember Thee.

When Jesus instituted the Sacrament, it was a glorious gift to man. It was *gracious*, freely given, as was His death: "Therefore doth my Father love me, because I lay down my life, that I might take it again. No man taketh it from me, but I lay it down of myself" (Jn 10:17–18). His grace is answered by the meekness of the believer, who accepts the gift he does not deserve. So the believer promises to fulfill the command to remember. Notice the emphatic position of the pronoun *this* and the unusual reversal of the verb and the subject: Not *I will do this* but *This will I do*. What is the great *this*, which merits such emphasis? The last line tells us. It doesn't seem like much. No heroic deed; but no heroic deed can match the death of Jesus. It's all he can do: *I will remember Thee.*

In the second, stanza Montgomery applies that remembrance to the Sacrament he now receives:

Thy Body, broken for my sake,
My Bread from heaven shall be;
Thy testamental Cup I take,
And thus remember Thee.

When the priest breaks the consecrated Host before consuming it, he reminds us of the body of Christ upon the cross, broken for us. That is "the bread which cometh down from heaven" (Jn 6:50). So too the blood: "This cup is the new testament in my blood, which is shed for you" (Lk 22:20). It is *testamental*—that is, it gives testimony, it is witness to the new covenant. The poet acknowledges that witness; and thus remembrance is a profession of faith.

In the next two stanzas, Montgomery brings us from the Last Supper to the agony in the garden, to the cross:

Gethsemane can I forget?
Or there Thy conflict see,
Thine agony and bloody sweat,
And not remember Thee?

When to the Cross I turn mine eyes
And rest on Calvary,
O Lamb of God, my Sacrifice,
I must remember Thee:

The rhetorical questions hit home. How can I forget *Gethsemane?* Notice the emphatic position—Gethsemane, of all places, how can I forget? And as if he has not the leisure or desire to insert himself into the stanza again, he resumes with the conjunction *or*, followed by what he sees in that garden, the *conflict*, the *agony and bloody sweat*. All the emphasis is on what Jesus suffered. How can we not remember that? Then comes the consummation, upon Calvary. The poet rests his eyes there, and recalls the words of the Baptist: "Behold the Lamb of God, which taketh away the sin of the world" (Jn 1:29). He calls Jesus *my Sacrifice*, and that possessive adjective is telling.

What does it mean to say, "Jesus is the Lamb of God, *my Sacrifice?*" The children of Israel, on the night of their deliverance from slavery in Egypt, slew the Passover Lamb of God. It is crucial to distinguish this sacrifice from the pagan sacrifices which it resembles, superficially. The Passover Lamb does *not* represent the sins of the people, for which they must atone; it is *not the scapegoat*, driven out into the wilderness (Lv 16:8–10). Instead it is a gift God provides, as when Abraham found the ram tangled in the thickets, and was commanded to sacrifice it instead of his son Isaac (Gn 22:13). So too the Suffering Servant prophesied by Isaiah. God provides the lamb led to the slaughter: "All we like sheep have gone astray; we have turned every one to his own way; and the Lord hath laid on him the iniquity of us all" (Is 53:6). It is but the astonishing fulfillment of these foreshadowings, that God Himself should dwell among us and *be the Sacrifice*. Christ is *my Sacrifice*, in this sense, because He sacrifices Himself *for me, on my behalf*. But there's more. We are partakers in the sacrifice. It is ours. "The bread which we break," says St. Paul, "is it not the communion of the body of Christ?" (1 Cor 10:16). We offer the Son to the Father, as "priests unto God" (Rv 1:6). All we have to offer is what God has given to us first: Himself, in love.

The fourth stanza did not end with a period; it races on to the fifth stanza, which sums up the determination the poet has expressed from the beginning:

Remember Thee, and all Thy pains,
And all Thy love to me;
Yea, while a breath, a pulse remains,
Will I remember Thee.

That is nicely done. The poet will remember, so long as he has breath in his lungs or a pulse in his heart. The verb *will*, in emphatic position (Montgomery could have written *I will remember Thee*), expresses more than a future state. It expresses *willingness*, resolution, desire. I will remember! What? *All Thy pains*, which show forth *all Thy love*. But more than that: I will remember *Thee*.

So far, the stanzas have all ended on the same phrase. Now Montgomery turns about. He places himself at Calvary in exactly the same position as Thomas Aquinas did, that of the repentant thief:

And when these failing lips grow dumb,
And mind and memory flee,
When Thou shalt in Thy kingdom come,
Jesu, remember me.

Here he imagines himself, like that thief, at the point of death. He's already declared that he will remember Jesus with every breath and pulse. But there will come a time when the lips can no longer confess that Jesus is Lord, when even the memory fades. At that point, we trust ourselves to memory—the loving remembrance of Jesus. "Lord," said the thief, "remember me when thou comest into thy kingdom" (Lk 23:42).

One of the oldest Eucharistic hymns in existence, attributed to the Irish monk St. Sechnall (d. 457), is the Latin *Sancti, venite, Christi Corpus sumite*. We know it in the translation of John Mason Neale as *Draw Nigh and Take the Body of the Lord*. It gives us, in concentrated form, Eucharistic lessons from all of Scripture, and it too does not shun the vision of Calvary. Here is Neale's version, complete:

Draw nigh, and take the Body of the Lord,
And drink the holy Blood for you outpoured,
Saved by that Body, hallowed by that Blood,
Whereby refreshed we render thanks to God.

Salvation's giver, Christ the only Son,
By that His Cross and Blood the victory won.

Offered was He for greatest and for least:
Himself the Victim, and Himself the Priest.

Victims were offered by the law of old,
That, in a type, celestial mysteries told.
He, Ransomer from death and Light from shade,
Giveth His holy grace His saints to aid.

Approach ye then with faithful hearts sincere,
And take the safeguard of salvation here.
He that in this world rules His saints and shields,
To all believers life eternal yields:

With heavenly Bread makes them that hunger whole,
Gives living waters to the thirsty soul.
Alpha and Omega, to whom shall bow
All nations at the doom, is with us now.

Most of the motifs we've seen in our two later Eucharistic hymns are here already: the bread from heaven; the living water; the fulfillment of the old sacrifices in the new; the victory of the Cross, whereon Christ the Lord was both victim and priest; the body broken for us; and the blood poured out. There are, however, a few things besides, also important in the tradition to follow.

Notice Neale's word *refreshed.* That's a good translation of the Latin *refecti*—food *remakes* us, *restores* us (the inner meaning of our words *refectory* and *restaurant*). The Eucharist is not just any food. It is *the refreshing food*: The food that makes us whole and fresh again. The language comes from Scripture: The law of the Lord refreshes or restores or revives the soul (Ps 19:7). St. Peter urges the people of Jerusalem to repent, that their sins might be blotted out "when the times of refreshing shall come from the presence of the Lord" (Acts 3:19).

Notice also Neale's title for Jesus, *Ransomer*, translating the Latin *redempti*, applied to the people receiving the Eucharist. To redeem is, literally, to buy back; to ransom, if we are bought back from slavery. A rich man might open his purse and ransom a good many slaves indeed. But the wonderful and terrible irony is that Jesus has come to ransom us slaves, not with gifts in His possession, but with His very self. The greatness of His love is to be seen in that humility. So he tells his disciples not to quarrel over who shall be greatest: "For even the Son of man came not to be ministered unto, but to minister, and to give his life a ransom for many" (Mk 10:45). St. Paul takes up the theme: "There is one God, and one mediator between God and men, the man Christ Jesus; who gave himself a ransom for all" (1 Tm 2:5–6).

But I think the final lines of the hymn are the richest of all. Says Jesus to John in the final vision of the Bible: "I am Alpha and Omega, the first and the last" (Rv 1:11). He is the Lord through whom all things were made. He is the Lord *for whom* all things were made, as their fulfillment and end. He will sit upon His throne of judgment, *at the Doom*. "And before him shall be gathered all nations: and he shall separate them one from another, as a shepherd divideth his sheep from the goats" (Mt 25:32). That Lord, who is coming again in glory—Latin *venturus*—is with us *now*, here, in this church, in the sacrament of the altar. All of time, from creation to the final judgment, is present *now*, in Jesus.

For a vision of all the promises of Scripture fulfilled in the Eucharist, it is hard to beat James Montgomery's *Shepherd of Souls*:

Shepherd of souls, refresh and bless
Thy chosen pilgrim flock
With manna in the wilderness,
With water from the rock.

"The Lord is my shepherd," says the psalmist (Ps 23:1), and "I am the good shepherd," says Jesus, "and know my sheep, and am known of mine" (Jn 10:14). The *chosen flock* are the Jews, pilgrims through the desert, making their way from Egypt to the Promised Land; and they foreshadow the new flock of Christ, "a chosen generation, an holy nation," summoned by God "out of darkness into his marvelous light" (1 Pt 2:9). The *manna* and the *water from the rock* are now spiritual realities: The Sacrament of the Lord's Supper.

The second stanza takes up the motif of food for the journey:

We would not live by bread alone,
But by Thy word of grace,
In strength of which we travel on
To our abiding place.

Montgomery shifts our attention to another time of hunger, when Jesus was tempted in the desert. "If thou be the Son of God," said Satan, "command that these stones be made bread" (Mt 4:3). The temptation is to locate our ultimate good in the body and its desires. But Jesus replies, "Man shall not live by bread alone, but by every word that proceedeth out of the mouth of God" (Mt 4:4). We now sing that reply. We *would not live by bread alone*—that is, *we do not wish* to live as if we were mere bodies to feed. We wish to live by Jesus' *word of grace*. That is our food, and in its strength, we journey forth, refreshed, *to our abiding place*. To *abide* is more than to *remain*, as so many dull modern translations of the Bible put it. It is to *dwell*, to make one's home, to rest, as in the heart of one's life. Montgomery has in mind the words of Jesus, "Abide in me, and I in you" (Jn 15:4), and, of course, the words of the psalm of the shepherd: "I will dwell in the house of the Lord for ever" (Ps 23:6).

Then we return to the Eucharist and to the risen Lord:

Be known to us in breaking bread,
But do not then depart;
Savior, abide with us, and spread
Thy table in our heart.

That is excellent. The scene is the inn on the way to Emmaus, on the day of the Lord's resurrection. The disciples with whom Jesus spoke on the road did not recognize Him as He explained the Scriptures, how they were fulfilled in the Messiah's death and resurrection. Then it grew late, and they said, "Abide with us: for it is toward evening, and the day is far spent," so Jesus entered the inn with them, "and it came to pass, as he sat at meat with them, he took bread, and blessed it, and brake, and gave to them. And their eyes were opened, and they knew him, and he vanished out of sight." But they returned straightaway to Jerusalem to tell the apostles "how he was known of them in breaking of bread" (Lk 24:29–31, 35). Here we pray that we too may know the Lord in the breaking of the bread. But we, who know what those disciples did not yet know, ask our Savior to abide with us, not at a village inn, but in the depths of our hearts—to abide *with us*. The final line echoes and inverts the words of the mistrustful Israelites, who muttered against God and Moses when they were sojourning through the desert. "Can God furnish a table in the wilderness?" they asked (Ps 78:19). Yes, He can—He did, sending manna from above. But there is a more deserted wilderness than the sands of Sinai. It is the human heart without God. There we ask for God to spread His Eucharistic table.

The final stanza binds together all the rest and sees in one glance the Last Supper, the Eucharist celebrated by the singers now, and the eternal Supper of the Lamb:

Lord, sup with us in love divine;
Thy Body and Thy Blood,
That living bread, that heavenly wine,
Be our immortal food.

"He that eateth of this bread," says Jesus, "shall live forever" (Jn 6:58).

Then let us turn to that great wedding of Christ and His Church. In the glorious hymn *At the Lamb's High Feast We Sing*, written by an unknown Latin poet and translated into English by Robert Campbell (1849), the whole of the life of Christ is seen in the light of the eternal day of resurrection, and the Eucharistic feast:

At the Lamb's high feast we sing
Praise to our victorious King,
Who hath washed us in the tide
Flowing from His pierced side;
Praise we Him, whose love divine
Gives His sacred blood for wine,
Gives His body for the feast,
Christ the victim, Christ the priest.

The melody *Salzburg*, harmonized by Bach, is a perfect match for the poem—strong half notes with marked intervals, no lilting, but rather the clarion call of trumpets. We see in the first stanza no fewer than six Eucharistic motifs, from everywhere in the New Testament. It is the *Lamb's high feast*: "Blessed are they which are called unto the marriage supper of the Lamb" (Rv 19:9). He has *washed us* in His blood: "[The saints] have washed their robes, and made them white in the blood of the Lamb" (Rv 7:14). The blood flowed from *His pierced side* (Jn 19:34). The brilliant George Herbert in "The Sacrifice," a poem we've glanced at before, places these words on the mouth of the crucified Lord:

Nay, after death their spite shall further go;
For they will pierce my side, I full well know;
That as sin came, so Sacraments might flow:
Was ever grief like mine?

The blood that washes us is also the blood of the Eucharist, given as wine, both now and forever:

> *Drink ye all of it; For this is my blood of the new testament, which is shed for many for the remission of sins. But I say unto you, I will not drink henceforth of this fruit of the vine, until that day when I drink it new with you in my Father's kingdom.* (Mt 26:27–29)

It is His body He gives: He is the giver and the gift. He does not sprinkle the temple walls with the blood of calves and goats, but offers Himself "without spot to God" (Heb 9:14) to make us clean and worthy to enter the true Holy of Holies, the presence of God.

The second stanza sees in the sacrifice of Christ the fulfillment of the deliverance of Israel from bondage:

Where the Paschal blood is poured,
Death's dark angel sheathes his sword;
Israel's hosts triumphant go
Through the wave that drowns the foe.
Praise we Christ, whose blood was shed,
Paschal victim, Paschal bread;
With sincerity and love
Eat we manna from above.

The poet does not pause to make a comparison. He is asserting an *identity*. He recalls the words of the Lord to Moses, instituting the Passover. The children of Israel were to eat the Passover Lamb with unleavened bread, sprinkling its blood upon their lintels and doorposts. Then, says the Lord, "When I see the blood, I will pass over you, and the plague shall not be upon you, when I smite the land of Egypt" (Ex 12:12). The sword of the angel of death did not strike the firstborn of the Israelites. But Christ, the only begotten Son of God, has become our *Paschal victim*, the unblemished Lamb of the sacrifice, and our *Paschal bread*, the bread of the Eucharist. He has conquered death—not delayed it for a time, as the Lord spared the Israelites from death at the hands of the Egyptians. He has conquered it definitively, by taking it to Himself, in a gift of total love. Then we, who are not just *like* the Israelites but *are Israel's hosts*, we the new Israel march triumphantly through the *wave that drowns the foe*. Those are deeper waters than the Red Sea ever knew: They are the waters of death itself, and our pursuing foe, death, is drowned in them. The line *sincerity and love* also expresses the difference between the old Israel and the new. The children of Israel grumbled against Moses and Aaron in the desert, complaining, "Ye have brought us forth into this wilderness, to kill this whole assembly with hunger" (Ex 16:3).

Then the Lord sent them *manna from above*, which they ate all through their sojourn, but which they grew weary of in turn. But our Eucharist is a meal of thanksgiving and joy.

The final two stanzas show us the definitive triumph of Christ and what that means for the faithful who unite themselves with Him:

Mighty victim from the sky,
Hell's fierce powers beneath Thee lie;
Thou hast conquered in the fight,
Thou hast brought us life and light:
Now no more can death appall,
Now no more the grave enthrall;
Thou hast opened paradise,
And in Thee Thy saints shall rise.

Easter triumph, Easter joy,
Sin alone can this destroy;
From sin's power do Thou set free
Souls new-born, O Lord, in Thee.
Hymns of glory, songs of praise,
Father, unto Thee we raise:
Risen Lord, all praise to Thee
With the Spirit ever be.

Again, we have a veritable tapestry of Scripture. "He must reign," says St. Paul, "till he hath put all enemies under his feet. The last enemy that shall be destroyed is death" (1 Cor 15:25–26). *Hell's fierce powers* are vanquished: Notice the insistent repetition of the words *now no more*, bracketed by the repeated declaration, *Thou hast*. Because of what Christ has done once and for all, death has been defeated. That is why the poet hammers at the adverb *now*, placed in the emphatic first position. "O death," cheers St. Paul, "where is thy sting? O grave, where is thy victory?" (1 Cor 15:55). Death can no longer *appall* us, literally, make us pale with fear and confusion. Nor can the grave *enthrall*—literally, make thralls of us, slaves, prisoners. Christ has descended to the dead and arisen, and "led captivity captive" (Eph 4:8; cf. Ps 68:18).

The phrase *Paschal victim, paschal bread* is now fulfilled, theologically, by the phrase that begins the last stanza: *Easter triumph, Easter joy*. The one leads to the other. Christ is the Lamb of God who takes away the sins of the world by His death on the Cross and His victory over death. What can spoil this joy? Only the slavery of sin, from which we pray that the Lord will free us, bringing us to a new birth in Him: "Except a man be born again, he cannot see the kingdom of God" (Jn 3:3).

So short this happy poem is, yet so full of significance; like the bread of the Sacrament itself, we might say. Small, yet comprehending infinity.

Chapter Eight

The Holy Spirit

WE'VE seen how often the early Christian poets ended their hymns with a doxology, a "glory-word" praising the Blessed Trinity. It may be a measure of our theological confusion and childishness that this tradition has been discarded. It's hard to meditate upon the Trinity when one is doting on the image in the mirror.

What's almost as bad is that the old hymns that honor the Trinity are seldom sung to their completion. The poor Holy Spirit is shut out in the cold, like a traveler who has arrived a minute too late. "I'm sorry, Mr. Paraclete," says the liturgical innkeeper, "but the rooms are full." It's a thoughtless offense to God, most of all: The doctrine of the Trinity is an awe-inspiring gift to us, revealing that the inner life of God is a communion of love. Why should we treat that gift so dismissively?

It is also an offense to sacred art. What work could a poet produce with two thirds of the alphabet? How would Beethoven's Ninth Symphony sound if we cut it off at some random point in the second of the four movements? What would Michelangelo's *Creation of Adam* look like if he had shrugged and left Adam without the arm extended toward God? How should we like traveling over half a bridge? What if the bridge spans not a river but the abyss between earth and heaven?

We need the Father, we need Jesus Christ, His Son, and we need the Holy Spirit, the Comforter, the indwelling life of Christ, the quiet Physician of the soul. If the Friday of Christ's death on the Cross is good only because of Easter, then Easter itself is only effectual because it is crowned with the birth of Christ's mystical body upon earth, the Church, at Pentecost. Then let us turn to hymns addressing that great Nativity and the Holy Spirit through whom alone do we come to know the Father and the Son.

First among these is the medieval plainsong hymn known as *The Golden Sequence*. The Latin text, *Veni, sancte Spiritus*, is often attributed to the thirteenth-century archbishop of Canterbury, Stephen Langton (r. 1207–28), a man whose importance in history should not go unnoted: He was a fierce enemy of the weak and corrupt King John and was a part of the ecclesial and aristocratic force that compelled the king to sign the Magna Carta in 1215. The Latin is noble in its terseness and simplicity. It consists of a series of three-line stanzas, each with seven syllables; the first two lines rhyme, and the third line always ends in *–um*, thus binding all the stanzas together. When Edward Caswall set his hand to translate it, he preserved the seven-syllable lines, so that they could be sung to the original melody—or rather the beautiful series of four mutually echoing melodies, one for every pair of stanzas in succession. He preserved the rhyme on the first two lines of each stanza. But English simply will not allow eight successive stanzas to end on the same rhyme, not without absurdity or burlesque. So Caswall hit on a compromise, rhyming the stanzas in four pairs, four of them, each pair sung to one of the four melodies, in order.

Here is the first pair, following the Latin:

Veni, Sancte Spiritus,
et emitte caelitus
lucis tuae radium.
Veni, Pater pauperum,
veni, dator munerum,
veni, lumen cordium.

Come, Thou Holy Spirit, come!
And from Thy celestial home
Shed a ray of light divine.
Come, Thou Father of the poor!
Come, Thou source of all our store!
Come, within our bosoms shine!

English can't match the potent compression of Latin, but Caswall has understood the poetry of the original quite clearly. He sees that the imperative verb is the key to the poem: *Veni! Come!* That is not redundancy. Is a second kiss redundant, because there has been a first? The repetition suggests urgency and fervor: The singer already burns with the flame of love that the Holy Spirit kindles within. We long to house the Holy Spirit within us because He is the *Father of the poor*, which is to say, He is our Father, because we have nothing without Him: He is the *source of all our store*, the giver of all good gifts.

The next pair of stanzas turns our attention to the Spirit as our Comforter:

Consolator optime,
dulcis hospes animae,
dulce refrigerium.

In labore requies,
in aestu temperies,
in fletu solatium.

Thou, of comforters the best;
Thou, the soul's most welcome guest;
Sweet refreshment here below;
In our labor, rest most sweet;
Grateful coolness in the heat;
Solace in the midst of woe.

A terrific translation. Caswall has preserved everything in the original. When he could not easily repeat the word *sweet* in the first three lines, he included it as the rhyming word in line four, to lay special stress upon it. English lacks the vocative case—the ending of *optime* in line one tells us that we are not describing the Comforter but addressing Him directly. So Caswall includes the personal pronoun, without a verb: *Thou*, tenderly repeated. The Holy Spirit comes to bring us rest, sweetness, coolness, solace. At the Last Supper, Jesus told His disciples that if they kept His commandments, He would pray to the Father, "and he shall give you another Comforter, that he may abide with you for ever; even the Spirit of truth; whom the world cannot receive, because it seeth him not, neither knoweth him: but ye know him; for he dwelleth with you, and shall be in you" (Jn 14:16–17). And when the Holy Spirit dwells within us, we are transformed, for "the fruit of the Spirit is love, joy, peace, longsuffering, gentleness, goodness, faith, meekness, temperance" (Gal 5:22–23).

Stanzas five and six present to us the divine Physician. In Tolkien's short story, "Leaf by Niggle," the title character, a man of middling virtue, is sent on a long journey—an allegory for the journey of death—and when he arrives at the train's terminus, he is found to be in a poor state. His heart doesn't work right, and his head is weak, since he had hardly ever thought—he'd hardly ever devoted himself to concentrated prayer. Niggle hears this diagnosis as coming from two voices, who deliver him over to a third, a severe physician, who gives him a bottle of a bitter but salutary medicine. This physician seldom speaks, but it is clear that all the treatment Niggle receives—treatment which includes ordinary manual labor, hours (or is it centuries?) of solitude and silence, harsh and healthful restoratives—works within him rather than simply upon him, healing the whole person, body and soul. We are like Niggle, with nothing of our own to boast:

O lux beatissima,
reple cordis intima
tuorum fidelium.
Sine tuo numine,
nihil est in homine,
nihil est innoxium.

O most blessed Light divine,
Shine within these hearts of Thine,
And our inmost being fill!
Where Thou art not, man hath naught,
Nothing good in deed or thought,
Nothing free from taint of ill.

The Latin *numine* is impossible to render in English. It suggests the inexpressible glory of the divine presence. Its rhyme with *homine*, "man," underscores our poverty, with the word *nihil* ringing in our ears: *Nothing*, which Caswall does well to repeat. The Latin *innoxium* suggests both bodily and spiritual harm, as of a slow poison: Hence Caswall's *taint of ill*.

If the poison of evil has infected us, we must call upon the doctor:

Lava quod est sordidum,
riga quod est aridum,
sana quod est saucium.
Flecte quod est rigidum,
fove quod est frigidum,
rege quod est devium.

Heal our wounds, our strength renew;
On our dryness pour Thy dew;
Wash the stains of guilt away:
Bend the stubborn heart and will;
Melt the frozen, warm the chill;
Guide the steps that go astray.

Caswall has had to supply phrases to bring out the meaning of the Latin, with its daring sequence of imperative verbs and the exactly repeated pattern of each noun clause to follow. Literally: *Wash what is filthy, soak what is dry, heal what is wounded, bend what is stiff, warm what is frozen, steer what is stray*. Caswall's solution is to preserve the imperative verbs: *heal, pour, wash, bend, melt (warm), guide*; and then to make those adjectives personal: *our wounds, our dryness, the stains of guilt, the stubborn heart, the steps that go astray*.

The inner meaning of the English word *heal* is to bring to a state of *wholeness*. To be healed is to be *hale, whole*, even *holy*. So this hymn ends with wholeness restored and raised to the divine:

Da tuis fidelibus,
in te confitentibus,
sacrum septenarium.
Da virtutis meritum,
da salutis exitum,
da perenne gaudium.

On the faithful, who adore
And confess Thee, evermore
In Thy sevenfold gift descend:
Give them virtue's sure reward;
Give them Thy salvation, Lord;
Give them joys that never end.

The poet prays for the seven gifts of the Holy Spirit: wisdom, understanding, counsel, fortitude, knowledge, piety, and fear of the Lord (cf. Is 11:2–3). They are pure gifts; note the insistent verb *give*, translating the Latin imperative *da*. Those gifts conform us to Jesus Himself, who grew "strong in spirit, filled with wisdom: and the grace of God was upon him" (Lk 2:40). One with Jesus, we will see the *joys that never end*; the life that is the Spirit Himself.

The Latin word *spiritus*, like the Greek *pneuma* and the Hebrew *ruah*, means *breath*: To be *inspired* is to be endowed with breath from without, to have knowledge or skill or vision breathed into one's soul. The idea is everywhere in Scripture: Consider the breath or spirit of God brooding above the waters of creation (Gn 1:2), or the breathing of God upon Adam, whence he became a living soul (Gn 2:7). When the prophet Elijah upon the mountain sought the presence of God, it was revealed to him not in the tempest or the whirlwind or the fire, but in the "still small voice" (1 Kgs 19:12), or, as some translations have it, a gentle rustling sound, as of a slight breeze. So the most momentous change in a man's life comes about, says Jesus, invisibly, as the wind is felt but not seen: "The wind bloweth where it listeth, and thou hearest the sound thereof, but canst not tell whence it cometh, and whither it goeth; so is every one that is born of the Spirit" (Jn 3:8). The birth of the Church was mysterious in that same way, to mark a new creation:

> *And when the day of Pentecost was fully come, they were all with one accord in one place.*
>
> *And suddenly there came a sound from heaven as of a rushing mighty wind, and it filled all the house where they were sitting.*
>
> *And there appeared unto them cloven tongues like as of fire, and it sat upon each of them.*
>
> *And they were all filled with the Holy Ghost [the Holy Breath], and began to speak with other tongues, as the Spirit [Breath] gave them utterance.* (Acts 2:1–4)

This scene of Pentecost, with the motif of the Holy Breath, is the subject of a beautiful poem by Harriet Auber (1773–1862), *Our Blest Redeemer*. It is sung to an Irish air, *Wicklow*, whose melody nicely reflects the pattern of the poem. Auber employs the ballad meter, with alternating rhyming lines of eight and six syllables, but with one important change: The last line of each stanza consists of only *four* syllables, slowing the tempo to stress those few words. Let me illustrate, marking melody lines with letters and the variation with an asterisk, and placing the final "rhyming" note in parentheses:

A (C)

Our blest Redeemer, ere He breathed

B (D)

His tender last farewell,

A (C)

A Guide, a Comforter, bequeathed

B* (D)

With us to dwell.

Notice how the form of the poem, echoed in the melody, focuses our attention upon the last words: *with us to dwell*. They make sense of the whole stanza. The Lord is about to leave us. But He does not leave us: He dwells with us more intimately than ever! So the risen Christ, appearing to the disciples, "breathed on them, and saith unto them, Receive ye the Holy Ghost" (Jn 20:22). He is the "Comforter, which is the Holy Ghost, whom the Father will send," to strengthen and direct, to "teach you all things, and bring all things to your remembrance" (Jn 14:26). So the gentle breath with which Jesus says His farewell is at one with the Holy Breath, the inspirited Paraclete, the quiet Teacher.

In the second stanza, Auber combines the account of Pentecost with Jesus' words to Nicodemus about the invisibility of the Spirit's action:

He came in tongues of living flame,
To teach, convince, subdue;
All-powerful as the wind He came,
As viewless too.

Auber begs us to consider at once that the Spirit is omnipotent and unseen—we may say, unseen because omnipotent. The world always associates might with prominence. It's why we erect statues in honor of great politicians, some of whom are no better than plagues upon mankind. But this Spirit comes not to overmaster us, like a despot. He comes quietly, to raise the lowly:

He came sweet influence to impart,
A gracious, willing Guest,
While He can find one humble heart
Wherein to rest.

The *influence* is *sweet*: It is life-giving, nourishing, but also gentle. Think of the English word *soothe*: Its inner meaning is in fact to make *sweet*. The Spirit is thus a *gracious Guest* in two senses: He brings gifts; and He brings them gently, courteously. He brings them to the humble dwelling places that can accept them; only in such hearts can this gentle Lord rest.

What does He do when He makes His abode within? Auber devotes her next two stanzas to describing the action of the Spirit, in words to make the faithful soul long for His presence:

And His that gentle voice we hear,
Soft as the breath of even,
That checks each fault, that calms each fear,
And speaks of heaven.

And every virtue we possess,
And every victory won,
And every thought of holiness
Are His alone.

The poetry here is itself a work of tact, of gentleness. A poor poet would never think of beginning so many lines with the connector *and*, but it is perfect, striking the ear like the lapping waves of a vast and calm sea. So too, the division of the third line of the first stanza into even parts, and the repetition of the adjective *every*. The Spirit speaks to us, quietly, of heaven. He gives life to our minds, so that thoughts of holiness, more profound than virtue and more wondrous than victory, are *His alone*.

The final stanza is a petition, welcoming the Spirit:

Spirit of purity and grace,
Our weakness, pitying, see:
O make our hearts Thy dwelling-place,
And worthier Thee.

We are not worthy that the Spirit should dwell within us. We pray that the Spirit Himself will make us so.

That is the petition animating a fifteenth-century Latin hymn by Banco da Siena, translated into English by R. F. Littledale (1867) as *Come Down, O Love Divine*:

Come down, O Love divine,
Seek Thou this soul of mine,
And visit it with Thine own ardor glowing;
O Comforter, draw near,
Within my heart appear,
And kindle it, Thy holy flame bestowing.

The pensive and delicate melody to which the hymn is commonly sung, Ralph Vaughan Williams' *Down Ampney* (1906), binds the two long lines together by "rhyming" them on exactly the same melody, without variation, providing nice closure to the whole. If we consider the words of the poem, we see how appropriate this is. The first three lines beg for the *ardor* of the Spirit, the *Love divine*. The second three lines make that ardor specific: It is the Pentecostal *flame* of the Holy Spirit drawing near, appearing within the heart, and setting it afire.

The second stanza builds upon the motif of the conflagration:

O let it freely burn,
Till earthly passions turn
To dust and ashes in its heat consuming;
And let Thy gracious light
Shine ever on my sight,
And clothe me round, the while my path illuming.

The Spirit of the Lord "is like a refiner's fire" (Mal 3:2). Fire cleanses—the basic meaning of *purge* and *purify*. "If any man's work shall be burned," says St. Paul, referring to the day of judgment, "he shall suffer loss: but he himself shall be saved; yet so as by fire." And he follows that prophecy of purgation with a reminder of the tabernacles we are to become: "Know ye not that ye are the temple of God, and that the Spirit of God dwelleth in you?" (1 Cor 3:15–16). This fire burns away all our dross. Worldly passions dry up and turn to dust. To understand the Spirit, we must hold simultaneously in mind these verses: "God is love" (1 Jn 4:8), and "Our God is a consuming fire" (Heb 12:29). God does not wish to quench our love. That love is ever too tame, too timid. It is lukewarm. Love itself, that consuming fire, will destroy what only passes for love. The worldly passions darken our hearts, but God's love sheds light as well as heat. It clothes us in light, and shows us the way we are to go.

The third stanza develops the image of clothing, associating it with the fire of charity that we show to the world, while humility dwells within us, even to the point of self-loathing. It is omitted from most hymnals:

Let holy charity
Mine outward vesture be,
And lowliness become mine inner clothing;
True lowliness of heart,
Which takes the humbler part,
And o'er its own shortcomings weeps with loathing.

Perhaps that last word is too strong for most tastes. But holy tears too are the work of the Spirit. Jesus declares that they who mourn will be blessed; and St. Paul writes through his tears to the Corinthians, recounting all the perils he has undergone in preaching Christ crucified, only to conclude: "If I needs must glory, I will glory of the things which concern mine infirmities" (2 Cor 11:30). That is indeed to take *the humbler part*, and give due thanks to God for all the good in us.

The final stanza is a paean to the power of this divine love, whose beauty can only be grasped from within:

And so the yearning strong,
With which the soul will long,
Shall far outpass the power of human telling;
For none can guess its grace,
Till he become the place
Wherein the Holy Spirit makes His dwelling.

It is the peace of God that passes understanding.

When the apostles heard that the people of Samaria—long hated by the Jews for their heresy—had come to believe in Jesus, they "sent unto them Peter and John: who, when they were come down, prayed for them, that they might receive the Holy Ghost" (Acts 8:14–15). And when Peter visited Cornelius the Roman, who had come to believe in Jesus, and preached to him and his household, "the Holy Ghost fell on all them which heard the word" (Acts 10:44), and they began to speak in tongues, glorifying God. The Holy Spirit is like an interior energy. He speaks through the prophets. He opens the eyes of the conscience. He confirms us in our faith, by sending its roots down deep in the heart and mind and soul. A seed that germinates in the earth is alive; so the person who has been baptized is alive in Christ. The Holy Spirit works within the seed to transform it into the strong tree it is to become.

Our prayers to the Holy Spirit, then, naturally beg for this quiet yet unmistakable transformation. One such prayer is *Holy Spirit, Truth Divine*, written by Samuel Longfellow (1864), the brother of the renowned poet Henry Wadsworth Longfellow. The stanzas consist of four lines of seven syllables each, in rhyming couplets. Each stanza begins by naming the Holy Spirit in a special way, to entreat Him to heal or guide or strengthen a particular faculty:

Holy Spirit, Truth divine,
Dawn upon this soul of mine;
Breath of God, and inward Light,
Wake my spirit, clear my sight.

The first name is *Truth*. But notice that truth is not reduced to facticity; to numbers that can be totted up, or to a bare description of some material property. This Truth is *divine*, glorious, filled with light. It shows us what is good and to be desired. It reveals a glimpse of the God from whom all reality depends. Thus it is like a *dawn* that quietly dispels the darkness. It is a divine *breath.* It is not a laser that dissects, but an *inward Light.* The breath of God awakes the *spirit* or breath of the poet; the light of God clears the haze from his soul, so that he may see.

The mysterious silence of the Spirit's working is reflected in the simplicity of Longfellow's lines, and in the peaceful suspension of the final note of the traditional English melody, *Lew Trenchard,* to which the hymn is commonly sung. Most melodies end on the tonic note, in a tonic chord—the note we would call "do." So a melody written in the key of C will almost always end on a C, with a C major chord. Our ears have been trained, in western music, to hear that as marking a fit closure; our expectations are satisfied. But *Lew Trenchard,* set in the key of C, ends instead on the "third" note, E (mi); and the chord, until the final stanza, is not C major but E major. In other words, the melody is not resolved, not yet; there is more to come.

So we move from stanza to stanza, from silent work to silent work:

Holy Spirit, Love divine,
Glow within this heart of mine;
Kindle every high desire;
Perish self in Thy pure fire!

Notice the progression of verbs. Longfellow entreats the Spirit to *glow* within his heart, and the verb suggests a quiet, warm light. But that light grows and acts: It will *kindle.* We may imagine a small spark that sets the fire going, but soon it is no mere flame, but a bonfire, great enough and hot enough to purify—to burn. So the third verb is a subjunctive, and marks a brave tossing away of all reserve: Let the self *perish* in the *pure fire,* the purgative fire, of the Holy Spirit.

Now we are ready to act in the world:

Holy Spirit, Power divine,
Fill and nerve this will of mine;
By Thee may I strongly live,
Bravely bear, and nobly strive.

Let's examine the words closely. Longfellow does not simply ask the Spirit to strengthen his will. Many a tyrant has had a strong will. Alexander the Great was resolute. Stalin was inflexible. Strength, by itself, is not the point: Strength in evil is, essentially, like a strong and raging disease destroying the soul. Longfellow asks the Spirit to *fill* his will before he asks for the muscles, the fiber, the *nerve*. His will is like an empty vessel. If the Holy Spirit fills it to brimming, then the poet may *live*. The final line describes the two principal actions of the human will: We *bear* the troubles that come our way, and we *strive* for the good we do not yet possess. The former is the will *against*, the latter is the will *for*. If we live *strongly*, in the strength of the Holy Spirit, then we will *bravely* bear adversity and *nobly* strive for the crown that God promises to His own.

The fourth stanza describes that life in terms of order:

Holy Spirit, Right divine,
King within my conscience reign;
Be my law, and I shall be
Firmly bound, for ever free.

Only when God is our King do we enjoy the "glorious liberty of the children of God" (Rom 8:21), because He is the Truth that sets us free. They who will not obey God obey men instead, or they obey worse and lower creatures in the order of being: Their baser passions or demons outright. When the Holy Spirit assumes the throne of our conscience, we can rely on His inner promptings. We need not waver. We are bound to Him, who is Love; and there is no love without the free gift of the self, entire and forever.

If the Spirit reigns within us, we need not trouble ourselves with wind and tempest:

Holy Spirit, Peace divine,
Still this restless heart of mine;
Speak to calm this tossing sea,
Stayed in Thy tranquility.

Longfellow recalls when Jesus and the disciples were in a boat on the Sea of Galilee, and a violent storm arose, threatening to capsize them. But Jesus was asleep, in the same peace for which Longfellow prays. The apostles awoke Him and cried, "We perish!" After rebuking them gently for their little faith, Jesus "rebuked the winds and the sea; and there was a great calm" (Mt 8:26). That was the Sea of Galilee, notorious for sudden and destructive tempests. But the Sea of Galilee is a puddle in the street compared with the surges and roiling of the human heart. Only if the Spirit of God dwells within can there be peace, *stayed* or made steadfast in His *tranquility*.

All now leads to the end for which the soul was made:

Holy Spirit, Joy divine,
Gladden Thou this heart of mine;
In the desert ways I sing,
"Spring, O Well, for ever spring!"

Such joy the world does not know, but the faithful soul knows it, even in the midst of the dry paths of our lives on earth. The Spirit is there with us, like the unseen underground spring, an inexhaustible well of life. And for this final stanza, the hymnals change the harmony slightly, and we end not on the expectant E major but on the tonic chord C major, resting in confidence.

The peace of the indwelling Spirit is well expressed in the last hymn we'll examine in this chapter, John Keble's *Blest Are the Pure in Heart* (1819), sung to a sweet and simple German melody, *Franconia*. Keble does not address the Holy Spirit, and yet all the quiet work of the Spirit is there, transforming the soul of the believer:

Blest are the pure in heart,
For they shall see our God;
The secret of the Lord is theirs,
Their soul is Christ's abode.

The words are those of Jesus: "Blessed are the pure in heart: for they shall see God" (Mt 5:8). What does that mean? Keble tries to explain in the following lines. When the heart is made pure, then Christ can make His abode there. "Abide in me, and I in you," says Jesus (Jn 15:4). To abide is to dwell, to continue in the presence of someone beloved. We may remain in a place, but we abide in a home. We abide with someone: "As the branch cannot bear fruit of itself, except it abide in the vine; no more can ye, except ye abide in me" (Jn 15:4). If Christ dwells in our hearts, we will know His *secret*—hidden from the indifferent or hostile multitude but brought to light by the Holy Ghost (Jn 14:26).

The next two stanzas make up one sentence, explaining why we should expect that only the humble would truly come to know Jesus:

The Lord, who left the heavens
Our life and peace to bring,

To dwell in lowliness with men,
Their pattern and their King;

He to the lowly soul
Doth still Himself impart;
And for His dwelling and His throne
Chooseth the pure in heart.

Only the humble heart is small enough to house the immensity of God's love. Only the humble heart will learn. So Jesus says:

> *I thank thee, O Father, Lord of heaven and earth, because thou hast hid these things from the wise and prudent, and hast revealed them unto babes.*
>
> *Even so, Father: for it seemed good in thy sight.*
>
> *All things are delivered unto me of my Father: and no man knoweth the Son, but the Father; neither knoweth any man the Father, save the Son, and he to whomsoever the Son will reveal him.*
>
> *Come unto me, all ye that labor and are heavy laden, and I will give you rest.*
>
> *Take my yoke upon you, and learn of me; for I am meek and humble of heart: and ye shall find rest for your souls.* (Mt 11:25–29)

Then, if we do not possess the Lord, we pray that He will come to us. But that is the same as praying for a humble heart:

Lord, we Thy presence seek;
May ours this blessing be;
Give us a pure and lowly heart,
A temple meet for Thee.

Chapter Nine

Penitence and Supplication

IF we are to follow Jesus, we must do something crucial first. We must *turn around.*

I use the word *crucial* advisedly. We find ourselves at a *crux viae*, a crossroads. One way leads to fame and glory and wealth and pleasure, or seems to; the other way leads into darkness, and life. One way leads to the grave of sin; the other way leads to the Cross. There is no third.

The tempter whispers into our ears, "Surely you deserve a little rest? A little of your own way, after having given so much? Look at all the people hustling down that path! They can't all be wrong, can they? What have you gotten for all your devotion?" So we look toward the lie. That is one way to describe sin: A turn of the heart away from God and life, toward illusions and death.

The poets who gave us our great treasury of hymns understood this. They knew too well how wretched and foolish we are, without the grace of God. Therefore they, like the psalmists, wrote hymns of supplication. We need Him; we cannot take one right step without Him; we cannot lift an arm in our own defense against evil. When we sin, we do evil to others and to ourselves, but it is God our Lord and friend whom we cast as our enemy. Then the aim of our songs of penitence is, first of all, to *turn back to Him*, which we can only do if He gives us the strength.

That is the message of the great Psalm 51, known also by its Latin name as the *Miserere mei*, and for centuries a mainstay for choral music sung during Holy Week. The Hebrew caption says that King David composed the psalm after he had been accused by the prophet Nathan of his adultery with Bathsheba. Here it is in its entirety:

> *Have mercy on me, O God, according to Thy lovingkindness: according unto the multitude of thy tender mercies blot out my transgressions.*
>
> *Wash me thoroughly from mine iniquity, and cleanse me from my sin.*
>
> *For I acknowledge my transgressions: and my sin is ever before me.*
>
> *Against thee, thee only, have I sinned, and done this evil in thy sight: that thou mightest be justified when thou speakest, and clear when thou judgest.*
>
> *Behold, I was shapen in iniquity; and in sin did my mother conceive me.*
>
> *Behold, thou desirest truth in the inward parts: and in the hidden part thou shalt make me to know wisdom.*
>
> *Purge me with hyssop, and I shall be clean: wash me, and I shall be whiter than snow.*
>
> *Make me to hear joy and gladness; that the bones which thou hast broken may rejoice.*
>
> *Hide thy face from my sins, and blot out all mine iniquities.*
>
> *Create in me a clean heart, O God; and renew a right spirit within me.*

Cast me not away from thy presence; and take not thy holy spirit from me.

Restore unto me the joy of thy salvation; and uphold me with thy free spirit.

Then will I teach transgressors thy ways; and sinners shall be converted unto thee.

Deliver me from bloodguiltiness, O God, thou God of my salvation; and my tongue shall sing aloud of thy righteousness.

O Lord, open thou my lips, and my mouth shall show forth thy praise.

For thou desirest not sacrifice; else would I give it; thou delightest not in burnt offering.

The sacrifices of God are a broken spirit; a broken and a contrite heart, O God, thou wilt not despise.

Do good in thy good pleasure unto Zion; build thou the walls of Jerusalem.

Then shalt thou be pleased with the sacrifices of righteousness, with burnt offering and whole burnt offering; then shall they offer bullocks upon thine altar.

This is a fascinating Hebrew poem, which says much and implies more. We are too accustomed to our worship of a God of love and righteousness to notice how the poem strikes to the heart of a new theological understanding. God, says David, does not desire sacrifice! That would have struck the worshipers of Zeus, Baal, Moloch, and all the other pagan gods with blank astonishment. What else does a god desire, if not that? If a man sins, he can work out an economic deal by slaughtering a bull in the god's honor. It is a shadow of the true repentance that God desires, but only a shadow. David says, instead, that the sacrifice God desires is *a broken and contrite heart*. That is because sin disrupts the relationship between God and man, which is deeply personal: *Against Thee, Thee only, have I sinned*, says David, repeating the pronoun, in an agony of sorrow.

When we are struck to the heart, knowing that we have repaid love with callous disregard, and favor with ingratitude, we know—we don't have to be told by theologians—that we are nothing. We are the *wretch* that John Newton proclaimed himself to be when he penned *Amazing Grace*. Newton knew it well, because he'd been a slave trader, selling his fellow human beings into misery. *Wretch* is not too strong a word for that, regardless of what our modern editors think when they blot it out and replace it with something bland and inoffensive. Nor does David spare himself: *Behold, I was shapen in iniquity; and in sin did my mother conceive me*. He doesn't mean there was something wrong with his mother and father, other perhaps than the wrong that we all suffer, as we are sinners all. He means that the rot of sin penetrates to the core of his being, and it has always been that way.

Then if he is to turn from his sin, he must call upon God to remake him: *Create in me a clean heart, O God; and renew a right spirit within me*. The word *create* is well chosen by the translators. It renders the Hebrew *bara*, the same word used in Genesis for God's creation of the heavens and the earth from nothing. David the sinner, then, must be transformed. He must be filled with the renewing breath of God: The *spirit*, translating the Hebrew *ruah*, which stirred above the waters of creation. David cannot even praise God unless God opens his lips. If you are looking for music that captures the sorrow of this psalm, shot through with grateful joy, find a copy of Gregorio Allegri's *Miserere*, sung by a choir of men and boy sopranos. For centuries it has been sung during Holy Week in the Sistine Chapel;

the young Mendelssohn heard it there and wrote that it made manifest the very essence of music.

The composers of the 1912 Anglican *Psalter* did a creditable job rendering the psalm into English verse:

God, be merciful to me,
On Thy grace I rest my plea;
Plenteous in compassion Thou,
Blot out my transgressions now;
Wash me, make me pure within,
Cleanse, O cleanse me from my sin.

My transgressions I confess,
Grief and guilt my soul oppress;
I have sinned against Thy grace
And provoked Thee to Thy face;
I confess Thy judgment just;
Speechless, I Thy mercy trust.

I am evil, born in sin;
Thou desirest truth within.
Thou alone my Savior art,
Teach Thy wisdom to my heart;
Make me pure, Thy grace bestow,
Wash me whiter than the snow.

Broken, humbled to the dust
By Thy wrath and judgment just,
Let my contrite heart rejoice
And in gladness hear Thy voice;
From my sins O hide Thy face,
Blot them out in boundless grace.

It is hard to imagine a more direct confession than the one that begins the third stanza: *I am evil.* The greatest saints and the greatest sinners understand it, no matter for the vast complacent middle. Since God desires that truth should dwell in our inmost parts, the poet begs God to teach His wisdom to his heart—and *that* is what it means to be renewed in spirit and washed whiter than snow. It is a complete re-creation, from the *dust* to which the sinner has been humbled, recalling the dust from which the first sinner came, and to which God declared he would return, "for dust thou art" (Gn 3:19). But there is a promise in this dust. The poet plays upon the meaning of the word *contrite*: To scour, to rub away to dust, to nothing. A contrite heart requires more than a pat and a smile. It requires the renewing power of the Creator.

Yet there are tremendously gentle poems of repentance, and rightly so, because though repentance is bitter, it is also sweet. It is the sweetness of restored love and gratitude, drowning all shame. The prodigal son tasted it when his father threw his arms about his neck and kissed him. We find this sweetness in Newman's quiet and subtle poem, *Lead, Kindly Light* (1833):

Lead, kindly Light, amid the encircling gloom,
Lead Thou me on;
The night is dark, and I am far from home;
Lead Thou me on;
Keep Thou my feet; I do not ask to see
The distant scene; one step enough for me.

I was not ever thus, nor prayed that Thou
Shouldst lead me on;
I loved to choose and see my path; but now
Lead Thou me on.

I loved the garish day, and, spite of fears,
Pride ruled my will; remember not past years.

So long Thy power hath blessed me, sure it still
Will lead me on
O'er moor and fen, o'er crag and torrent, till
The night is gone;
And with the morn those angel faces smile
Which I have loved long since, and lost awhile.

Most impressive are Newman's pauses, placed with great tact, in the middle of the long pentameter lines. They give us the effect of lines-within-lines, echoing one another, tinting one another, so to speak, with a different color, a different feeling. In the first stanza, each of the long lines is suspended in the same position, after the fourth syllable:

Lead, kindly Light
The night is dark
Keep Thou my feet
The distant scene

That is fine indeed. Newman begs the Light to lead him, because *the night is dark*. What does it mean to be led by the Light? It means that we are led in every step we take: *Keep Thou my feet*. The destination is distant. Newman cannot see it, in the dark. Yet it is there. He does not even pray to see it, now: *One step enough for me*, he concludes the stanza, a terse, elliptical sentence omitting the verb *is*. What kind of terrain is he traversing? We don't know yet. All we know is that a foreboding gloom surrounds him, and—now turning to simple language that even a child can understand—he is *far from home*. That is all we need to know.

The second stanza turns from the present journey to the past. Newman now varies the position of his pauses, lending the verses a meditative effect, as he ponders the person he used to be. Again we may place beside one another the lines-within-lines:

I was not ever thus
I loved to see and choose my path
I loved the garish day
Pride ruled my will

How powerful and sad the progression is! Newman begins line after line with the personal pronoun *I*—and it was just because he once led his whole life according to the *I*, with pride ruling his will, that he went astray. That pronoun is set against the familiar *thou*. I once led myself, but I do not wish to do so anymore; please, *you* lead me now, it's *you* I trust and not myself. Notice the ironic power of the verbs: *I loved to see and choose; I loved; pride ruled*. It is as Augustine said: *Amor pondus meum*, "My love, my weight." Our desire is like a weight on a pulley that throws us in one direction and not another. Newman loved, but loved badly; he loved his own way, his own path. He wanted to *see*. That doesn't mean he wanted to understand. He wanted his future to be laid plain before him. He wanted to be the decider of his fate. He wanted to bask in the glare of the day. But now he begs the Lord to forget that foolish past. If we thought that the darkness was merely that of sin, we are mistaken. It is also the darkness of trust in the Lord, giving ourselves utterly to His providence, declining to insist that we know all the specifics of our journey beforehand.

The third and final stanza makes the journey more concrete for our imaginations. It is as if Newman were walking through a vast English wilderness, crossing the moors and the fens, fording the swift rivers; dangerous in the night. But the night will not last forever. The day will dawn, and when it does, the night will be *gone*, once and for all. The morning will shine with the faces of angels, those which the repentant Newman now tells us he once loved, a long time ago, but which he had *lost awhile*. The words are simple, and steeped in honest shame. How could he have lost such beauty? But the word *awhile* tempers the shame. Yes, he did lose them; but he did not lose them forever.

In 1865, the hymnodist John Dykes composed a most unusual and lovely melody for this poem. It is called *Lux Benigna*, a Latin translation of Newman's *kindly light*. Its complex interlacing structure helps to bring out the lines-within-lines and the power of the short lines, which Dykes stresses by slowing the melody down, lengthening the notes. Let me try to illustrate the structure, with boldface and doubled letters for the slow phrases, and an asterisk to denote a variation:

A	B	**CC**
Lead, kindly Light,	*amid the encircling gloom,*	*Lead Thou me on;*
A	B	**CC***
The night is dark,	*and I am far from home;*	*Lead Thou me on;*
A*	B*	
Keep Thou my feet;	*I do not ask to see*	

A**	B/C**
The distant scene;	*one step enough for me.*

Musically, we "hear" the similarity in meaning between the general prayer, *Lead Thou me on*, and its specific application for the benighted traveler, *Keep Thou my feet*. The final phrase, too, is a musical variation of both the previous B and C phrases, so that we return, in song, to the heart of the poem: The prayer that God will lead us.

It may be difficult to imagine a more heartfelt plea for mercy; but the old hymnodists will not disappoint us. Newman was a nineteenth-century Anglican priest who converted to the Roman Catholic Church; Charles Wesley, with his brother John and their friend George Whitefield, began the Methodist movement in England in the eighteenth century, stressing personal holiness and an ever-deepening relationship with Jesus Christ. I believe that Newman and Wesley would have understood one another on that score. And Charles Wesley, like Newman, has bequeathed to us some of the finest hymns in the English language.

One of my favorites is *Jesus, Lover of My Soul* (1740), set by Joseph Parry to the minor key Welsh melody *Aberystwyth* (1879):

Jesus, lover of my soul,
Let me to Thy bosom fly,
While the nearer waters roll,
While the tempest still is high:
Hide me, O my Savior, hide,
Till the storm of life be past;
Safe into the haven guide,
O receive my soul at last.

Newman presented to us the quiet and ominous danger of an English moor. Wesley's metaphor is more dramatic: We are on a stormy sea, in imminent danger of foundering. Wesley has in mind the words of David:

> *Save me, O God; for the waters are come in unto my soul.*
> *I sink in deep mire, where there is no standing; I am come into deep waters, where the floods overflow me.*
> *I am weary of my crying: my throat is dried; mine eyes fail while I wait for my God.* (Ps 69:1–3)

The verb *hide*, too, is rich in scriptural resonance. Again the psalmist:

> *Cause me to hear thy lovingkindness in the morning; for in thee do I trust: cause me to know the way wherein I should walk; for I lift up my soul unto thee.*
> *Deliver me, O Lord, from mine enemies: I flee unto thee to hide me.* (Ps 143:8–9)

> *One thing have I desired of the Lord, that will I seek after; that I may dwell in the house of the Lord all the days of my life, to behold the beauty of the Lord, and to inquire in his temple.*
> *For in the time of trouble he shall hide me in his pavilion: in the secret of his tabernacle he shall hide me; he shall set me up upon a rock.* (Ps 27:4–5)

Notice that the psalmist seeks the Lord not simply as a refuge, but as the beloved. To *hide* with the Lord, then, is not to cower in trembling but to dwell in what Wesley calls the *haven*: The home port for the sailor, or the cleft in the rock for the dove. He also calls it the *bosom* of the Lord: The shelter of His love.

In the second stanza, Wesley makes the plea more urgent still and explains why it must be so:

Other refuge have I none,
Hangs my helpless soul on Thee;
Leave, ah! leave me not alone,
Still support and comfort me!
All my trust on Thee is stayed;
All my help from Thee I bring;
Cover my defenseless head
With the shadow of Thy wing.

The psalmist again:

> *Be merciful unto me, O God, be merciful unto me: for my soul trusteth in thee: yea, in the shadow of thy wings will I make refuge, until these calamities be overpast.*
>
> *I will cry unto God most high; unto God, that performeth all things for me.* (Ps 57:1–2)

Let us see with what craft Wesley has transformed the images and the language of the psalms into his poetic prayer in English. Consider what the first line means: "I have no other refuge." But Wesley has reversed the normal word order. A poor poet does so because he finds himself hemmed in by meter and rhyme. But a poet like Wesley uses the necessity to great advantage. The reversal lays special stress on the adjective *other* and the pronoun *none*, as if to say, "*Other* refuge? There is *none*." That hollow word rhymes with *alone*: For there are only two choices.

Either God is our refuge or we are utterly *alone*, in the midst of this tempestuous life, with not a prayer for our salvation.

That explains the power of the strange verb *hangs* in the second line, also stressed by the reversed syntax. It is the meaning of the word *depend*—but how pallid the line would be, if Wesley had merely said, "My helpless soul depends on Thee." For that word *depend* has become wholly abstract for us. A theorem depends on a postulate. A commuter depends on the bus to arrive on time. That is not the spiritual and personal dependence we are trying to describe. The soul *hangs* upon God: like a child clinging to the Father's arms. We hang for dear life. The soul is *helpless*; Wesley means, of course, incapable, but also *without help*, because our help is in the name of the Lord, who made heaven and earth (Ps 121:2). The psalmist makes this clear. God does more than help us. *He is our help*:

> *Unless the Lord had been my help, my soul had almost dwelt in silence.*
>
> *When I said, My foot slippeth; thy mercy, O Lord, held me up*. (Ps 94:17–18)

The goddess Athena *helps* her favorite, Odysseus, but she does so as a shrewd conspirator and a wry observer of what Odysseus will do, when he is clinging naked to a rock in the midst of a roaring sea or when he is outnumbered by the crowd of men suing for his wife's hand in marriage. Odysseus must help himself; Athena's help is conditional upon that. But when we turn to the Lord, we do not ask for a helping hand for a moment. We ask for a Savior. Hence the emphasis that Wesley lays upon the pronoun *all*, contrasting with the pronoun *none* in the first line. *All my trust on Thee is stayed*, he says, meaning fixed in one place, steadfast. My enemies have compassed me about, cries

David, but the Lord drew me out of the waters, the Lord was *my stay* (Ps 18:18).

Wesley ends the poem with a surprising turn. He cries out not for less water but for even more:

Plenteous grace with Thee is found,
Grace to cleanse from every sin;
Let the healing streams abound,
Make and keep me pure within.
Thou of life the fountain art,
Freely let me take of Thee:
Spring Thou up within my heart,
Rise to all eternity.

The waters of calamity recede into insignificance. Now we see the waters of salvation: The living waters Jesus promised to the Samaritan woman at the well. Whoever drinks of this water, said Jesus, pointing to the well, shall thirst again, "but whosoever drinketh of the water that I shall give him shall never thirst; but the water that I shall give him shall be in him a well of water springing up into everlasting life" (Jn 4:14). It is the water that John saw flowing in heaven from the throne of God and the Lamb (Rv 22:1).

Wesley has chosen his words most precisely. God's grace is *plenteous*—literally, it *fills*, as water fills the well. That grace, that water, cleanses and heals. So he prays that its streams will *abound*, that their waves will overflow the banks! Thus the grace of God is not tamer than the tempest. It is more abundant, more exuberant. The initial words of the last four lines are strongly stressed: *Thou, freely, spring, rise. Thou of life the fountain art: Thou*, and no other. *Freely let me take of Thee. Freely*—that is, largely, bounteously, as much as I will, echoing the words of Jesus: "Freely ye have received, freely give" (Mt 10:8). What do we freely take from God, but God? It is the indwelling God Himself whom we desire to *spring* within our hearts, like the river bursting forth in the midst of a new Eden, springing, and rising, for all eternity.

Wesley knew that we sinners can never know joy unless we turn to God in our distress. We must be converted. The very word *conversion* suggests a turning-about: We turn from our old ways and seek to walk in the ways of God. We have seen the motif in Psalm 51 above: *Then will I teach transgressors Thy ways; and sinners shall be converted unto Thee.* It is a common one in Scripture. When the young Solomon prayed at the dedication of the new Temple, he entreated the Lord to forgive His people even if they should sin and be dragged into captivity. If they come to their senses, confessing, "We have sinned, and have done perversely, we have committed wickedness; and so return unto [God] with all their heart," then He will hear them and forgive them and bring them home (1 Kgs 8:47–50). Notice that the promise is held forth not just for an individual sinner here and there, walking in the night, but for the whole people: They too require the prayer of penitence.

In the New Testament, this conversion or turning-back is extended to all people, everywhere. It is the commission that Jesus gives to St. Paul, sending him to the Gentiles, "to open their eyes, and to turn them from darkness to light, and from the power of Satan unto God, that they may receive forgiveness of sins" (Acts 26:18). We should not suppose that such preaching is no longer necessary, because almost everyone in the world has at least heard of Jesus. When Christians say that man is a sinner, they mean more than that John or Sarah commits sins. They mean also that the whole human race, *as a race*—for man is a social creature—turns toward evil, and needs conversion.

In 1916, during the misery of the brutal First World War, the German composer Gustav Holst asked a poet named Clifford Bax to compose the penitential hymn we know as *Turn Back, O Man*:

Turn back, O man, forswear thy foolish ways.
Old now is earth, and none may count her days,
Yet thou, her child, whose head is crowned with flame,
Still wilt not hear thine inner God proclaim,
"Turn back, O man, forswear thy foolish ways."

The melody to which this poem is sung, *Old Hundred Twenty Fourth*, composed by Louis Bourgeois (1551), is stately and solemn, each of the five lines a variation upon the same theme. We saw how John Dykes, understanding the nuances of Newman's poem, wrote a melody that would bring the nuances out. Bax had to do the reverse. The melody was already there, so he had to write verses that would fit the music. In this case it was not easy to do. Most of the hymns we've looked at use short lines of three and four strong beats (six or eight syllables), common in English ballads. But these lines have five beats (ten syllables), and there are five of them in a row, each one reflecting the others. Bax's solution is ingenious. He doesn't delay the rhymes: The second line rhymes with the first, the fourth line rhymes with the third. But what about the odd fifth line? There would seem to have been three choices. The first is not to rhyme at all; and that might work, if the music of the fifth line were markedly different from the music of the other lines—then its particularity would stand out. But that would strain against the melody as it is—for the fifth line echoes all the other lines. The second choice would be to rhyme once more on the third line. That would give us a couplet—lines one and two—followed by a triplet—lines three through five. But that would leave us with an awkward imbalance, and again, it isn't suggested by the melody. The third choice would be to rhyme on the first and second lines. That might do, but we should remember that this is a hymn we are singing, not just a poem we read on the page. We can't really *see* the lines simultaneously; we have to *hear* their reflections upon one another in time, as we sing. It's a wide gap to bridge, then, those thirty syllables that would link the rhyme in line two to the rhyme in line five.

So Bax chooses something else, something to provide a stronger link than any of those options can provide. *He repeats the first line entirely*, but in a different context. When we first sing the line, *Turn back, O man, forswear thy foolish ways*, it is in our own person, appealing to mankind generally and to ourselves in particular. But when we sing the same line at the end of the stanza, it is in the voice of the indwelling Holy Spirit, the *inner God*, who commands us, *Turn back, O man, forswear thy foolish ways.* The command is necessary because—although we enjoy the benefits of our intellectual nature, our heads *crowned with flame*, and have done so for ages upon ages, because *old now is earth* and so are we—we still are deaf to God's call.

The other stanzas of this short poem follow the same pattern:

Earth might be fair, and all men glad and wise.
Age after age their tragic empires rise,
Built while they dream, and in that dreaming weep:
Would man but wake from out his haunted sleep,
Earth might be fair, and all men glad and wise.

The first line is bittersweet: Notice that little word *might.* It might be so, but man persists in his dreaming. It's a nice reversal of perspective. The bustlers in this world think they have a grasp upon reality, while the people on their knees in prayer are the dreamers. Quite the contrary. The sleep of sinful man is *haunted* with dreams of power, with *tragic empires* rising and falling to the dust. All paganism ends in despair; but when the paganism attaches itself to the idol of empire, or of the all-healing State, the despair is most dreadful because the fall is most catastrophic.

In the final stanza, the modal *might* is replaced by *shall*:

Earth shall be fair, and all her people one;
Nor till that hour shall God's whole will be done.
Now, even now, once more from earth to sky
Peals forth in joy man's old, undaunted cry,
"Earth shall be fair, and all her people one!"

I reserve judgment on that. Perhaps Bax meant to turn our attention to the kingdom of God, which man longs for, but which man—and the poet is not clear about this—cannot bring to pass on his own. In any case, the mood of penitence merges with a cry that anticipates the triumph of God's church on earth, in time, or at the end of time.

If one wishes a more vigorous penitential prayer for the cleansing of both the individual soul and the world, the great essayist, novelist, and poet G. K. Chesterton will oblige us. His poem *O God of Earth and Altar* (1906) sounds many a note that is utterly missing from our contemporary hymnals. For Chesterton sees that the wrath of God is more merciful than the indulgent apathy of the world; and the mercy of God is more searing than is the cruelty of the world. Ralph Vaughan Williams set the poem to a bold, masculine English melody,

King's Lynn, with a straightforward interlocking structure: A B / A* B* / A* B* / A B. Here is the first of its three stanzas:

O God of earth and altar,
Bow down and hear our cry,
Our earthly rulers falter,
Our people drift and die;
The walls of gold entomb us,
The swords of scorn divide,
Take not Thy thunder from us,
But take away our pride.

Chesterton desires to surprise us into thought. He does not say, *O God of heaven and altar*, even though that would fit the meter. Why *earth*, and why is that placed beside *altar?*

We should remember what an altar is. Man rears up a stone table, an earthen structure resting upon the earth, to send up a sacrifice to God in heaven. But our God is not a distant despot, waiting for the sweet smell of burnt flesh to please the nostrils. He is a *God of earth*, intimately involved in the lives of men, and a God of the *altar*, as the writer to the Hebrews testifies of Jesus:

> *This man, because he continueth ever, hath an unchangeable priesthood.*
>
> *Wherefore he is able also to save them to the uttermost that come unto God by him, seeing he liveth ever to make intercession for them.* (Heb 7:24–25)

We ask then that God will more powerfully exercise His kingship among us and within us. The possessive *our* is crucial: The God of earth must save us, because *our* rulers on earth are ineffectual and *our* people, our flock, wander away and die.

We are in a parlous state. We are entombed in *walls of gold*: Such joy does our pursuit of wealth bring. We are divided by *swords of scorn*: Such fellowship does worldly righteousness bring. Chesterton is thinking of the admonitory words of Jesus: "Think not that I am come to send peace on earth: I came not to send peace, but a sword" (Mt 10:34). The sword of Jesus will not let men rest in their sluggish sin, in the despair that looks like peace because it no longer acknowledges any transcendent good for which to fight. The sword of Christ divides father from son and daughter from mother, because there can be no true communion between those who shoulder the Cross and those whose lives are dedicated—if that is the right word to describe self-serving apathy—to avoiding that love at all costs. What do people need from God when they are divided by their own scorn for one another? Not a clear calm day, but *thunder*. Do not take that away from us, pleads the poet. That would be to abandon us to our folly. Instead *take away our pride*.

The second stanza casts a keen glance upon the ways of the world—the political world, which ever rises up as a mighty-looking alternative to worship of the true God:

From all that terror teaches,
From lies of tongue and pen,
From all the easy speeches
That comfort cruel men,
From sale and profanation
Of honor, and the sword,
From sleep and from damnation
Deliver us, good Lord!

That is an extraordinary progression of evils: terror, mendacity, demagoguery, cruelty, treachery, *sleep*, and damnation. What is the odd item, the one Chesterton wishes us particularly to notice? *Sleep*, no doubt. Sleep—what does that mean? How can someone who must listen to the jabbering of politicians, who must look upon the strutting tyrant, who must share a drink with a mercenary who has sold his soul and his honor for worldly advancement, how can that person *sleep?* But that's exactly the point. Only the sleep of the soul will allow it. Only sleep can explain how we Americans can have allowed our public culture to degenerate into an open cesspool of the venal, the imbecilic, and the obscene. We stumble to damnation like sleepwalkers. *Deliver us, good Lord*, Chesterton cries, from that deadly sleep!

The final stanza presents us with the alternative of holiness:

Tie in a living tether
The prince and priest and thrall,
Bind all our lives together,
Smite us and save us all;
In ire and exultation,
Aflame with faith, and free,
Lift up a living nation,
A single sword to Thee.

That is no holiness as the world considers it, winking wisely and saying, "Well, it's nice that some people sit in their rooms and pray all day long. We'll let them do that, they're harmless enough." Holiness, Chesterton saw, is the most revolutionary thing in the world. It wakes us up. It binds *our lives together*. It transforms the scattered pursuers of worldly goods into an army bound by the *living tether* of the love of God. It is far from painless! The world seeks an anodyne, but the ache remains, because we are made for God, and nothing else can fill the yawning abyss of the human soul. God cannot save us without smiting us; then let Him do so! Let us be afire with joy and with *ire*, the just anger of God against evil. Only then will we be liberated: Notice how Chesterton has bound by alliteration the three words *flame, faith*, and *free*. Those words echo one another because the things they name are one. *Faith* is not a cool assent to a theological proposition. It is *aflame* with love for God. It does not sink us into inaction. It sharpens all our faculties. It helps us to become the saints God has destined us to be. It sets us *free*. Not as self-seekers, meandering at will, but together, raising a *single sword* to God.

So does the soul in penitence pray.

Chapter Ten

The Church Militant

MOST hymnals today evince a strange contradiction. They're filled with songs that focus upon the self or upon the wonderfulness of the people singing, but almost all songs celebrating the heroism of the saints who have gone before us, as shining examples of faith and hope and love, have been removed. Thus are our congregations deprived of poetry that stirs them to bold and even dangerous action. That such hymns appeal especially to young men makes the loss all the more to be decried, as the Church must then lose their considerable energy and combativeness, and see those capacities either dissipated or turned to worldliness or vice.

So let's begin with a rousing call to action, John Bunyan's spirited *Who Would True Valor See* (also known, in altered form, as *He Who Would Valiant Be*), from *Pilgrim's Progress*—sung equally well to the melodies *St. Dunstan* and *Monks' Gate*:

Who would true valor see,
Let him come hither;
One here will constant be,
Come wind, come weather.
There's no discouragement,

Shall make him once relent
His first avowed intent,
To be a Pilgrim.

Whoso beset him round
With dismal stories,
Do but themselves confound;
His strength the more is.
No lion can him fright,
He'll with a giant fight,
But he will have a right,
To be a Pilgrim.

Hobgoblin, nor foul fiend,
Can daunt his spirit:
He knows, he at the end
Shall life inherit.
Then fancies fly away,
He'll fear not what men say,
He'll labor night and day
To be a Pilgrim.

This short poem is the official hymn of a few boys' schools in England; no surprise. But I first heard it sung at a most solemn occasion. It was the recessional hymn for the Mass in which a friend of mine was ordained a priest. The church fairly shook with joy.

I won't claim that this is great poetry. It is very good poetry, bold and forthright, for a great hymn. Bunyan doesn't engage in subtleties, yet even so there's more going on here than we might suspect. The valiant man—Mr. Valiant-for-Truth in the novel—is like a fearless sailor in a tempest. What do rough winds and storms matter to him? He is as constant as the northern star. He has an *avowed intent*, the object of a sacred oath. He is going to be a *pilgrim*.

The motif of the pilgrim is common in Scripture and in the annals of Christian history. Abraham, who followed the call of God to leave his home in Ur of the Chaldees and go to a far-off land of promise, was a pilgrim, a stranger in a strange land. Moses led the pilgrim Israelites through the desert all the way to the banks of the Jordan. Jesus commands His apostles to go forth and make disciples of all nations. St. Paul took that command to heart and voyaged all over the Mediterranean world. A wanderer has gone astray, and doesn't know where his path will lead him. A tourist has a destination, but one that he wishes to put in his pocket—the experience as a souvenir. But the pilgrim, whose destination is a holy place, engages in a real adventure, because he has a definite aim for whose love he will give all he has.

In the second stanza, the threats to the pilgrim are not physical but spiritual, and far more dangerous. Enemies beset him, not with pikes and swords, but with *dismal stories*, tales of failure, of abandonment, of despair. He flings them aside—all they do is make him more determined to press on. We might attribute to him the high-hearted daring of a boy who actually *wants* to meet a lion or a giant in his path; and that boyishness, that high-heartedness, is certainly there. But Bunyan is also thinking of the warnings of Scripture. Be sober and watchful, says St. Peter, "because your adversary the devil, as a roaring lion, walketh about, seeking whom he may devour" (1 Pt 5:8). We must resist him with steadfast faith. As for the giant, we may think of Goliath but, better still, the mysterious Gog and Magog of the Apocalypse, who are to go forth with Satan to deceive the earth, before they are finally thrust into hell forever (cf. Rv 20:8).

The last verse, with fine insouciance, reduces the prince of darkness to a bugbear that frightens people in the dark—a *hobgoblin*, a *foul fiend*. But the valiant man remains undaunted. He trusts not in his own strength but in the promises of Christ: that in the end he will inherit everlasting life. So then, what are all the demons? Nothing but *fancies*, phantasms, specters. And what of the ridicule of our fellow men in the know? Or the whimpers of people too frightened to move? But who cares what people say? He'll labor night and day *to be a pilgrim*.

We should never be embarrassed to appeal to the soldier, for Jesus Himself has said, "Greater love hath no man than this, that a man lay down his life for his friends" (Jn 15:13). Compared against the religious leaders of His time and the lawyers and the politicians—the Pharisees, the scribes, and the Roman officials—the common soldiers and the centurions in the New Testament come off fairly well. Perhaps it's because the soldier puts his life in danger for something other than personal gain; or perhaps it's because the soldier is accustomed to obedience. "I also am a man set under authority," said the centurion, humbly expressing his faith that Jesus need not enter his unworthy house, but need only say a single word to heal his dying servant (Lk 7:6–8).

The New Testament abounds in imagery of spiritual warfare. Devotion to Christ becomes the standard of a new manliness. "Watch ye," says St. Paul, in his parting words to the church at Corinth, "stand fast in the faith, quit you like men, be strong" (1 Cor 16:13). "Let us put on the armor of light," he says, because the day is at hand (Rom 13:12). They who preach of Christ crucified must comport themselves without blame, proving themselves by suffering and by the purity of their love, by "the word of truth, by the power of God, by the armor of righteousness on the right hand and on the left" (2 Cor 6:7). The children of darkness sleep in their drunkenness, but "let us, who are of the day, be sober, putting on the breastplate of faith, and love; and for an helmet, the hope of salvation" (1 Thes 5:8). Indeed, Paul develops the analogy at great length, thinking of the *hoplite*, the Greek foot soldier. An infantryman who is fully armed possesses, literally, a *panoply*, everything that he needs:

> *Put on the whole armor [panoply] of God, that ye may be able to stand against the wiles of the devil.*
>
> *For we wrestle not against flesh and blood, but against principalities, against powers, against the rulers of the darkness of this world, against spiritual wickedness in high places.*
>
> *Wherefore take unto you the whole armor [panoply] of God, that ye may be able to withstand in the evil day, and having done all, to stand.*
>
> *Stand therefore, having your loins girt about with truth, and having on the breastplate of righteousness;*
>
> *And your feet shod with the preparation of the gospel of peace;*
>
> *Above all, taking the shield of faith, wherewith ye shall be able to quench all the fiery darts of the wicked.*
>
> *And take the helmet of salvation, and the sword of the Spirit, which is the word of God.* (Eph 6:11–17)

They who do so will be "more than conquerors" (Rom 8:37). They will be able to say, with St. Paul as he awaited execution, "I have fought a good fight" (2 Tm 4:7).

That is the context for Charles Wesley's hymn of zeal, *Soldiers of Christ, Arise* (1749), sung to the cheerful march-tune *Silver Street*:

Soldiers of Christ, arise,
And put your armor on,
Strong in the strength which God supplies
Through His eternal Son.

Strong in the Lord of hosts,
And in His mighty power:
Who in the strength of Jesus trusts
Is more than conqueror.

Wesley alludes to the verse from Romans and all those verses generally wherein St. Paul urges his fellow Christians to ready themselves for the fight. But the allusions are compressed into two stanzas of great power. The key words are *strong* and *strength*, each repeated, with *strong* in a position of particular emphasis, especially at the beginning of the second stanza. We are to be *strong* but not in our own *strength*: rather in the power of the Lord of *hosts*—that is, *armies*. Jesus shall "put all enemies under his feet," and "the last enemy that shall be destroyed is death" (1 Cor 15:25–26), so that we may cry out with St. Paul, "O death, where is thy sting? O grave, where is thy victory?" (1 Cor 15:55).

In the third stanza, Wesley picks up the favorite imperative of St. Paul, *stand*:

Stand then in His great might,
With all His strength endued,

And take, to arm you for the fight,
The panoply of God.

Again, we have the word *strength*, grappling this stanza to the ones before. We are *endued* with the strength of God, and the word has a double meaning. We are *endowed* with it, freely given to us by God; and we *put on* that strength, we *don* it, as a man straps armor to his back. It is the *panoply* or *whole armor of God*, both the whole armor devoted to God, and the whole armor given by God to the foot soldier for the coming battle.

Then Wesley echoes that magnificent verse from the psalms, "On they go from strength to strength" (Ps 84:7), and applies it to the terrible wrestling with powers and principalities that St. Paul says every Christian soldier must endure:

From strength to strength go on,
Wrestle, and fight, and pray:
Tread all the powers of darkness down,
And win the well-fought day.

Notice the series of imperative verbs in the second line: *wrestle, fight, pray*. The first two clearly have to do with warfare, but the third? That too, and more than the others! If we are to go *from strength to strength*, then prayer encompasses all our wrestling and fighting; it is our most dreaded weapon. If we do indeed *wrestle, and fight, and pray*, we will, in the strength of Jesus, fulfill the commands of the imperative verbs to follow: We will *tread down* the evil, and we will *win* the day.

The final stanza gives us the picture of the soldier victorious:

That, having all things done,
And all your conflicts past,

Ye may o'ercome, through Christ alone,
And stand complete at last.

The verb that sums up the hope of the soldier returns for the final line: To *stand*. But now it does not mean to stand guard, to stand against the approaching enemy, to stand fearless in battle. Now it means to *stand complete*, to stand in entirety, in fulfillment. Again Wesley alludes to the words of St. Paul, this time to the Christians at Colossae: "Epaphras, who is one of you, a servant of Christ, saluteth you, always laboring [wrestling] fervently for you in prayers, that ye may stand perfect and complete in all the will of God" (Col 4:12).

Perhaps the only soldierly hymn that remains in many hymnals today is the mighty *For All the Saints*, because All Saints' Day requires some hymn or other and that one is an obvious choice. But what's done to it is so shameful, so petty, that it would be more honest to leave it out entirely. Let's look at the hymn as it was actually composed, by William How (1864):

For all the saints, who from their labors rest,
Who Thee, by faith, before the world confessed,
Thy name, O Jesus, be forever blest.
Alleluia, alleluia!

One of the dismaying things about teaching old poetry to students raised on modern poetry is that they will often assume that poets don't have to be grammatical—poets can toss things into the pot at their pleasure, and the stew will have a general taste to it, without anybody being able to tell exactly what's in it and what one ingredient has to do with another. But *no English poem written before 1900 is like that*. How has written a perfectly grammatical sentence with a precise meaning. The key word is the pronoun *Thee*. That is in the accusative case; it is the *object* of the verb *confessed*. The saints didn't just *confess*—that doesn't make sense. One cannot, in English, confess, without confessing something or professing something or professing someone. Here is what the sentence means:

For [the sake of] all the saints, who rest from their labors, who by faith confessed Thee before the world, [may] Thy name, O Jesus, be blest forever.

But why didn't How just lead off with the subject of the sentence, thus?

Thy name, O Jesus, be forever blest,
For all the saints, who from their labors rest,
Who Thee, by faith, before the world confessed.

Because he knew what he was doing, that's why. He is writing in a form that invites surprise in the final line, or climax. We expect one line to rhyme with a previous line; that's common enough. But a triplet, three rhymes in a row, is not common; and the long pentameter (five-beat, ten syllable) lines, relatively unusual in a hymn, also serve to highlight that final rhyme. The poet wanted to begin not with the subject of the sentence but the topic of the whole poem, the saints; and he wanted to end with the emphatic praise of the holy name of Jesus.

The second stanza, in but three lines, weaves together a wealth of images from the psalms, the letters of Paul, and the gospels:

Thou wast their rock, their fortress, and their might:
Thou, Lord, their Captain in the well-fought fight;
Thou, in the darkness drear, the one true light.
Alleluia, alleluia!

"The Lord is my rock, and my fortress, and my deliverer," says the psalmist, "my God, my strength, in whom I trust" (Ps 18:1). "For it became [was worthy of] Him," says the writer to the Hebrews, "for whom are all things, and by whom are all things, in bringing many sons unto glory, to make the Captain of their salvation perfect through sufferings" (Heb 2:10), in the good fight. "I am the light of the world," says Jesus. "He that followeth me shall not walk in darkness, but shall have the light of life" (Jn 8:12).

Again, we may ask, given that the lines may be rearranged without damage to the grammar, why How has placed them in this order. The first line, echoing the many psalms that speak of the Lord as the rock, places the saints in the position of guards upon the battlements of a fortress. They are being protected. But in the second line, we have engaged the battle, under the leadership of Christ the Captain. In the third line, we are actually following Christ through the darkness. He is the one light shining upon the fearful darkness of the field. Thus do we move from the general state to the specific action, and from the shelter of the fortress to the danger of the fight. The emphatically repeated pronoun *Thou* focuses our devotion and attention upon Christ. Notice how the force would be dissipated if we "corrected" the "unnecessary" repetition, thus:

Thou wast their rock, their fortress, and their might,
Their Captain also in the well-fought fight,
And in the darkness drear, the one true light.
Alleluia, alleluia!

In the third stanza, we apply the example of the fighting saints to ourselves:

O may Thy soldiers, faithful, true, and bold,
Fight as the saints who nobly fought of old,
And win, with them, the victor's crown of gold.
Alleluia, alleluia!

We pray to be inspired by those saints, the brave men and women who sallied forth before us, so that we too may enjoy the victory. The crown is ours by virtue of the kingship of Christ: "And I looked, and behold a white cloud, and upon the cloud one sat like unto the Son of man, having on his head a golden crown" (Rv 14:14).

The poet repeats the vocative interjection *O* to link the fourth stanza with the third, for we and the saints of old, fighting the same fight, are soldiers in the same army:

O blest communion, fellowship divine!
We feebly struggle, they in glory shine;
Yet all are one in Thee, for all are Thine.
Alleluia, alleluia!

The second and third lines explain the first. We profess the communion of the saints, meaning that we understand that we and the saints are not divided by the abyss of death. We enjoy their fellowship even now. The pronouns show us how that can be. *We* struggle on, *they* shine in glory, but *all* of us are *one*. One, that is, in *Thee*, Lord, for *all*—the saints of the Church Triumphant and the soldiers in the Church Militant upon earth—*all are Thine*. The whole meaning is embraced by the personal: We are not one because of something God has planned but because we all belong to God Himself, who loves us. We are His.

The foolish editors of the hymnal *Glory and Praise* couldn't abide the old pronouns, nor, apparently, the ghost of something masculine suggested by the scriptural word "fellowship," so they butchered the stanza:

O blest communion, family divine!
We feebly struggle, they in glory shine;
Yet all are one within God's great design.

The word *family* was chosen because it's got three syllables—that's all. When we think of a divine family, we think of the Trinity, or of the Holy Family, Jesus, Mary, and Joseph. So the word simply confuses. The buildup of the pronouns, *we* and *they* united in *Thee*, here falls with a thud. There's nothing personal or heartwarming about a *design*. Builders and plotters have designs; God has designs; the devil has designs. That wasn't the point. At least these editors left the word *feebly* as it was. Other editors haven't been so kind. Believing that the adjective doesn't give us enough credit, they have amended the line to read:

We live and struggle, they in glory shine.

And that implies that to shine in glory is to be dead.

The fifth stanza—frequently omitted, as too martial—binds us and the saints together in the music we hear:

And when the strife is fierce, the warfare long,
Steals on the ear the distant triumph song,
And hearts are brave again, and arms are strong.
Alleluia, alleluia!

We can well imagine the scene. We are soldiers slogging through the mud, bearing upon our bucklers the brunt of the enemy's swords, yet carrying on, when all at once—do you hear that?

Yes, there it is! The clarion of victory, coming from the far city of God. And all at once we take heart, and our arms swing with the greater force. They no longer sag from our shoulders, but strike boldly. Is it not so? Again, the editors of *Glory and Praise* couldn't abide it, so they amended it thus:

And when the strife is fierce, the conflict long,
Then from the distance comes the triumph song,
And hearts are brave again, and courage strong.

Now there's a stanza to get you right—where? All's been rendered abstract, nerveless.

The final three stanzas take us from the calm evening of death to the morning of the eternal day, as Christ, the King of Glory, marches in triumph through the gates of the New Jerusalem, and all the saints join in his train, singing their hymn of praise:

The golden evening brightens in the west;
Soon, soon to faithful warriors cometh rest;
Sweet is the calm of paradise the blest.
Alleluia, alleluia!

But lo! there breaks a yet more glorious day;
The saints triumphant rise in bright array;
The King of glory passes on His way.
Alleluia, alleluia!

From earth's wide bounds, from ocean's farthest coast,
Through gates of pearl streams in the countless host,
Singing to Father, Son, and Holy Ghost,
Alleluia, alleluia!

The repetition of the adverb *soon* is deliberate, as if someone were to throw an arm around a weary soldier and say, "Friend, we're almost there! It won't be long now, it won't be long at all." What they look forward to is the restful sunset, the blessed end of life in this valley of tears, blessed not because we despise life but because we await the life of life, the consummation of our battles in victory. Then we may join our voices with those of the saints, singing to the Holy Trinity. What do they sing? Notice that for the final stanza the poet does not end the triplet with a period. They sing, "Alleluia, alleluia!"—"Praise the Lord, praise the Lord!" It is the Alleluia Chorus of eternity, so magnificently set to music by Handel: "And I heard as it were the voice of a great multitude, and as the voice of many waters, and as the voice of mighty thunderings, saying, Alleluia: for the Lord God omnipotent reigneth" (Rv 19:6).

Well did the old poets know, too, that the Christian warrior must fight his most dangerous battles within. St. Athanasius tells us of the terrible demonic attacks that St. Anthony the hermit endured in the desert. Christian asceticism—from the Greek *askesis*, the exercise drills of a soldier or a champion athlete in training—is intended to strengthen us by subduing the body, the will, and the imagination to the commands of the soul. Therefore one of the strategies of the Evil One is to scoff at that exercise, so that in the day of trial we will be soft and flabby and uncertain and timid. With that in mind, let's look at the poem *Christian, Dost Thou See Them?*, ascribed to St. Andrew of Crete (660–732), and translated into English trochaic meter—a meter that begins with a strong beat, well suited for marches—by John Mason Neale:

Christian, dost thou see them
On the holy ground,

How the powers of darkness
Rage thy steps around?
Christian, up and smite them,
Counting gain but loss,
In the strength that cometh
By the holy cross.

Notice the strong appeal made by the direct address: *Christian!* The first half of the stanza, in the form of a question, is a summons, a clarion—look! "Why do the heathen rage?" asks the psalmist (Ps 2:1), and here the heathen are *powers of darkness* themselves. They have dared to set their accursed feet upon *holy ground*: "And there was war in heaven: Michael and his angels fought against the dragon; and the dragon fought and his angels" (Rv 12:7). What are we to do when these filthy beings rise up about our steps, leering, mocking, snapping? The answer is given in the second half of the stanza. The poet repeats the direct address: *Christian!* Swing the sword! Have at them! Follow the example of St. Paul, whose brave words St. Andrew has echoed: "What things were gain to me, those I counted loss for Christ" (Phil 3:7). St. Paul gloried in his infirmities, deriving all his strength from the cross of Christ. "For we preach Christ crucified," said he (1 Cor 1:23).

Both melodies to which this poem is commonly set, *Sohren* and *St. Andrew of Crete*, are unusual, and highlight the division in the stanza between the trial and the call to victory. The first half of the melody is set in a minor key; the second half, in the corresponding major key. The first half is expressive, musically, of trouble; the second, of high-hearted confidence. This division is especially marked in *St. Andrew of Crete*, because for the first two lines of the stanza there is no melody at all—just a monotonous drumming upon one note, while the harmony lines below it provide the alteration that makes the monotony into music, a menacing kind of music indeed. So when the major key breaks in, like the dawn upon a dark night, the joy of a delightful melody breaks in with it, with a note that is almost—almost—too high to sing.

The second stanza shows that the battlefield is the soul itself:

Christian, dost thou feel them,
How they work within,
Striving, tempting, luring,
Goading into sin?
Christian, never tremble;
Never be downcast;
Gird thee for the battle,
Watch and pray and fast.

Those first four lines show that good poetry is true poetry: It helps us see what we already know, but in a new way, or it makes us aware of what we would know, if only someone were to bring it to our attention. Those participles, *striving, tempting, luring, goading,* are downright terrifying. The poet asks me if I've felt them, and I answer, yes, I feel them even now. They aren't always the same. Sometimes it's a wrestling match; sometimes a trial; sometimes a fruit of evil hanging low upon the tree, its fragrance luring the unwary fellow to nibble just a little, to taste; and then sometimes it's the whip and the spur, the horrible and hated compulsion. How do we respond? St. Andrew says, *Never be downcast.* We're to don the armor of God, but here it is the armor of the ascetic—to do as Jesus did when the devil tempted Him in the desert. We are to *watch and pray and fast.*

Ah, but then the devil attempts to turn our prayer too into a temptation. Here I imagine him as a benign churchman, up-to-date, willing to please, and secretly cutting the heart right out of the Christian soldier, not with direct hatred, but with gentle mockery, urbane laughter, and false compassion:

Christian, dost thou hear them,
How they speak thee fair?
"Always fast and vigil?
Always watch and prayer?"
Christian, answer boldly:
"While I breathe I pray!"
Peace shall follow battle,
Night shall end in day.

That's a deft bit of conversation. *Always, always*, repeated, as if to stress the dreariness of prayer. Why, it's interminable! You—note that the pronoun is suppressed, as is the object of the prayer, God—deserve better, you do. The devils thus *speak fair* to the Christian sentry. You're all right as you are. You should take a rest. Tsk, tsk, what you're doing isn't reasonable. A little break wouldn't hurt. You've earned it. Then the answer breaks in, with defiance. "Do you think that I pray too much?" says the Christian. "*While I breathe I pray!*" Never mind the times set aside for prayer, now and then. I will pray so long as I am breathing. And do not try to deceive me about times. The battle shall not last forever, for the day is coming.

The final stanza, as we have seen in other hymns, both fulfills and breaks the pattern of the stanzas before it. Again the Christian is addressed, but not by the poet:

"Well I know thy trouble,
O my servant true;
Thou art very weary,

I was weary too.
But that toil shall make thee
Someday all mine own,
And the end of sorrow
Shall be near my throne."

These are the words of Jesus. They *comfort*, in the old sense of the word: They make us firm, they give us fortitude. We know no troubles that Jesus did not know before us. He gives us honorable toil, to draw us the nearer to Him, that we may hear Him say, "Well done, thou good and faithful servant!" (Mt 25:21). The soldier, his robe washed white in the blood of the Lamb, will be one of those "which came out of great tribulation" and now stand "before the throne of God, and serve him day and night in his temple: and he that sitteth on the throne shall dwell among them" (Rv 7:14–15).

Chapter Eleven

Consolation

DESPISERS of the faith often claim that people believe because otherwise they could not endure a life full of suffering and ending in death. Faith is a crutch. That is on Tuesday. But on Monday they claim that the challenges of the Christian faith are too difficult for the ordinary man. The mountain is too steep, the air too thin, and the path too strenuous. On Wednesday, they will complain that the faith saps the strength of men who should be warlike and bold, shaming them for their natural aggressiveness and turning them meek instead. By Thursday morning they will have forgotten all about that, and will decry the Christian for being too much of a soldier. The only constant, besides inconstancy, is opposition.

But Christians should not be ashamed of the consolations of the faith. For the secularist hugs his consolations too, such as they are. He will clutch at the touchingly naïve hope that even though his own life is empty and dreary, the general lot of mankind is improving, because of better medicine, indoor plumbing, automobiles, and television. Those things don't really console, because they don't touch the heart. They don't address the question, "Where are you going? What will your life have meant, when you have returned to the dust, along with all those who could recall your name?"

There are only two mature ways to address suffering and death. One is to scorn them, with the brusque contempt of the Stoic or the cool aloofness of the Buddhist. It grants death the field, while claiming a moral victory in the courage of the defeated. That is not the Christian way. The Christian way is to enter into suffering and death with Christ. We see that He did not dismiss our suffering with contempt, but took it to Himself, embraced it, and fathomed the depths of desolation upon the Cross. "If we be dead with Christ," says St. Paul, "we believe that we shall also live with him: knowing that Christ being raised from the dead dieth no more; death hath no more dominion over him. For in that he died, he died unto sin once; but in that he liveth, he liveth unto God" (Rom 6:8–10). He has broken the bonds of sin and death—death, not just the cessation of physical powers, but alienation from God. The Christian then looks forward to liberation. It is not so much liberation *from* a world to be rejected, as the Buddhist rejects the wheel of desire; it is a liberation *into* a world to be desired.

So the best Christian hymns of consolation acknowledge both the trials of this world and the joys of the true world, for which this world, pronounced good by the Lord at creation, prepares us. Let us examine a few of these, beginning with Henry Lyte's beloved *Abide With Me* (1847):

Abide with me: fast falls the eventide;
The darkness deepens; Lord, with me abide:
When other helpers fail and comforts flee,
Help of the helpless, O abide with me.

We see here again the allusion to that Easter walk to Emmaus, now applied to the individual's state of life. The *eventide* is falling for *him*; the *darkness deepens* because he is growing old. Who will help him? Notice the insistent changes rung upon the word *help*, used as a noun. What can help us? The brash potentates of this world who seem to prosper dwell in fortresses of sand: "How are they brought into desolation, as in a moment! They are utterly consumed with terrors" (Ps 73:19). Nothing will help us, not riches, not battle-horses, not princes; all these flee. Only the Lord will *abide* with those who abide in Him: "If ye keep my commandments, ye shall abide in my love; even as I have kept my Father's commandments, and abide in his love" (Jn 15:10). The poet longs for more than external assistance to meet his difficulties. He longs for Christ the friend, who will not leave him alone in the wayside inn, awaiting death.

The next stanza applies our experience of age to the state of the whole physical world:

Swift to its close ebbs out life's little day,
Earth's joys grow dim, its glories pass away,
Change and decay in all around I see;
O Thou who changest not, abide with me.

Lyte is thinking of the anguish of the afflicted Job: "[Man] cometh forth like a flower, and is cut down: he fleeth also as a shadow, and continueth not" (Jb 14:2). Also of the sad resignation of the Preacher: "All go unto one place; all are of the dust, and all turn to dust again" (Eccl 3:20). But "I am the Lord," says God, "I change not" (Mal 3:6). We may understand this declaration in two ways. The first is simple enough: All created things owe their existence to God, not to themselves. They need not have been at all. Therefore they are subject to change or decay.

Bodies do not endure forever. The sun will grow dark; the earth will grow cold. Beings endowed with intellect can turn away from the fount of their knowledge; they can turn toward non-being, toward evil. But there is no such change in God. That first understanding implies the second: God does not change *toward us*. "O give thanks unto the Lord," cries the psalmist, "for he is good: because his mercy endureth for ever" (Ps 118:1). Amid the storms of change, we beg the Lord to abide with us, because He alone is constant.

In the third stanza we turn to that possibility of moral decay, not as an abstraction to analyze, but as an urgent threat we all experience, especially in times of frailty:

I need Thy presence every passing hour;
What but Thy grace can foil the tempter's power?
Who, like Thyself, my guide and stay can be?
Through cloud and sunshine, Lord, abide with me.

I need Thee every hour, sings another lovely hymn: Every hour. Not now and then but always, because every pulse of our hearts is like the beat of a drum as we march closer to the end and to eternity. At every hour the tempter assails us, sometimes flaring up with hatred impossible to miss, sometimes speaking to us sweetly with sickly enticements, sometimes lulling us into sloth and apathy. On our own we always fail. Nothing but the grace of God can frustrate the tempter. Nothing and no one can be our *guide and stay*—our *guide*, who leads us along the path of right, and our *stay*, our support, our prop, who gives us the strength to stand our ground. In good times and bad, *through cloud and sunshine*, we need the Lord.

All these passing days, sunny or dark, lead us on to the end:

I fear no foe, with Thee at hand to bless;
Ills have no weight, and tears no bitterness.
Where is death's sting? Where, grave, thy victory?
I triumph still, if Thou abide with me.

"The Lord is my light and my salvation; whom shall I fear?" (Ps 27:1). With the Lord near to bless us, afflictions do not press us down; they have *no weight*. The renowned biologist Francis Collins, working in a cancer ward, was astonished by that weightlessness among his Christian patients who were dying, yet whose spirits were not crushed. Even their tears had *no bitterness*, and this brought Collins to Christ. The poet Lyte understands: So long as the Lord is with us, who or what can really be against us? We can cry out boldly with St. Paul: "O death, where is thy sting? O grave, where is thy victory?" The sting of death is in sin, says Paul, but Christ has conquered sin, and we are forgiven: "Thanks be to God, which giveth us the victory through our Lord Jesus Christ" (1 Cor 15:55–57). The key word in this stanza—easy to miss, because we aren't in the habit of thinking as poets think—is the little adverb *still*. What has happened to all the change and decay, the fleeing, the vain shadows, and the swift fall of the evening? All that change is defeated by the constancy of God, and the poet can claim, "I triumph *still*"—that is, "I triumph even so, in spite of all that"—and "I triumph *still*"—that is, "I triumph again and again, I triumph always," because God is with me.

Even the moment of death is a triumph:

Hold Thou Thy cross before my closing eyes;
Shine through the gloom, and point me to the skies;
Heaven's morning breaks, and earth's vain shadows flee:
In life, in death, O Lord, abide with me.

The novelist Sigrid Undset, in *Kristin Lavransdatter*, gives us a most moving portrayal of a Christian death. The patriarch of the family, Lavrans, is dying. He is, or was, a man of immense physical strength and stamina. He was also a man of generous heart and incorruptible integrity. His body is racked with spasms; his breath rattles in his chest. He has bid farewell to all his friends, and now his family gathers round him, with his friend the priest Eirik praying at his side. When the moment of death comes, Lavrans is wide-eyed and conscious, and Eirik holds a cross before the eyes of his friend: That, the cross, is his last sight in this world, and Lavrans prays with the priest, "Into your hands, O Lord, I commend my spirit," the words of Christ upon the Cross. The Cross is our comfort. Whatever stupidities the devil may hurl at us—stupidities of wealth, lust, doubt, terror—we may turn to that Cross and say, "I don't care, I want to be with Him, He is my guide, because if I know nothing else in this world, I know that He is good, and life without Him might as well be death!" He is with us as we die, because He died: He drank that cup to the dregs.

So the everlasting Easter breaks through the *gloom*—the word here is used in its old sense of twilight (cf. *gloaming*). The dim light of the earth is swallowed up in the brightness of heaven.

Is death something to fear? Jesus wept when He stood before the tomb of Lazarus. The psalmist cries in his trouble, "Let not the pit shut her mouth upon me!" (Ps 69:15). We know that Christ has conquered death, the ultimate enemy to be destroyed, and that is one reason why the old painters placed a skull at the base of the Cross. Yet we still experience this severance of the body from the soul as violent or wrong; we sense, with our openness to the infinite, that we are not made for annihilation. And though we trust in the salvation that Christ brings, we do not cease to be human on that account. Far from it. We should not fear death. But we should not fear the fear of death, either. Never in all of Scripture is someone condemned for that fear.

The poets understood that Jesus, entering our human condition, took all our sins and our frailties upon His shoulders. When they write about the approach of death, then, it is with a mingled sympathy for the dying, and confidence. That combination makes for poems that are utterly unlike pagan treatments of death, with their scornful defiance, or their quiet despair. Let us take a look at one of the best of these Christian hymns on dying. It is by the great Isaac Watts, *There Is a Land of Pure Delight* (1709), sung to the traditional English melody *Mendip* or, better still, the lilting *Capel*, the latter arranged by Ralph Vaughan Williams (1906):

There is a land of pure delight,
Where Saints immortal reign;
Infinite day excludes the night,
And pleasures banish pain.

There everlasting spring abides,
And never-withering flowers;
Death, like a narrow sea, divides
This heavenly land from ours.

The adverb *there*, beginning the second stanza and echoing the first, is crucial. *There* is not *here*. Here, delight is not pure. Here, despots and charlatans reign. Here, the night falls. Here, every pleasure is shot through with pain; the spring passes, and the flowers wither. But *there*, the day *excludes the night*, and Watts is playing upon the literal meaning of the word. To be excluded is to be shut out, to have the door closed against you; it's as if night were barred from entry at the gates of heaven. That image is confirmed in the next line. Pleasures *banish pain*: They order them to get out of town, to leave the land forever.

Watts then turns to images from nature. Heaven is a land of *everlasting spring* and *never-withering flowers*: "The grass withereth, the flower fadeth," says the prophet, "but the word of our God shall stand for ever" (Is 40:8). St. Peter, thinking of that same verse from Isaiah, says that our merciful God has "begotten us again unto a lively hope by the resurrection of Jesus Christ from the dead, to an inheritance incorruptible, and undefiled, and that fadeth not away, reserved in heaven for you" (1 Pt 1:3–4). For "all flesh is grass, and all the glory of man as the flower of grass" (1 Pt 1:24), but we have been "born again, not of corruptible seed, but of incorruptible, by the word of God, which liveth and abideth for ever" (1 Pt 1:23). In other words, what divides one land from the other is this new birth in Christ—and death.

That's why Watts portrays death not as a vast ocean but as a *narrow sea*, like the waters of birth—so narrow that we might be able to see, in the distance, the shores we approach:

Sweet fields beyond the swelling flood
Stand dressed in living green;
So to the Jews old Canaan stood,
While Jordan rolled between.

Some modern hymnals emend Watts' *sweet* to read *bright*, and that's not bad, as it broaches the motif of what we can or cannot see from our side. But *sweet*, the more unusual adjective in this context, is better. It suggests the promise of Canaan. "I am come down to deliver them out of the hand of the Egyptians," says the

Lord to Moses, "and to bring them up unto a good land and a large, unto a land flowing with milk and honey" (Ex 3:8). The Jews knew the bitterness of bondage in Egypt and the privations of their sojourn through the desert, and sometimes they grumbled against God and wanted to return to Egypt, where at least their bellies were full. But when the time came, they stood at that river and beheld the Promised Land.

The word *sweet* alliterates with *swelling*, and that is not coincidental. Watts echoes a phrase from Jeremiah, "the swelling of Jordan" (Jer 12:5), referring to when the river runs high at harvest time. That was when Joshua was to lead the Israelites across, into Canaan, "for Jordan overfloweth all his banks all the time of harvest" (Jb 3:15), but the Lord wrought a miracle as when Moses and the Israelites crossed the Red Sea. In other words, they were not overwhelmed by those swelling waters. They crossed them in safety; they reached those *sweet fields* under the banners of Joshua, whose name we know in the New Testament as Jesus. Joshua led the Jews to *old Canaan*, but Jesus leads His followers to a new Canaan, the true Promised Land.

What then delays us? We are frail:

But timorous mortals start and shrink
To cross this narrow sea,
And linger shivering on the brink,
And fear to launch away.

Watts puts us right on the shore. We feel the cold wind blowing from off the water. We feel it piercing to our bones. We *shrink*, we *shiver*. Where we stand is aptly called the *brink*: The border between two completely different realms of being. We hesitate to step forth onto the boat that will take us across the water.

In the last two stanzas, Watts addresses us directly—not *they* but *we*—and appeals to our love and to the faith that sees:

O could we make our doubts remove,
Those gloomy doubts that rise,
And see the Canaan that we love
With unbeclouded eyes!

Could we but climb where Moses stood,
And view the landscape o'er,
Not Jordan's stream, nor death's cold flood,
Could fright us from the shore!

To *doubt* is, literally, to waver, to teeter this way and that. Here the doubts are like a mist rising from the waters to cloud our vision. Let faith then whisk that mist away, and let our eyes, *unbeclouded*, see what we long for. Let us *climb*—the verb implies determination and energy—*where Moses stood.* Watts alludes to Moses' vision upon the summit of Mount Pisgah. The Lord allowed him to see the Promised Land but not to enter it (Dt 34:1–4). If we could climb our own Mount Pisgah, nothing should frighten us then, not the narrow Jordan River, or even the cold waters of death.

Death brings us closer to our Savior. Death brings us closer to our Judge. Well it is for us that our Judge is our Savior. "For we have not an high priest which cannot be touched with the feeling of our infirmities; but was in all points tempted like as we are, yet without sin," says the writer to the Hebrews. "Let us therefore come boldly unto the throne of grace, that we may obtain mercy, and find grace in time of need" (Heb 4:15). Let's now look at two hymns of approach to that throne.

The first is the thirteenth-century Latin hymn by Thomas of Celano, the famous *Dies Irae*, translated by William J. Irons (1849): *Day of Wrath*. You won't find it in any modern hymnal. I'm tempted to say that it is too deeply founded in Scripture for that: The Scripture that warns us that the path to salvation lies through the valley of repentance, and that God's mercy is not our indifference or weak resolve or sentimentality. God does not pretend that we are good. He *makes* us good, and that will require refining. "Who may abide the day of his coming?" asks Malachi, referring to the Messiah. "And who shall stand when he appeareth? For he is like a refiner's fire, and like fullers' soap" (Mal 3:2). The heat of the flame and the caustic bite of the lye are the passageway between the wickedness of the world and the pure joys of heaven. Therefore the wrath of God is most just and most merciful at once. "The sun shall be turned into darkness, and the moon into blood, before the great and terrible day of the Lord come" (Jl 2:31), says the prophet Joel, and the Baptist echoes these warnings when he tells that the Messiah is near: "He shall baptize you with the Holy Ghost, and with fire: whose fan is in his hand, and he will thoroughly purge his floor, and gather his wheat into the garner; but he will burn up the chaff with unquenchable fire" (Mt 3:11–12).

The *Dies Irae* takes up these warnings and applies them to the individual Christian approaching the Day of Judgment. The meter of the poem is perfect for the theme—a thundering trochaic tetrameter—four strong beats per line, always beginning with a stress. The stanzas are rhyming *triplets*, allowing the poet opportunity to use the third line for a surprising turn on the first two, or a powerful summation. It is not a meter for an easy walk in the park.

The poem is sung to a plainsong sequence also known as *Dies Irae*, and this too requires some explanation. Old Catholic and Anglican hymnals used to be filled with *sequences*, long melodies that carried the singers through long texts. These melodies usually included some internal repetition; a portion of the melody might be repeated before the singers would move to the next section of the melody. The *Dies Irae* melody as printed in the Episcopalian *1940 Hymnal* (a more difficult and haunting version appears in the 1933 *English Hymnal*) is really five separate melodies, echoing one another. The first two verses of the poem are sung to the first melody. The next two, verses three and four, are sung to the second melody. The two following, verses five and six, are sung to the third melody. Then the singers return to the first melody for verses seven and eight, and so on, until verse eighteen, which is cast in a new melody entirely, and the final verse, nineteen, which echoes the end of the first (and principal) melody quite strongly, but is not identical with it. When a good choir sings this poem with different voices taking up different melodies—say, the men alone, women and boys alone, and all together—the effect is unforgettable.

The poem begins with a trumpet blast:

Day of wrath! O day of mourning!
See fulfilled the prophet's warning,
Heaven and earth in ashes burning!

O what fear man's bosom rendeth
When from heaven the Judge descendeth,
On whose sentence all dependeth!

Our sweet Lord would never speak like that, would He? But He does: "And then shall appear the sign of the Son of man in heaven: and then shall all the tribes of the earth mourn, and they shall see the Son of man coming in the clouds of heaven with power and great glory" (Mt 24:30). Notice the tension that the insistent rhythms build, and the power of the final lines. Why are the nations mourning? What did the prophet warn of? *Heaven and earth in ashes burning*. Why should fear rend our hearts when we see the just Judge descending? Because on His sentence everything depends.

The next two stanzas combine the admonitory words of Jesus with the prophecy in Revelation:

Wondrous sound the trumpet flingeth;
Through earth's sepulchers it ringeth;
All before the throne it bringeth.

Death is struck, and nature quaking,
All creation is awaking,
To its Judge an answer making.

"And he shall send his angels with a great sound of a trumpet," says Jesus, "and they shall gather together his elect from the four winds" (Mt 24:31). "And I saw a great white throne," says John, "and him that sat on it, from whose face the earth and the heaven fled away; and there was found no place for them. And I saw the dead, small and great, stand before God" (Rv 20:11–12). It is the resurrection of the dead, to judgment. *Death is struck*, says the poet—in the Latin original, *mors stupebit*, "death will be stupefied," death will gape in amazement. We see the war between life and death brought to its crisis: Life triumphs, and a living death will swallow those who gave themselves to the works of death. The Latin rhymes in the fourth stanza are terrifying in their implication: *natura, creatura*, "nature, creature," but then *responsura*, "will have to respond," *will answer* the Judge.

But they will not be able to lie. "*There* is no shuffling," says the tormented king in *Hamlet*, bitten with remorse for the murder of his brother. There, at the judgment, we ourselves will be

. . . . compelled,
Even to the teeth and forehead of our faults,
To give in evidence.

For the book will be opened, "which is the book of life: and the dead were judged out of those things which were written in the books, according to their works" (Rv 20:12). No denials then:

Lo! the book, exactly worded,
Wherein all hath been recorded:
Thence shall judgment be awarded.

When the Judge his seat attaineth
And each hidden deed arraigneth,
Nothing unavenged remaineth.

"To me belongeth vengeance, and recompense," says God to Moses (Dt 32:35), and when the Son of Man returns, says Jesus, "there is nothing covered, that shall not be revealed; and hid, that shall not be known" (Mt 10:26). We can hide our deeds from one another. We can hide them from ourselves—we're good at that. We can hide nothing from God. All will be made manifest; all is written down exactly.

What are we to do? The hymn returns to the first melody, and with this turn the poem becomes acutely personal:

What shall I, frail man, be pleading?
Who for me be interceding,
When the just are mercy needing?

King of majesty tremendous,
Who dost free salvation send us,
Fount of pity, then befriend us!

Perhaps Michelangelo had these verses in mind when he painted his *Last Judgment* upon the sanctuary wall in the Sistine Chapel. There, Christ the Judge raises His right arm as if to draw all mankind out of their graves; yet the gesture appears threatening too, and the saints who approach Him, carrying evidence of their devotion or their martyrdom, do so in an attitude of fear. If St. Peter himself pleads for mercy, what about me? How can I plead? I am *miser*, in the Latin, a poor pitiable wretch. I beg then that the King Himself will save me; that salvation is *free*, in Latin *gratis*, unearned, a pure gift of God's grace. Jesus' generosity is like a spring welling up with life, a *fount of pity*, giving, not according to our merits, but according to His mercy.

Why should Jesus have mercy upon us? The poet turns not to what we have suffered for Jesus, but to what Jesus has already suffered for us:

Think, good Jesus, my salvation
Cost Thy wondrous incarnation;
Leave me not to reprobation!

Faint and weary, Thou hast sought me,
On the cross of suffering bought me.
Shall such grace be vainly brought me?

Jesus took to Himself all the weaknesses of the flesh. He sought out the lost sheep and traversed a hard and weary path to do it, for "foxes have holes, and birds of the air have nests; but the Son of man hath not where to lay his head" (Lk 9:58). He has *bought* the sinner back—that is the meaning of the Latin *redemisti*, "redeemed"—by His suffering upon the cross. Should all that *labor*—the word in the Latin, here rendered as *grace* that is brought at great trouble—be in vain?

Let it not be so! The poet begs for forgiveness, in the ashes and sackcloth of a repentant soul:

Righteous Judge! for sin's pollution
Grant Thy gift of absolution,
Ere the day of retribution.

Guilty, now I pour my moaning,
All my shame with anguish owning;
Spare, O God, Thy suppliant groaning!

It seems to be a rule of spiritual growth. Saints are keenly aware of their sins; but sinners have a pretty good opinion of themselves. If we consider mere human righteousness, which is no better than a filthy rag to cover our shame, most of us are all right; as a person hobbling on a crutch is better off than someone who has to crawl. But God is a *righteous Judge*. That is a different matter altogether.

So the poet recalls others whom Jesus forgave:

Thou the sinful woman savedst;
Thou the dying thief forgavest;
And to me a hope vouchsafest.

Worthless are my prayers and sighing;
Yet, good Lord, in grace complying,
Rescue me from fires undying!

"Go, and sin no more," said Jesus to the woman caught in adultery (Jn 8:11). "Today shalt thou be with me in paradise," He said to the repentant thief (Lk 23:43). Then I too may beg for forgiveness, not on my own account, because my very sighs are worthless, but on account of the grace of God:

With Thy favored sheep O place me,
Not among the goats abase me,
But to Thy right hand upraise me.

While the wicked are confounded,
Doomed to flames of woe unbounded,
Call me with Thy saints surrounded.

"And he shall set the sheep on his right hand, but the goats on the left" (Mt 25:33). The goats, those condemned, will depart "into everlasting fire, prepared for the devil and his angels" (Mt 25:41). It's interesting here that the poet does *not* claim any merit for being set with the sheep. He does not say, "I fed you when you were hungry, I clothed you when you were naked!" All he has, at this moment, is sorrow. "I abhor myself, and repent in dust and ashes," says Job, confronted with the majesty of God (Jb 42:6). That is the sacrifice that pleases God best: "A broken and contrite heart, O God, thou wilt not despise" (Ps 51:17). It is all the poet has:

Low I kneel, with heart submission;
See, like ashes, my contrition;
Help me in my last condition.

Now come the last two stanzas, in different meters, to bring us back to the beginning of the poem but also to sum it up in the plea for mercy, for all mankind:

Ah! that day of tears and mourning!
From the dust of earth returning,
Man for judgment must prepare him;
Spare, O God, in mercy spare him!

Lord, all-pitying, Jesus blest,
Grant them Thine eternal rest. Amen.

But there is more than forgiveness when, in faith, we meet our Maker. There is comfort for the way, because every moment in our lives is a providentially given by God, to draw us nearer to Him. When the Titanic was sinking, and all the lifeboats had been filled and set forth, the brave men of the band remained on board and played music to comfort the people who would soon die. We are told that they played the beautiful hymn *Nearer, My God, to Thee*, whose first verse sums up what a Christian may see in the suffering that comes his way:

Nearer, my God, to Thee,
Nearer to Thee!
E'en though it be a cross
That raiseth me:
Still all my song would be,
"Nearer, my God, to Thee,
Nearer to Thee!"

Most hymnals set Sarah Adams' poem (1841) to the melody *Bethany*, which doubles the second last line, so that in the first verse alone we sing out the adverb *nearer* five times, always in emphatic position. The melody *Horbury*, by the hymnodist J. B. Dykes, is to my ear even lovelier, setting off the phrase *nearer to Thee* with a quiet modulation in a simple three-note span, rather like chant.

This trust in God, even as death approaches, expressed so boldly by Mrs. Adams, assumes a mysterious calm in *I Know Not What the Future Hath*, by the American poet John Greenleaf Whittier (1867):

I know not what the future hath
Of marvel or surprise,
Assured alone that life and death
God's mercy underlies.

And if my heart and flesh are weak
To bear an untried pain,
The bruised reed He will not break,
But strengthen and sustain.

God's mercy *underlies* both life and death, as a quiet underground stream nourishes the land above. The future may bring us wonders; but it may bring us *surprise*, a word that had not yet acquired its current color of festivity. A man walking alone at night is *surprised* or, literally, snatched from below, by thieves; or a platoon is *surprised* by an ambush. We are assured only of the mercy of God. And if our hearts are weak? Whittier turns to Scripture, and these words applied to the quiet and gentle, even surreptitious, coming of the Messiah: "A bruised reed shall he not break, and smoking flax shall he not quench, till he send forth judgment unto victory" (Mt 12:20, citing Is 42:3). But here the poet—or the singer of the hymn—is the *bruised reed*. We are reeds in our weakness, and bruised at that. It is hard to imagine anything feebler than a reed shaking in the wind (cf. Mt 11:7). But the gentle mercy of God will not break that bruised reed; rather, will give it strength and will *sustain* it, shoring it up from below.

The bruised reed can't brace up the wall of a house. Its lightness, its insubstantiality suggests the lightness of the human soul, which has nothing to give God but God's own gifts, and no love for God but God's first gift of love:

No offering of my own I have,
Nor works my faith to prove;
I can but give the gifts He gave,
And plead His love for love.

If that sounds self-abasing to our ears, it is because we haven't been listening too closely to the saints. The nearer we draw to God, the more acutely do we feel that He is all, and we are dust; and we glory that He is all, and that we are dust He has chosen to form in His image, to love, and to exalt. Even our love for God is not of our own making, but is an answer to God's grace. So if we wish to *plead* our case before God—the verb, along with *prove*, suggests a scene at a court of law—we had better make evident His love for us, and let that stand for our love. "We love him," says St. John, "because he first loved us" (1 Jn 4:19).

The final two stanzas of the poem place us at the seashore, awaiting the boat that will take us to a land we cannot see:

And so beside the silent sea
I wait the muffled oar;
No harm from Him can come to me
On ocean or on shore.

I know not where His islands lift
Their fronded palms in air;
I only know I cannot drift
Beyond His love and care.

An inattentive reader might accuse Whittier of sentimentality. It isn't so. He has chosen all his words precisely. The sea is *silent*—why? The silence is soothing but also strange: The sea will not divulge its secrets. The oar is *muffled*—why? The boat approaches quietly but also inexorably: We will look up from the sands one day, and it will be there, waiting for us to enter. The words *harm* and *Him*, alliterating, nearly rhyming, are set next to one another to underscore their contradiction: No *harm* can come from *Him*, not on the shores of this life where he stands waiting, and not on the vast ocean to come.

The boat will take him to a paradise, sweetly imagined as islands of God in the south sea, raising their green palm trees to the skies. Our own south seas were dangerous sailing even in the days of Whittier, but there is no need to worry. The poet doesn't know where he is going, but he does know that he cannot possibly *drift*—think of a ship that has lost its sails and its masts—beyond the love and the *care*—the word denotes not sentiment but action; to *care* is to take pains for someone, especially someone in need of a *cure*, as a doctor cares for a patient or a priest cares for a soul—of God.

How, finally, do we commemorate the death of a loved one? What shall we sing at a funeral?

I'm fond of noting the final corporal work of mercy, to bury the dead. It shows the high regard Christians have for the body, which isn't a husk to be shucked away, but the flesh our Savior took on and sanctified, and which will be raised again.

Contemporary songwriters don't often think of funerals and burials. In Catholic churches, the most popular hymn for funerals is the effeminate *On Eagle's Wings*, which transforms the soldierly strength of those who trust in the Lord into the insubstantiality of a puffball borne upon the "breath of dawn," whatever that means. That at least is an attempt at sacred music. But some people request secular songs to commemorate their loved one's passing to judgment before God: *Danny Boy*, for instance, or Frank Sinatra's obnoxious *My Way*.

A good rule to follow: If Satan could sing it, it doesn't belong in church.

But Christian poets have never been cowed by the prospect of death. Let's look at one hymn for the departed, one that combines tenderness with a confident trust in the mercy of the Father. It's John Ellerton's *Now the Laborer's Task is O'er* (1870), set to the extraordinarily peaceful melody *Requiescat*:

Now the laborer's task is o'er;
Now the battle day is past;
Now upon the farther shore
Lands the voyager at last.
Father, in Thy gracious keeping
Leave we now Thy servant sleeping.

The last two lines are the refrain for each of the stanzas, with the word "sleeping," sung at the tonic note, middle C, taking up a full six beats—music and meaning thus in harmony. The *now* of the sorrowful moment in the church or at the graveyard is also the *now* of an event we cannot see—the arrival of the voyager, the wayfaring Christian, upon the farther shore.

Here we weep, but not there:

There the tears of earth are dried;
There its hidden things are clear;
There the work of life is tried
By a juster judge than here.

There the penitents, that turn
To the cross their dying eyes,
All the love of Jesus learn
At His feet in paradise.

The repetition of the adverb links one clause to the next and builds them up to the lovely climax. *There*, in the new Jerusalem, every tear shall be wiped away, and that in turn gives us eyes to see, as there is nothing hidden that shall not be brought to light. The meaning of our works in life is hidden to us, but that too will be made clear, and by a just judge.

Christ cannot be swayed by false witness or bribes. But even those whose good works have been despised by the world confide not in their works, but in the judge's mercy. So Ellerton places the departed, and by implication the faithful mourners too, in the position of the penitent thief dying on the cross beside Jesus. With our last words, with the last longing gaze of our dying eyes, we turn to the cross and pray the words of the thief, and hear that reply of ineffable solace: "This day you shall be with me in paradise."

That means that *there*, we find no shadow but only light. There is no wolf in the fold, no prowling lion:

There no more the powers of hell
Can prevail to mar their peace;
Christ the Lord shall guard them well,
He who died for their release.

What a concentration of scriptural verses did the old poets give us! Scripture was their meat and drink, the air they breathed, the sky above their heads and the ground beneath their feet. The gates of Hell shall not prevail against the church of Christ, whereof the faithful soul is a triumphant member. Who is the guardian against hell's predators? Christ Himself, no hireling, but the Good Shepherd who lays down His life for the sheep. He died that they might live, and live abundantly; not that they would survive another winter, but that they would triumph with Him over the final enemy, death. Death shall have no dominion. For Christ died to release the faithful from death's bonds. He took captivity captive.

Not with dull despair or resignation do we sprinkle earth upon the coffin as it is lowered into the grave, but with the virtue that no pagan can ever know—hope:

"Earth to earth, and dust to dust,"
Calmly now the words we say;
Left behind, we wait in trust
For the resurrection day.

"I look forward to the resurrection of the body," declares the final sentence of the Nicene Creed, "and the life of the world to come." Dust returns to dust, but what is sown in corruption arises in incorruption, and the corn of wheat that enters the earth in mortality bears the fruit of immortality. The hymn is oriented not toward what was, but toward what will be. We wait. To the faithful heart, every pulse brings us closer to our ultimate gain. Yes, death is a fearful thing, and we need not be ashamed of the fear. But we are not alone. There, at our side, is Jesus.

Chapter Twelve

The Glory of God

I was glad when they said unto me, Let us go into the house of the Lord. (Ps 122:1)

And I beheld, and I heard the voice of many angels round about the throne and the beasts and the elders . . . saying with a loud voice, Worthy is the Lamb that was slain to receive power, and riches, and wisdom, and strength, and honor, and glory, and blessing. And every creature which is in heaven, and on earth, and under the earth, and such as are in the sea, and all that are in them, heard I saying, Blessing, and honor, and glory, and power, be unto him that sitteth upon the throne, and unto the Lamb for ever and ever. (Rv 5:11–13)

WHY should we praise or thank God, since God needs nothing from us? But need is not the point. Love is. God made the world from nothing, needing nothing from the world, and our response to this grace is grateful praise—the response of a loving heart to the God who loves. We are most like God the Creator when we praise and thank Him, because then we enter most closely into the freedom of giving, and "the glorious liberty of the children of God" (Rom 8:21). That is the way to understand heaven. It is not the place where God grants our desires, whatever those may happen to be. It is the place where our desire for God is granted, a desire inherent in our beings as creatures capable of intellect and love. It is a place of reveling in the glory of God.

In this chapter, then, I shall look at hymns that direct our gaze, in gratitude and awe, to the glory of God. Many old hymnals begin with a large selection of these, understanding that praise is our highest form of approach to the Almighty. We depend on God, we ask His assistance, and we beg that He will forgive our sins; and yet most fundamental of all is the prayer of thanks and praise, Hallowed be Thy name.

Why should we praise God? Here is one reason: Because in His unsurpassable wisdom He made the heavens and the earth. That is the message of Walter Chalmers Smith's glorious hymn, *Immortal, Invisible, God Only Wise* (1867):

Immortal, invisible, God only wise,
In light inaccessible hid from our eyes,
Most blessed, most glorious, the Ancient of Days,
Almighty, victorious, Thy great Name we praise.

The dactylic meter of the poem thunders along, strong beats followed by two short beats: *im-MOR-tal, in-VIS-i-ble, GOD on-ly WISE, in LIGHT in-ac-CESS-i-ble HID from our EYES.* It is quite well done; the adjectives *immortal, invisible*, and *inaccessible* echo one another in form and sound and suggest a connection in meaning too, as the poet will go on to show, for there are good reasons why God is *invisible* to us. The lines also unite many motifs from Scripture. The opening echoes St. Paul: "Now unto the King eternal, immortal, invisible, the only wise God, be honor and glory for ever and ever" (1 Tm 1:17). Later in the same letter to Timothy, Paul applies that praise to Christ, in words that Smith echoes in his second line: "[He] only hath immortality, dwelling in the light which no man can approach unto" (1 Tm 6:16), rendered in some translations and in Milton's *Paradise Lost* as "inaccessible light." The unity between immortality and dwelling in unapproachable light is suggested again in the third line, where God is given the title *Ancient of Days*, alluding to Daniel's apocalyptic vision of the triumph of God over the empires of the world:

> *I saw in the night visions, and, behold, one like the Son of man came with the clouds of heaven, and came to the Ancient of days, and they brought him near before him. And there was given him dominion, and glory, and a kingdom, that all people, nations, and languages, should serve him; his dominion is an everlasting dominion, which shall not pass away, and his kingdom that which shall not be destroyed.* (Dn 7:13–14)

That is the prophecy Jesus applied to Himself at His trial before the Sanhedrin: "Hereafter shall ye see the Son of man, sitting on the right hand of power, and coming in the clouds of heaven" (Mt 26:64).

In the second stanza Smith sharpens our understanding of what it means for God to be *invisible*. It is not just that God is a spiritual being. It is that God's wisdom is *beyond* our understanding in its greatness, and *beneath* our understanding in its intimacy. We cannot see such greatness; nor can we see such smallness:

> *Unresting, unhasting, and silent as light,*
> *Nor wanting, nor wasting, Thou rulest in might;*

Thy justice like mountains high soaring above
Thy clouds, which are fountains of goodness and love.

Let's pause to appreciate the brush strokes of the artist. Notice how the first two lines of this stanza echo one another *and* the first two lines of the opening stanza: The immortality and invisibility of God are related to His being both *unresting*—He is always in act—and *unhasting*—He is always at rest, never hurried. He is a God of exuberant abundance—He is not *wanting*—yet all things work together in His providence—He is not *wasting*. The paradoxes are brilliantly expressed in the rhymes: God is as *silent as light*; and yet He rules *in might*. In the opening stanza, the light was too bright for man to approach; now the light is *silent*, gentle, and invisible because we do not notice its work. That quiet light manifests the power of God in a way the world finds at once too great and too small to perceive.

So too are His justice and His goodness. The ways of the Lord are beyond our comprehension, yet they work intimately to bring about His merciful will. Smith has adapted the language and the meaning of these verses from Isaiah:

> *For my thoughts are not your thoughts, neither are your ways my ways, saith the Lord.*
>
> *For as the heavens are higher than the earth, so are my ways higher than your ways, and my thoughts than your thoughts.*
>
> *For as the rain cometh down, and the snow from heaven, and returneth not thither, but watereth the earth, and maketh it bring forth and bud, that it may give seed to the sower, and bread to the eater:*

> *So shall my word be that goeth forth out of my mouth: it shall return unto me void, but it shall accomplish that which I please.* (Is 55:8–11)

Smith's verse suggests that we cannot see the justice of God because it is hidden from our sight by His quietly working *goodness and love*, the gentle clouds that shed their fruitful rain upon us. It is a magnificent and theologically suggestive analogy.

In the third stanza, Smith turns from the immortal God to mortal man:

> *To all life Thou givest, to both great and small;*
> *In all life Thou livest, the true life of all;*
> *We blossom and flourish, like leaves on the tree,*
> *Then wither and perish; but naught changeth Thee.*

God *gives* life to all things, the great and small; that is a measure of His might. But He also *is the life* of all things, the silent light of life working upon them from within; that is a measure of His might, too, His might as His mercy. Everything that a creature has and is comes from God and through God. What are we, in our own right? The last two lines tell us. Notice the very fine internal rhyme, *flourish* and *perish*. The two are meant to be considered together. To *flourish* is, literally, to put forth a flower; but flowers fade all too soon. The lines allude to Isaiah again, another Messianic prophecy:

> *The voice said, Cry. And he said, What shall I cry? All flesh is grass, and all the goodliness thereof is as the flower of the field:*
>
> *The grass withereth, the flower fadeth: because the spirit of the Lord bloweth upon it; surely the people is grass.*

The grass withereth, the flower fadeth; but the word of our God shall stand for ever. (Is 40:6–8).

By ourselves we are grass that withers, the flower that perishes. But they who believe in Christ, says St. Peter, citing the same verses, will endure, "being born again, not of corruptible seed, but of incorruptible, by the word of God, which liveth and abideth for ever" (1 Pt 1:23).

The life we long for is one of praise, in the light of God's countenance:

Great Father of glory, pure Father of light,
Thine angels adore Thee, all veiling their sight;
All laud we would render: O help us to see
'Tis only the splendor of light hideth Thee.

All the motifs of "seeing" now unite. Why is God invisible to us? For the same reason why the angels themselves must veil their eyes in His presence. It is the *light*: that which works silently, but also blazes forth in glory. We want to praise God rightly, so we ask Him to help us *see*. What shall we see? The word now means to *understand*; to grasp with the mind and heart and soul. We *see* that it is only the *splendor of light* that hides God from us: God is hidden, because His glory is infinitely and immortally manifest.

We praise and thank God for the mighty creation around us: He is the maker of heaven and earth, "clothed with honor and majesty" (Ps 104:1). That is the theme of Psalm 104, "Bless the Lord, O my soul," and of Robert Grant's rousing hymn, *O Worship the King*, wherein we sing the psalmist's verses as people redeemed and looking forward to the resurrection of all flesh.

Grant employs a four-line stanza, with rhyming couplets, but his lines are long—the first two have ten syllables, the second two have eleven. We have seen how short, terse lines are consistent with slow tempo; similarly, long lines induce us to speed up the tempo, especially when most of the syllables are unstressed. Consider the following lines:

The galloping horses race down the ravine

The old mule plods on the dry road

The first line has eleven syllables in it, the second only eight. But the subject of the first line is well rendered by the racing of all those syllables, while the subject of the second line is rendered by the stop-start plodding of those short, slow words.

Grant's lines race, and they well might race out of control, but he has bound them together with interior rhymes as well as rhymes at the ends of the lines. Here in the first stanza Grant calls us to worship God whose power and love are one:

O worship the King, all glorious above!
O gratefully sing His power and His love!
Our shield and defender, the Ancient of Days,
Pavilioned in splendor, and girded with praise.

I bless thee, O Lord, says the psalmist, "who coverest thyself with light as with a garment" (Ps 104:2). What can that mean? Let's not suppose that the poetry is primitive, or merely emotive. The first of God's creatures was light; and that created light proceeds from the uncreated light, for, as St. John says, "God is light" (1 Jn 1:5). We need clothing to hide our nakedness. But God is "clothed" with what at once makes Him manifest and hidden, as we've seen. It is intrinsic to His being. Hence His very dwelling place is a pavilion of splendor, and He is "girded with praise," touching the mystery that praise belongs to God essentially, and not just by virtue of the wonders He has wrought for us.

The second stanza continues this simultaneous praise of who God is and what God has done:

O tell of His might! O sing of His grace!
Whose robe is the light, whose canopy space.
His chariots of wrath the deep thunderclouds form,
And dark is His path on the wings of the storm.

Again the images of light and dark accentuate one another and compel us to consider God's glory in terms that shatter any possibility that we might reduce Him to a comfortable object of admiration. Notice that the *might* and the *grace* of God are celebrated in exactly parallel exclamations. Somehow, both might and grace are shown forth in the light of God's being and the darkness of His path—in both the vast reaches of the universe, and the *chariots of wrath*, the mighty roll of the thunder and the storm.

Grant then devotes his next two stanzas to each pole of the hymn, the first to the might of God, which stuns us with wonder, and the next to His grace, for which we sing in gratitude. His might is gracious, and His grace is mighty:

The earth, with its store of wonders untold,
Almighty, Thy power hath founded of old,
Hath stablished it fast by a changeless decree,
And round it hath cast, like a mantle, the sea.

Thy bountiful care, what tongue can recite?
It breathes in the air; it shines in the light;

It streams from the hills; it descends to the plain,
And sweetly distils in the dew and the rain.

The first stanza presents us a world that is settled in order. It is *stablished*, fixed fast in one place, by a *changeless decree*. The mantle of the sea girds it round and provides it a boundary not to be breached. Yet the second stanza shows the great love of God breaking through the mantle, so to speak—and that is signaled by the break in the syntax, the sudden rhetorical question of the first line. No tongue can tell of all the abundant, overflowing care of God. Here the power is shown forth in the quiet and intimate things. Note the series of verbs: God's care *breathes, shines, streams, descends, and sweetly distils*. The storm of the second stanza is now the silent dew and the gently falling rain, watering the earth beneath and bringing life.

We are neither as great as God, nor as "small" as God; we need both His power and His grace. So they unite again for the final stanza, but here given personal intensity:

Frail children of dust, and feeble as frail,
In Thee do we trust, nor find Thee to fail;
Thy mercies, how tender! how firm to the end!
Our Maker, Defender, Redeemer, and Friend!

That's a brilliant counterpoint of the motifs of the poem. We are *frail*—note that the word brackets us; our feebleness is both physical and moral, and we recall the words of God to the fallen Adam: "Dust thou art, and unto dust shalt thou return" (Gn 3:19). But that word sets off the absolute trustworthiness of God, marked by the repeated pronoun *Thee*. The third line, split into two exclamations, echoes the two exclamations of the second stanza. Let me put them side by side:

O tell of His might! O sing of His grace!
Thy mercies, how tender! how firm to the end!

Again we have the identity of might and grace, of strength and tenderness. His mercies are tender (cf. Lk 1:78) but firm, unshakable, not subject to the chances and changes of time. Hence the succession of names for God in the final line. He made us; He defends us; He has redeemed us from the grave; and, to sum it all up in a way that only the revelation of Jesus Christ makes possible for us, He is our Friend.

For a resounding trumpet call to the power of God, we could hardly do better than Henry Lyte's *Praise, My Soul, the King of Heaven* (1834), sung to the melody *Lauda Anima*, written specifically for it. This is a joyous song, each stanza punctuated with alleluias before the final summative line. The text is based on Psalm 103: "Bless the Lord, O my soul: and all that is within me, bless his holy name" (Ps 103:1). That is the key—*all that is within me*, all we are and all we have unite in blessing the Lord.

Lyte employs the four beat line with strong stresses beginning each line, rhyming on alternate lines, with the "alleluia" of the fifth line unrhymed but binding all the stanzas together. The first stanza is a series of hearty imperatives:

Praise, my soul, the King of heaven;
To His feet thy tribute bring;
Ransomed, healed, restored, forgiven,
Evermore His praises sing:
Alleluia! Alleluia!
Praise the everlasting King.

Praise, bring, sing, praise! Why should we do so? The series of participles in the third line tell us—our souls have been *ransomed, healed, restored,* and *forgiven.* Lyte is following the order set forth by the psalmist:

> *Bless the Lord, O my soul, and forget not all his benefits:*
> *Who forgiveth all thine iniquities; who healeth all thy diseases;*
> *Who redeemeth thy life from destruction; who crowneth thee with lovingkindness and tender mercies.* (Ps 103:2–4)

Yet those benefits are braced before and after with the best reason to praise God: He is *the everlasting King.*

In the second stanza, Lyte turns with the psalmist toward the specific mercies of God to His people. The Lord "made known his ways unto Moses, his acts unto the children of Israel," and He is "slow to anger, and plenteous in mercy" (Ps 103:7–8). We are prey to time, but "the mercy of the Lord is from everlasting to everlasting" (Ps 103:17):

> *Praise Him for His grace and favor*
> *To our fathers in distress;*
> *Praise Him still the same as ever,*
> *Slow to chide, and swift to bless:*
> *Alleluia! Alleluia!*
> *Glorious in His faithfulness.*

Notice how Lyte coordinates his lines so that the second pair interprets the first pair. *Our fathers in distress* were sinful and unreliable, but God is *still the same as ever*: He does not swerve, even when we have. "He will not always chide: neither will he keep his anger for ever" (Ps 103:9). His sameness is not altered when He punishes or when He forgives, since, in both the one and the other, He is faithful.

Such faithfulness, even when God appears to change toward us, is the soul of His fatherly love:

> *Like as a father pitieth his children, so the Lord pitieth them that fear him.*
>
> *For he knoweth our frame; he remembereth that we are dust.* (Ps 103:13–14)

> *Fatherlike He tends and spares us;*
> *Well our feeble frame He knows;*
> *In His hand He gently bears us,*
> *Rescues us from all our foes.*
> *Alleluia! Alleluia!*
> *Widely yet His mercy flows.*

What remains for us but to join the heavenly hosts in song?

> *Bless the Lord, ye his angels, that excel in strength, that do his commandments, hearkening unto the voice of his word.*
>
> *Bless ye the Lord, all ye his hosts; ye ministers of his, that do his pleasure.*
>
> *Bless the Lord, all his works in all places of his dominion: bless the Lord, O my soul.* (Ps 103:20–22)

> *Angels, help us to adore Him;*
> *Ye behold Him face to face;*
> *Sun and moon, bow down before Him,*
> *Dwellers all in time and space.*

Alleluia! Alleluia!
Praise with us the God of grace.

"O sing unto the Lord a new song," cries the psalmist, "for he hath done marvelous things" (Ps 98:1). When we praise the glory of God, we praise Him for what He is and for what He has wrought in love. What is God in Himself but the three Persons of the Holy Trinity, united in a communion of love? Then it makes sense to praise the Holy Trinity while giving thanks to God for His loving care.

Most contemporary hymns avoid the Trinity, or relegate the three Persons to three ways of thinking about God. That is a dire heresy, and makes nonsense out of Jesus' claim to be *the* Son of God, rather than just a fine teacher of whom God approves. But if we want a hymn of praise to the Trinity that is also a hymn of gratitude and petition for the loving care of the Trinity, we can hardly do better than to turn to the ancient Irish poem known as "Saint Patrick's Breastplate," attributed to the Saint himself. The poem was translated into English by Cecil Frances Alexander (1889), on request for inclusion in an Irish hymnal, and is known as *I Bind Unto Myself*. It is sung to a minor key Irish melody called *St. Patrick*; the melody possesses a martial beauty, and can hardly be sung *unless* with the energy of a full heart. We see why that is so as soon as we read the first verse:

I bind unto myself today
The strong name of the Trinity,
By invocation of the same,
The Three in One, and One in Three.

The singer is strapping to his breast the armor of God (Eph 6:11), epitomized by the *strong name*, as we make across our breasts the sign of the Cross, in the name of the Father, the Son, and the Holy Spirit. Now that he has invoked the Trinity, he binds to himself the great deeds of the Trinity, in Christ:

I bind this day to me forever,
By power of faith, Christ's incarnation;
His baptism in the Jordan River;
His death on cross for my salvation;
His bursting from the spiced tomb;
His riding up the heavenly way;
His coming at the day of doom:
I bind unto myself today.

The stanzas are now doubled in length, and allow for a series of tremendous power: *His baptism, His death, His bursting, His riding, His coming*. The possessive *His* is balanced against the first person pronouns *I, me, myself*: I have nothing, says the poet, so I bind to *myself*, by the might of faith, what *He* has, what *He* has done. The events take us to the brink of judgment: Christ is born, He is baptized, He dies, He rises, He ascends, He comes again. All this vast span of time is concentrated in this moment: *Today*, the final word of the stanza, magnificently returns us to the beginning. All these wonders I bind unto myself, as a soldier fastens his armor, and as a lover embraces his beloved.

"I am crucified with Christ," says St. Paul, "nevertheless I live; yet not I, but Christ liveth in me" (Gal 2:20). So the glory of the incarnate Word is made manifest in the lives of the angels and the saints, lives of praise:

I bind unto myself the power
Of the great love of cherubim;
The sweet "Well done" in judgment hour;

The service of the seraphim;
Confessors' faith, apostles' word,
The patriarchs' prayers, the prophets' scrolls;
All good deeds done unto the Lord,
And purity of virgin souls.

These lives compose a symphony of praise in heaven; the deeds do not die but live still, as the Lord says to His own, "Well done, good and faithful servant! Enter thou into the joy of thy lord" (Mt 25:23). The list of the loving and marvelous works of Jesus prepares us for this list of our fellow worshipers, spanning the centuries, spiritual and bodily beings, those who awaited Christ's coming and those who saw Him in the world and those who witnessed to Him afterward by faith, old people and young, men and women, all displaying the great power of love.

Creation, too, joins in praise:

I bind unto myself today
The virtues of the starlit heaven,
The glorious sun's life-giving ray,
The whiteness of the moon at even,
The flashing of the lightning free,
The whirling wind's tempestuous shocks,
The stable earth, the deep salt sea,
Around the old eternal rocks.

That too is a power to bind to the breast. The poet recalls the words of the psalm:

Praise ye the Lord. Praise ye the Lord from the heavens: praise him in the heights.

Praise ye him, all his angels: praise ye him, all his hosts.

Praise ye him, sun and moon; praise ye him, all ye stars of light.

Praise him, ye heavens of heavens, and ye waters that be above the heavens. (Ps 148:1–4)

It is God's world we see round us, mighty and dangerous. So then the poet turns to God for guidance through this world, especially since we are beset with a prowling enemy:

I bind unto myself today
The power of God to hold and lead,
His eye to watch, His might to stay,
His ear to hearken to my need;
The wisdom of my God to teach,
His hand to guide, His shield to ward;
The word of God to give me speech,
His heavenly host to be my guard,

Again the series of possessives: *His* eye, *His* might. Here the nouns are linked to infinitive verbs: *watch*—that is, to keep vigil, as a sentry upon the battlements; *stay*, to hold the ground against the enemy's onslaught; and *hearken*, to hear my cry of distress amid the fight. I have nothing of my own: I pray instead to be filled with God. Let Him *teach, guide, ward*; I have nothing even to say, unless the word of God will *give me speech*. Even so I am in danger, but His angel guardians assist me always.

The next two stanzas are omitted from most hymnals. That's a shame, because they specify what the battle is about:

Against the demon snares of sin,
The vice that gives temptation force,
The natural lusts that war within,

The hostile men that mar my course;
Or few or many, far or nigh,
In every place and in all hours,
Against their fierce hostility
I bind to me these holy powers.

Against all Satan's spells and wiles,
Against false words of heresy,
Against the knowledge that defiles,
Against the heart's idolatry,
Against the wizard's evil craft,
Against the death wound and the burning,
The choking wave, the poisoned shaft,
Protect me, Christ, till Thy returning.

Notice the syntax of that first stanza, how the poet has delayed the subject and the verb until the final line. That is an extraordinary variation upon the pattern of the previous stanzas: Instead of beginning with *I bind*, we end with it, after having listed the threats that assail us, introduced by the preposition *against*, and summed up by the same preposition in the next-to-last line. The repeated word thus brackets those threats. They are ranged like platoons of enemies attacking, bearing different weapons, moving from the spiritual to the earthly and alternating between attacks from without and from within. The *demon snares* are laid in our path by the fallen angels, but our inner *vice* supports those temptations; then, too, we must fight against *natural lusts* that cause strife within us, and, returning outside the self, the *hostile men* who would thwart us on our journey to God. Then the poet, with a brave gesture of dismissal, declares that it does not matter to him how many they are or how few, how near they are (as near as our sinful hearts) or how far. Against them all he binds the holy powers he has named before.

That stanza is followed by another of the same structure: The preposition *against* begins the long sentence, and the subject and verb enter only in the final line. This time, though, the preposition is repeated *six times*, in a crescendo of evils. Some of these are spiritual, some are intellectual, some are physical—all are expressed in phrases pregnant with meaning. Satan is suggested by the word *wizard*, one who weaves *spells*. We should not attribute that to superstition. The language is Scriptural, recalling St. John's vision of the fall of Babylon, the great whorish anti-kingdom: "And the light of a candle shall shine no more at all in thee; and the voice of the bridegroom and of the bride shall be heard no more at all in thee: for thy merchants were the great men of the earth; for by thy sorceries were all nations deceived" (Rv 18:23). Sorcery is evil, true, but the point here is that evil *is sorcery*—a cheat, an illusion. It is like the pseudo-knowledge that Adam and Eve gained when they fell to Satan's trick, a *knowledge that defiles*, as the poet puts it; that makes us ignorant.

The last line of the stanza breaks the pattern of the previous stanzas: Now it is a direct address to Christ, begging for His protection until He comes again in glory. That leads us to this remarkably simple prayer:

Christ be with me, Christ within me,
Christ behind me, Christ before me,
Christ beside me, Christ to win me,
Christ to comfort and restore me,
Christ beneath me, Christ above me,
Christ in quiet, Christ in danger,

Christ in hearts of all that love me,
Christ in mouth of friend and stranger.

How far this is from the self-absorption of so many contemporary hymns! The poet—shall we just call him St. Patrick?—is not now strapping on the breastplate of faith in Christ. Christ Himself is that breastplate; He is the protection against the poisoned arrow shot in the dark; He is the strength of the heart beating within; He is the strong soldier at my side; He is the consoler in peace and war; He is the one I see and hear in friends and strangers.

One can go no further. So the poet returns to the beginning, in a cry of praise to the glorious Trinity, the God who made all things, and who redeems mankind:

I bind unto myself the Name,
The strong Name of the Trinity;
By invocation of the same,
The Three in One, and One in Three.
Of whom all nature hath creation;
Eternal Father, Spirit, Word:
Praise to the Lord of my salvation,
Salvation is of Christ the Lord.

Some of our most joyous hymns celebrate all that God is and all that God has done, placing one thing next to another so that we can see the harmony between creation and redemption, or between the song of the Church on earth and the song of the saints in Heaven or between our lives in time and the eternal life to come. James Montgomery (1771–1854), the Methodist poet we have met already (*Go to Dark Gethsemane*), wrote a splendid hymn that rouses us to do now what we long to do forever in the presence of God: *Songs of Praise the Angels Sang.*

The poem is composed of rhyming couplets, seven syllables to the line, beginning on the strong beat—a good martial rhythm. When it is sung to the sprightly melody *Riley*, two stanzas are sung together as one, and, as we will see, that is fitting, since the pairs belong together:

Songs of praise the angels sang,
Heaven with Alleluias rang,
When creation was begun,
When God spake and it was done.
Songs of praise awoke the morn
When the Prince of peace was born;
Songs of praise arose when He
Captive led captivity.

The first birth is that of the world, "when the morning stars sang together, and all the sons of God shouted for joy" (Jb 38:7), when God "spake, and it was done; he commanded, and it stood fast" (Ps 33:9). The second birth is more wondrous still, and songs illumine the morning of the nativity of the *Prince of peace* (Is 9:6). But the birth of the world and the birth of the Christ child bring us to that grand moment when man himself is born anew, when Christ "ascended up on high, [and] he led captivity captive, and gave gifts unto men" (Eph 4:8). Therefore, says St. Paul, we should redeem the time, encouraging one another "in psalms and hymns and spiritual songs, singing and making melody in [our] heart to the Lord" (Eph 5:19).

What can come next but the time we await, the consummation of the world:

Heaven and earth must pass away,
Songs of praise shall crown that day;

God will make new heavens and earth,
Songs of praise shall hail their birth.
And will man alone be dumb
Till that glorious kingdom come?
No, the Church delights to raise
Psalms and hymns and songs of praise.

Montgomery is a true artist. The first stanza *began* with the key phrase, *songs of praise*. This stanza ends upon it, citing the command of St. Paul. But before we come to the final line, we have sung that phrase twice, not at the beginning of a couplet, but in the *second* line. Consider this alteration:

Songs of praise shall crown the day
Heaven and earth shall pass away.
Songs of praise shall hail their birth
When God makes new heavens and earth.

Now that is not bad, but it's too programmatic, merely repeating the pattern of the first stanza. There's no surprise. By *reversing* the order, Montgomery throws into relief the dramatic events of the end times, *and surprises us* by declaring that, of all things, *songs of praise* will crown them. "Heaven and earth shall pass away," says Jesus, "but my words shall not pass away" (Mt 24:35). Jesus describes their dissolution as a time of great dread, like the flood in the days of Noah (Mt 24:38), but Montgomery caps his line with a declaration of joy, turning beyond time to the creation of a new heaven and earth (Rv 21:1). So then, shall we now remain silent? Not at all! We in the Church on earth rejoice to raise in time the songs that will resound in eternity. In the final stanza, Montgomery unites the choir on earth with the choir in heaven:

Saints below, with heart and voice,
Still in songs of praise rejoice;
Learning here, by faith and love,
Songs of praise to sing above.
Hymns of glory, songs of praise,
Father, unto Thee we raise;
Jesu, glory unto Thee,
Ever with the Spirit be.

And that gives us one delightful way to look upon our lives on earth. They are a singing school!

List of Hymns Referenced

Chapter 1

All People That on Earth Do Dwell, William Kethe (1561)
Pleasant Are Thy Courts Above, Henry Lyte (1834)
O God, Our Help in Ages Past, Isaac Watts (1719)
The King of Love My Shepherd Is, Henry W. Baker (1868) (Track 10)

Chapter 2

Creator of the Stars of Night, John Mason Neale (tr. 1852)
—*Conditor Alme Siderum*, Anon. (9th cent.)
Vexilla Regis Prodeunt, Venantius Fortunatus (569)
At the Name of Jesus, Caroline Noel (1870)
Let All Mortal Flesh Keep Silence, Gerard Moultrie (1864) (Track 6)
Crown Him With Many Crowns, Matthew Bridges (1851)

Chapter 3

The Glory of These Forty Days, Anon. (6th cent.)
Go to Dark Gethsemane, James Montgomery (1825)
The Story of the Cross, Edward Monro (1864)
Praise to the Holiest in the Height, John Henry Newman (1865)

Chapter 4

Of the Father's Love Begotten, John Mason Neale (tr. 1854) (Track 7)
—Prudentius (Latin Original; 4th cent.)
In the Bleak Midwinter, Christina Rossetti (1872)
Dost Thou in a Manger Lie?, Jean Mauburn (1494)
While Shepherds Watched Their Flocks by Night, Nahum Tate (1700)
Hark, the Herald Angels Sing, Charles Wesley (1739)

Chapter 5

Ah, Holy Jesus, Robert Bridges (tr. 1899) (Track 1)
—*Herzliebster Jesu* (German original), Johann Heermann (1630)
O Sacred Head, Sore Wounded, Robert Bridges (tr. 1899)
Christ the Lord is Risen Today, Charles Wesley (1742)

Chapter 6

O Sons and Daughters, John Mason Neale (tr. 1852)
—*O filii et filiae*, Jean Tisserand (1494)
Jesus, Priceless Treasure, Catherine Winkworth (tr. 1863) (Track 4)
—*Jesu, Meine Freude*, Johann Franck (1650)
Jesus, the Very Thought of Thee, Edward Caswall (tr. 1849)
—Anon. (11th cent.)
Savior! Thy Dying Love (Words: S. D. Phelps, 1862) Robert Lowry (1871)
My Spirit Longs for Thee, John Byrom (1773)
I Sought the Lord, Anon. (19th cent.)

Chapter 7

Lost, All Lost in Wonder, Gerard Manley Hopkins (tr.)
—*Adoro Te*, St. Thomas Aquinas (13th cent.)
Draw Nigh and Take the Body of the Lord, John Mason Neale (tr. 1861)
—*Sancte venite, Christi Corpus sumite*, St. Sechnall (5th cent.)

Shepherd of Souls, James Montgomery (1825)
At the Lamb's High Feast We Sing, Robert Campbell (tr. 1849) (Track 2)
—Anon. Latin Poet (4th cent.)

Chapter 8

Come, Thou Holy Spirit, Edward Caswall (tr. 1849)
—*Veni, Sancte Spiritus*, Stephen Langton (13th cent.)
Our Blest Redeemer, Harriet Auber (1829)
Come Down, O Love Divine, R. F. Littledale (tr. 1867) (Track 3)
—(Latin Original), Banco da Siena (15th cent.)
Holy Spirit, Truth Divine, Samuel Longfellow (1864)
Blest Are the Pure in Heart, John Keble (1819)

Chapter 9

Psalm 51 *Miserere mei*
—(rendered into English verse for 1912 Anglican *Psalter*)
Lead, Kindly Light, John Henry Newman (1833) (Track 5)
Jesus, Lover of My Soul, Charles Wesley (1740) (Track 17)
Turn Back, O Man, Clifford Bax (1916)
O God of Earth and Altar, G. K. Chesterton (1906) (Track 13)

Chapter 10

Who Would True Valour See, John Bunyan (1684) (Track 12)
Soldiers of Christ, Arise, Charles Wesley (1749) (Track 8)
For All the Saints, William How (1864)
Christian, Dost Thou See Them?, John Mason Neale (1862) (Track 16)
—(Original Greek), St. Andrew of Crete (7th–8th cent.)

Chapter 11

Abide With Me, Henry Lyte (1847)
There Is a Land of Pure Delight, Isaac Watts (1709) (Track 11)

Day of Wrath, William J. Irons (tr. 1849)
—*Dies Irae*, Thomas of Celano (13th cent.)
Nearer, My God, to Thee, Sarah Adams (1841) (Track 15)
I Know Not What the Future Hath, John Greenleaf Whittier (1867)
Now the Laborer's Task Is O'er, John Ellerton (1870)

Chapter 12

Immortal, Invisible, God Only Wise, Walter Chalmers Smith (1867)
O Worship the King, Robert Grant (1833)
Praise, My Soul, the King of Heaven, Henry Lyte (1834) (Track 14)
I Bind Unto Myself, Cecil Frances Alexander (1889)
—*Saint Patrick's Breastplate*, attr. St. Patrick
Songs of Praise the Angels Sang, James Montgomery (1819) (Track 9)

Audio Download & Track Listing

Scan QR code
with mobile device
to access audio tracks

1. Ah, Holy Jesus (Herzliebster Jesu) (Ch. 5)
   Text: Johann Heermann, 1630;
   trans. Robert S. Bridges, 1899
   Tune: Johann Crüger, 1640
2. At the Lamb's High Feast (Salzburg) (Ch. 7)
   [cid:ii_15792f15556d173a]
   Descant by Rev. Scott A. Haynes, S.J.C., 2016
3. Come Down, O Love Divine (Down Ampney) (Ch. 8)
   Text: Bianco of Siena, 15th cent;
   trans. Richard F. Littledale, 1867, alt.
   Tune: Ralph Vaughan Williams, 1906
   Descant by Rev. Scott A. Haynes, S.J.C., 2016
4. Jesus, Priceless Treasure (Jesu, Meine Freude) (Ch. 6)
   Text: [cid:ii_15792f297ebb7165]
   Tune: [cid:ii_15792f2fa0355c9f]

5. Lead, Kindly Night (Lux Benigna) (Ch. 9)
   Text: John Henry Newman, 1833
   Tune: John B. Dykes, 1865
6. Let All Mortal Flesh Keep Silence (Picardy) (Ch. 2)
   [cid:ii_15792f3eff5e3e73]
7. Of the Father's Love Begotten (Divinum Mysterium) (Ch. 4)
   Text: Marcus Aurelius C. Prudentius, 4th c.;
   tr. John M. Neale (1818-1866)
   Tune: Plainsong, 13th c.
8. Soldiers of Christ Arise (Silver Street) (Ch. 10)
   [cid:ii_15792f495f9d480a]
9. Songs of Praise the Angels Sing (Riley) (Ch. 12)
   Words: James Montgomery, 1819
   Music: Martin Shaw, 1915
10. The King of Love My Shepherd Is (St. Columba) (Ch. 1)
    [cid:ii_15792f5a2546999a]
11. There Is a Land of Pure Delight (Capel) (Ch. 11)
    Music: Traditional English Melody
    Arr. Ralph Vaughn Williams, 1906
    Text: Isaac Watts, 1709
12. Who Would True Valor See (Monks Gate) (Ch. 10)
    Music: Sussex Folk Song
    Arr. Ralph Vaughn Williams, 1906
    Text: John Bunyan [1628-1688]
13. O God of Earth and Altar (King's Lynn) (Ch. 9)
    Music: Traditional English Melody
    Arr. Ralph Vaughn Williams, 1906
    Text: Gilbert Keith Chesterton, 1906
14. Praise, My Soul, the King of Heaven (Lauda Anima) (Ch. 12)
    Music: John Goss, 1868
    Text: Henry Francis Lyte, 1834
    Descant by Rev. Scott A. Haynes, S.J.C., 2016
15. Nearer, My God, to Thee (Horbury) (Ch. 11)
    Text: Sarah Flower Adams, 1841
    Music: John Bacchus Dykes, 1861

16. Christian, Dost Thou See Them (St. Andrew of Crete) (Ch. 10)
    Text: [cid:ii_15792fd647341cc6]
    Music: John B. Dykes, 1868
17. Jesus, Lover of My Soul (Aberystwyth) (Ch. 9)
    Text: Charles Wesley, 1738
    Tune: Joseph Parry, 1876
18. What Star Is This? (Puer Nobis)
    [cid:ii_15792fea445b6796]

* Musicians: St. Cecilia Choir, St. John Cantius Church, Chicago
* Director: Rev. Scott A. Haynes, S.J.C.
* Organist: Walter Whitehouse
* Audio Engineer and Producer: Mark Essick
* Musical Advisor: Terry Sullivan

ABOUT THE AUTHOR

PROFESSOR Anthony Esolen holds a Doctorate in Renaissance English Literature from the University of North Carolina at Chapel Hill. He is a Professor of English at Providence College, located in Providence, Rhode Island. He is the translator of the celebrated three-volume Modern Library edition of Dante's *Divine Comedy* (Random House). He is a Senior Editor for *Touchstone: A Journal of Mere Christianity*, and his articles appear regularly in *First Things*, *Catholic World Report*, *Magnificat*, *This Rock*, and *Latin Mass*.